A Nearly Infallible
History of the Reformation

'I simply taught, preached, and wrote God's Word; otherwise I did nothing. And while I slept, or drank Wittenberg beer with my friends . . . the Word so greatly weakened the papacy that never a prince or emperor did such damage to it. I did nothing. The Word did it all.'

Martin Luther

'The Reformer is always right about what's wrong. However, he's often wrong about what is right.'

G.K. Chesterton

A Nearly Infallible
History of the Reformation

Commemorating 500 years of Popes, Protestants,
Reformers, Radicals and Other Assorted Irritants

Nick Page

HODDER

First published in Great Britain in 2017 by Hodder & Stoughton
An Hachette UK company

This trade paperback edition first published in 2018

1

Most of the illustrations are from the author's collection. Additional
sources: Alamy 14/Heritage Image Partnership Ltd, 52/classicpaintings,
150/Interphoto, 345/Chronicle.

A CIP catalogue record for this title is available from the British Library

ISBN 978 1 444 74970 0
eBook ISBN 978 1 444 74971 7

Typeset by Palimpsest Book Production Ltd, Falkirk, Stirlingshire
Printed and bound in the UK by Clays Ltd, St Ives plc

Hodder & Stoughton policy is to use papers that are natural, renewable
and recyclable products and made from wood grown in sustainable forests.
The logging and manufacturing processes are expected to conform to the
environmental regulations of the country of origin.

Hodder & Stoughton Ltd
Carmelite House
50 Victoria Embankment
London EC4Y 0DZ

www.hodderfaith.com

Contents

Introduction: The fastest-selling Playmobil® figure ever

'That change I have here in this Story unfolded is such that no man who does clearly understand it can think of it without the utmost degree of Admiration and Wonder. Its beginning was small and almost contemptible; and one man alone, a while, bore the hatred and violence of the whole World.'

So begins the first 'official' history of the Reformation. It was written by a man called Johannes Sleidanus or Sleidan.* Sleidan had studied at various universities and became a fully paid-up subscriber to the reformist cause. Not that he was ever really fully paid up himself. Although he had been appointed a kind of 'Official Historian of the Reformation' by Philip of Hesse – one of the leading reformed princes – his work brought him nothing but poverty and hardship and even abuse.† His great history was finally published in 1555. He died the next year in poverty and, according to one biographical sketch, 'plunged into a deep melancholy, with such a total loss of memory, as that he did not know his own children'.

In his history he'd made every effort to be fair to the various sides.

---

* His real name was Johann Philippson. The name Sleidanus came from his home town of Schleiden in Luxembourg. Which at that time was part of the Netherlands. Which at that time was owned by Spain. Just to warn you, it doesn't get any less complicated from here.

† His only portrait shows him with his left eye closed. Either he's winking, or the work took a toll on his eyesight as well.

So, naturally, everybody hated it.

Remind me again, why am I doing this?

———※———

That's the thing about histories of the Reformation. It is hard to remain impartial. Like it or not, we have all been affected by it. Anyone who has grown up in a church – or outside, come to that – has grown up in a culture deeply shaped by the language, ideas, traditions, rituals, expectations and attitudes which originated in that turbulent period.

The Reformation affects the way we define ourselves: Protestant, evangelical, Lutheran, Calvinist, Arminian, reformed, Baptist. Even Roman Catholic. It affects our ideas about heaven, hell, death, life. But it also affects the way we view our society. It defined so much that today we take for granted – ideas of sovereignty and individuality, of the nation state, of democratic rights. It reshaped the map of Europe and energised empires and nations. It gave us the 'Protestant work ethic' (which today is often neither Protestant nor ethical). It created our modern print media, and invented advertising and PR.

And, for Sleidan at least, it all began with one man: 'There lived at that time, in Wittenberg upon the Elbe, a City of Saxony, one Martin Luther, a Doctor of Divinity, and an Augustine Fryer; who . . . began to advise Men to be Wise . . . And this happened in the Year of our Lord one thousand five hundred and seventeen.'

On the desk in front of me is a Playmobil® figure of Martin Luther. I'll be honest, I don't think it's an exact replica. I mean, apart from anything else, he hasn't got a nose.* The figure was released to mark '500 years of Reformation' and here's a bit from the little brochure accompanying it:

---

* Hence the famous Catholic joke, 'Martin Luther's got no nose' / 'How does he smell?' / 'He's a heretic, therefore he smells of sulphur and the flames of hell.' It loses a bit in translation.

'In the beginning was the Word', we are told in the Gospel of St John. If this is the case, then the beginning of the Reformation was a thesis. Indeed, the ninety-five theses which Martin Luther nailed to the door of the castle church in Wittenberg on 31 October protesting against the sale of indulgences . . .

Frankly, it's a bit of a dodgy connection between the opening of John's Gospel and Martin Luther's Ninety-five Theses. But it's significant that the toymakers thought Luther important enough to make a figure of him in the first place. Clearly what Luther did five hundred years ago in Wittenberg has elevated him to the Playmobil® Hall of Fame. As far as I can find out, the only other historical characters they have ever done are Cleopatra, Caesar and the Butterfly Fairy.* And amazingly, the Luther figurine became Playmobil®'s fastest-selling figure, ever, with some 34,000 of the tiny plastic toys selling out within seventy-two hours.

Not bad for a five-hundred-year-old theologian.

The event celebrated by the Playmobil® figure has been called 'the hammer blow that launched the Reformation'.

Here's the story as it's commonly recounted. Catholic salesmen are making a killing selling indulgences – basically vouchers for time off in purgatory. Luther, outraged, writes down his Ninety-five Theses. Then, on 31 October – All Saints' Eve – 1517, he strides to the door of the Wittenberg church and nails his Theses to the door. A crowd gathers. 'Guten Tag!'; 'Achtung Spitfire!'; 'Vorsprung Durch Technik,' they exclaim. 'Es ist der Reformation!'

The scales fall from their eyes. There are cheers and tears and everyone goes home to be Protestant and be righteously happy ever after.

Suffice to say it didn't happen like that – indeed, it probably didn't happen at all. It's just one of those myths which cluster around Luther. (Of which more later.) Certainly, Luther was the crucial, pivotal figure of the Reformation. But the Reformation

* And Dürer, actually. Of whom, more later.

didn't begin with him and it didn't begin that October day in 1517. He wasn't the first person to call for a Reformation of the Church, or to object to the sale of indulgences, or to deny the Catholic theory of transubstantiation. His wasn't the first translation of the Bible into German. And he wasn't even the first person to invent the idea of justification by faith . . .

—⁓—

One day in the early sixteenth century, one man came to understand that the righteousness of Christ could be 'given and imputed unto us, as being graft into Christ, and having put on Christ'. He went on to develop this idea, declaring that Christians had to rely 'upon the justice of Christ given and imputed to us, and not upon the holiness and grace that is inherent in us'. This insight brought him a great relief: 'I was changed from great fear and suffering to happiness,' he wrote.

His name was . . .

Actually, his name was Gasparo Contarini, *Cardinal* Gasparo Contarini, and this was Easter Saturday 1511. Around seven years before Luther came up with the same idea.

Contarini was a Venetian from a noble family, and was the same age as Luther. Just a bit quicker off the mark. What Contarini didn't do, though, was to stretch this idea and use it to knock away at the established practices of the Catholic Church. He was a cardinal after all. And he spent the rest of his life trying to reconcile Catholic teaching with this idea of justification, rather than rebelling. We'll hear more of Contarini later.

You see, it wasn't necessarily that Luther got there first. In fact Christianity throughout its history has been a religion of renewal and reform. 'Reformation' – which comes from the Latin *reformatio* – is the lifeblood of the Church. It's there in the pages of the Bible. In the Old Testament the faith of the Patriarchs is renewed by the Law of Moses. King Josiah rediscovered the Torah and reformed the worship of his day. Ezra came back from exile with a plan of reform. The prophets called for continual refor-mation. Paul changed the relationship of Christianity and Judaism.

And beyond that, the history of Christianity up until Luther's day saw a constant churning of renewal and reform movements from the desert fathers to medieval mystics like Meister Eckhart, to reforming monks like Francis of Assisi. Luther himself wouldn't have said he was preaching new ideas. To Luther it was the medieval Western church, with its hierarchies and elaborate ritual, its superstition and its venality, that was a departure from the norm. Luther was a radical, in the true sense of the word: he wanted to get back to the roots.

But if he wasn't the first, then how come it's him who gets a Playmobil® figure?

Simple: he was the right man, in the right place, at the right time.

The right time, because there was technology available to make it happen. As we shall see, the story of Luther and the Reformation is largely bound up in the exciting new medium of the printed book. Luther wrote unmissable, unforgettable and often unedi-fying prose. Other people had similar ideas to him in previous years, but Luther had the printing press. And he was a one-man publishing industry.

The right place, because he was in an empire which, as the century went on, was unable to impose its political will as it once had. Luther lived in Wittenberg in Electoral Saxony, and the leaders of that place protected him. Had he been in Rome, or England, or France, it's doubtful he would have lived long enough to write all those books.

Most of all, perhaps, he was the right man. Unlike Contarini, for example, Luther took these ideas and ran with them. He refused to be cowed or silenced. George Bernard Shaw wrote that 'all progress depends on the unreasonable man'. And, believe me, in the whole history of human civilisation, you have to go a long way to find a more unreasonable man than Martin Luther.

Of course, there are many more reasons why the European

Reformation stuck, and there are many more people who played a significant part in its success.

But none of them are as important as Martin Luther.

And that's why (a) they don't get their own Playmobil® figure and (b) why he, more than anyone else, is the 'star' of the tale you are about to read.

First, though, some terms and conditions . . .

—∿—

It's a problem, when talking of the reformers and their ideas, to work out what to call them.

A term like 'protestant', for example, did not denote a religious grouping at the time; it was a political grouping of rebel states and cities. Of which, more later. Martin Luther preferred 'evangelical' (German, *evangelisch*) but when I use that term in this book please don't think that they were like modern, twentieth- and twenty-first-century evangelicals. He also tended to use the word 'Christian' – much to the annoyance of his opponents, all of whom considered themselves equally, if not more, Christian than Luther. Meanwhile, followers of Calvin and Zwingli preferred the word 'reformed' (*réformé* in French). Other terms changed their meaning over the course of the Reformation. Puritan, for example, started out as a term of abuse, but came to be a badge of honour.

Talking of abuse, there are sections in this book which are not for those of a nervous disposition. Some bits, I'm sorry to say, are quite rude and sweary.* In my defence, it's not me doing the swearing, for once, but people like Luther and . . . well, just Luther actually. During the past five centuries a great many myths grew up around people such as Luther, Calvin and others, not least the idea that they were nice. We like our heroes heroic, and our villains villainous. Particularly in Victorian times, but still,

---

* Well, not *that* sorry actually. It makes for a more entertaining book.

a little, today, biographies of Luther portray the principled man who stood alone against hatred and villainy, while rather ignoring the potty-mouthed, anti-Semitic, abusive man, with his bowel problems and his uncanny ability to fall out with virtually anyone. They praise the austere, philosophical, disciplined Calvin, the writer of beautiful prose, rather than the man who engineered his opponents' exile and even death, who could not bear to be contradicted and who was so unpopular in his own city that its inhabitants tried to empty their chamber pots onto him. We get the humanist Zwingli, who systematically preached the New Testament and radically transformed the nature of Christian worship, rather than the man who drowned his enemies in the river.

Some of their deeds were glorious. Some of their deeds were appalling. There is more than enough moral ambiguity in this tale to go around.

They were human beings, and, like the rest of us, they were, for the most part, just muddling along. As with all major historical shifts, nobody at the time realised that they were starting the Reformation.

But they were. And this is how it happened.

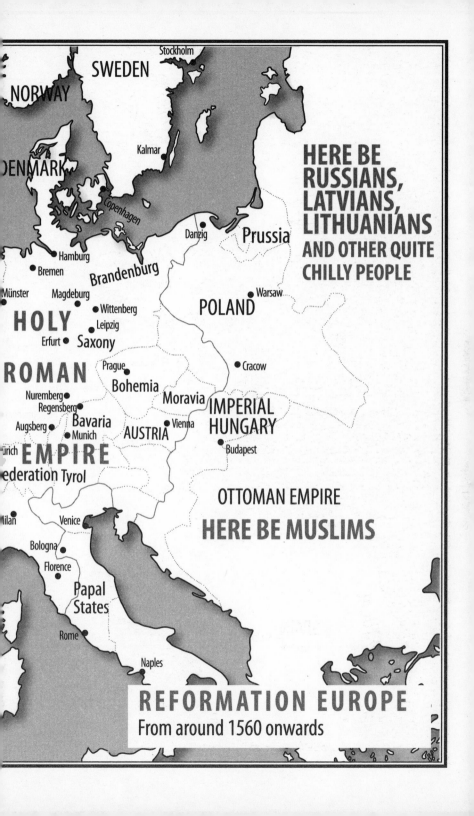

SWEDEN

NORWAY

Stockholm

DENMARK

Kalmar

Copenhagen

Hamburg

Bremen

Brandenburg

Danzig

Prussia

HERE BE
RUSSIANS,
LATVIANS,
LITHUANIANS
AND OTHER QUITE
CHILLY PEOPLE

Münster

Magdeburg

Wittenberg

Warsaw

POLAND

HOLY

Leipzig

Erfurt

Saxony

Prague

Cracow

ROMAN

Nuremberg

Regensberg

Bohemia

Moravia

IMPERIAL
HUNGARY

Augsberg

Bavaria

Munich

AUSTRIA

Vienna

zürich

EMPIRE

Budapest

ederation Tyrol

OTTOMAN EMPIRE

Milan

Venice

HERE BE MUSLIMS

Bologna

Florence

Papal
States

Rome

Naples

REFORMATION EUROPE
From around 1560 onwards

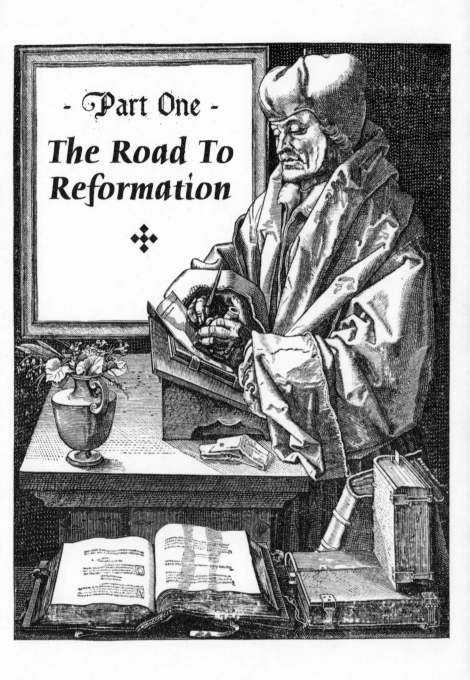

- Part One -
The Road To Reformation

❖

1 The medieval mindscape

Joen the painter

In 1516, a year before Luther published his Ninety-five Theses, a Dutch painter died during an outbreak of the plague. His name was Jheronimus van Aken, his neighbours knew him simply as 'Joen the painter', but he signed his works Jheronimus Bosch.

Bosch spent most of his life in the strangely named town of 's-Hertogenbosch (hence his assumed surname) where he lived in a house on the north side of the market square.* Bosch's life and paintings offer a unique, powerful and, some would say, borderline-insane glimpse into the medieval mind. His paintings contain some of the most mind-bogglingly bizarre creatures ever imagined. He painted heaven and hell and everything in between. (Actually, now I come to think of it, a lot of heaven and most of the in-between bits still look slightly hellish. Even his 'realistic' people are often grotesque, but then perhaps there's nothing more nightmarish than real people.)

When one looks at Bosch, one is tempted to think that he spent his life smoking a lot of the same stuff that his modern compatriots do. But Bosch's imagination – though unique – was inhaling nothing more mind-altering than medievalism. He was painting,

---

* That's not a typo. It really is 's-Hertogenbosch. The city's name is a contraction of the Dutch phrase *des Hertogen bosch* – 'the Duke's forest'. It would be like calling Shepherd's Bush, 's-Bush.

13

in fact, the landscape and the mindscape of the world in which Luther grew up.

Which probably explains a lot.

One of his paintings, *The Wayfarer*, depicts a peddler of some sort, a man just trying to scrape a living. He is getting old. He is gaunt, grey-haired, stubble on his chin. His back is bowed under the weight of his wicker pack. In his left hand he carries a hat to ward off the rain or the harsh sun. The other hand wields a walking stick, with a bulbous, cudgel-like end with which he is trying to ward off a dog. One of his legs is bandaged, suggesting that he has already been bitten. There is a hole in the knee of his trousers. He has lost one of his shoes and is having

Bosch, *The Wayfarer*

to wear a slipper instead. Today he would probably feature in a number of hipster magazines, but, in his world, he is *not* having a good day.

Behind the man, in the distance, there is a house. Underwear is hanging from the window, a woman and a soldier are kissing in the doorway. Another woman can be seen upstairs. A sign hangs on the house – an image of a swan: it's an inn, and a brothel.* Round the corner, a man is relieving himself against the wall of the house.

This is a fairly basic world. It is cold and muddy and hard. It is a place of danger and disease and temptation. What could make it better for this poor man? Only one thing. In the distance, through a gate which currently bars his way, there is a hill.

And on that hill is a tall, spindly cross.

Another world

Christian belief, its rites and rituals, completely shaped life in medieval Europe. The year was organised around the Christian calendar: Advent and Lent and Easter and Christmas. The weeks had a common pattern, with fasting on Friday and Sabbath on Sunday. There were feast days and holy days which celebrated local saints or commemorated events – real or imagined – in the life of Jesus and Mary. Such holy days provided a bright spot in lives which were, for the most part, sheer, unremitting hard grind.

Life was tough. It was whatever the opposite of a bowl of cherries is. (I'm not sure what that is, but I'm pretty sure Bosch painted it somewhere.) This was a world of uncertainty and anxiety. Sickness could snuff out your life at a moment's notice, and no one had a clue why. The Black Death had ravaged Western Europe in the mid-fourteenth century to such an extent that by

---

* The sign is significant: male swans are rare among fowl for having penises. Entertaining *and* informative, that's me.

1450 the population had declined from its 1350 levels by between 60 and 75 per cent.* Faced with such incomprehensible events, people needed reassurance that there was a better life available somewhere, somehow. And the Church gave them that. The Church held out the hope of salvation, rest, paradise – of a future life which was a great deal less muddy, cold and generally dung-coloured than the one around them.

Churches themselves were designed to make all this clear. Today we are used to rather austere churches (a consequence of Reformation ideas) unless you go to a cathedral, or one of those with the smoke machine and the lights and the worship leader with the rockstar complex. Mostly everything is plain and dull-coloured, not least the vicar. But in Bosch's day, entering a church was to enter somewhere covered in colour and dripping with decoration, its doorways filled with painted sculptures, its walls painted with stories from the Bible, or the lives of popular saints. The stained-glass windows glowed with light. Candles flickered. The air was thick with incense.

As well as the setting, the whole service was designed to give you a tantalising glimpse of another world. The sounds of the choirs, the priests in their colourful and often sumptuous robes, all gave the impression of otherworldly beauty and mystery. And 'mystery' was the word: for one thing, the liturgy was in Latin, a language which few people understood (sometimes not even those reciting the words). And there was a screen across the middle of the church which closed off some of the more sacred moments to ordinary lay people.† One day, of course, you would be able to participate fully in the mysteries. In heaven. But here on earth, you could look, but you could not touch.

* Florence lost between 45 and 75 per cent of its population. Venice lost around 60 per cent within the first eighteen months of the outbreak.
† The screen contained images of Christ on the cross, flanked by images of Mary and John. The Anglo-Saxon word for the cross was the rood. Hence the screen is known as a 'rood screen'. This is different to a rude screen, which in my youth was a cinema that showed certain 'European' films.

And, actually, even the promise of heaven was heavily guarded. I mean, you couldn't just let anyone in. No, even then, there were procedures, border patrols, immigration. There was a gate through which you had to pass, and that was guarded by the Church. The Church which controlled who would, and who wouldn't, be saved. And it administered this salvation through the sacraments.

Seven sacraments and other hocus pocus

A sacrament is a special, sacred act of the Church. Seven sacraments had been defined: baptism, confirmation, the Mass or Eucharist, penance, marriage, ordination and extreme unction (anointing with oil on your deathbed).* Five of these – baptism, confirmation, Eucharist, confession and extreme unction – were for everyone, priests and laity. One – marriage – was specifically for the laity.† And the final one – taking holy orders – was obviously only for the clergy.

All Christians were baptised soon after birth. Everyone in Europe was born into the Church. Later on you underwent the sacrament of confirmation, meaning that your membership of Christendom was rubber-stamped.

Then there was confession. This was a kind of spiritual MOT. At least once a year Christians would confess their sins and be

---

* Over the centuries what was and wasn't a sacrament had changed. In the early church there were two: baptism and Eucharist. Catholic theology enlarged this to seven, adding confirmation, penance, taking holy orders, marriage and anointing for the last rites. But this list only dates from around 1150 and was only formally adopted in 1439 at the Council of Florence. Nowadays, many churches add 'coffee drinking' and 'reading the church notices' to the list.

† Marriage had not always been out of bounds for the clergy: it was only officially declared so after AD 1139, mainly to stop inheritance disputes over church property. It was only in the eleventh and twelfth centuries that the Western church began to promote the idea that marriage was a sacrament.

prescribed a course of penance leading to absolution. Christians had to confess their sin 'on pain of damnation' (which seems a bit pointless, since if you didn't confess your sins you were damned anyway).* Mandatory private confession was only officially introduced in the Fourth Lateran Council in 1215, which declared it to be good for the soul. Not that it always was, actually. Sometimes it was more confusing than anything else. For those who took it really seriously, there was always the issue of whether you had confessed everything. Was there anything you had forgotten? In the fifteenth century, Margery Kempe, a woman in Norfolk, recorded how she left her confession so disturbed that she imagined devils around her, pawing and clawing at her as she walked home.

Then there was the Eucharist or Mass.† This was the centrepiece of Christian worship. From the moment you entered the church, your eye was drawn to the altar, on which Christ's body would be sacrificed to God. The Mass was the preserve of priests: the people would generally only get to partake once a year, and even then they would not get any wine. As to what happened during Mass, that was a matter of hotly contested debate.

According to the Bible, when Jesus had handed out the bread and the wine he said, 'this is my body' and 'this is my blood'.

---

* Sometimes people chose not to confess to the priest, but to a friar. Pope Boniface VIII had issued a ruling in 1300 that allowed friars to hear confessions. Friars were members of a religious order who were dedicated to preaching and ministering among the laity. The word comes from the Latin word *frater*, meaning brother. Unlike the monk, who was enclosed within a monastery, the friar was mobile and could be called out to wherever he was needed. He was a mobile monk. They took similar vows to monks – vows of poverty, chastity and obedience – and they were mendicants: people who supported themselves by begging. The key thing is that friars weren't local people. They were often just passing through. Confessing to a visiting stranger was much less embarrassing than confessing to your parish priest.

† The word Eucharist comes from the Greek word for thanksgiving; Mass is a Western nickname for the event. It comes from the Latin dismissal at the end of the service – *ite missa est* ('go, it is sent') – although precisely who or what goes or is sent has had liturgists arguing for centuries.

But what, exactly, did he mean? Jesus wouldn't lie. Obvs. So he must have meant that the bread and the wine were, in some way, *really* his body and blood. But how? Because it didn't look or taste any different. Medieval Catholic theologians found the answer with the help of a very ancient Greek. Aristotle had suggested that everything has an outward appearance and an inner, or deeper reality. The inner reality was termed the 'substance'; the outer appearance was known as the 'accidents'.

A theologian called Thomas Aquinas applied this idea to the bread: its 'substance', its fundamental nature, was the very *breadiness* of bread, while the 'accidents' meant the qualities of an individual piece, e.g. shape, size, density, number of poppy seeds, etc. What happened during the Mass, then, was that the *accidents* – the outer appearance – remained the same, but the *substance* of the bread – its inner reality – was altered. So it still looked like bread on the outside, but inside it was solid Jesus. Its *breadiness* had become *Jesusness*. The 'substance' was now the body of Christ. Hence the term, transubstantiation. It was Jesus, only shaped like a bun. That change occurred when the priest raised the bread and spoke the Latin phrase, *Hoc est corpus meum* ('This is my body'). Church bells would ring and the bread would be transformed. And if it seemed like a magic trick, well maybe that's why later generations changed the words *Hoc est corpus meum* into the more fairy-tale hocus pocus.

The final sacrament in the life of the ordinary believer – and I do mean final – was extreme unction. Extreme unction was not some kind of medieval extreme sport. It refers to the end-of-life anointing and confession, a full-service valet cleaning before your soul departed for heaven.* It's 'extreme' because there is a real danger of dying, and 'unctuous' because the priest anointed the sick person with oil. Like extreme sports, though, timing was

---

* Extreme unction was one of the 'last rites', which refers to three sacraments received on your deathbed: *extreme unction*, final confession and the *viaticum* – a special, presumably quicker, Communion for those about to pop off.

crucial. Timing your departure from life is rarely straightforward, but it's especially difficult in a society where you could be struck down by the plague, or warfare, or just a mug of some particularly dodgy mead.

All these sacraments were methods of sin management. And that was the most important task facing a Christian. Because as everyone was constantly reminded, sinners went to hell.

Hell, purgatory and the Devil

Bosch is perhaps best known for his visionary, nightmarish, surreal pictures of hell. But medieval people did not think hell was surreal: they thought it was only too real. Bosch inhabited a world where demons were real and dangerous, where kings wrote treatises on witchcraft and where Martin Luther could calmly record that it was the Devil who caused 'all the maladies which afflict mankind' and who drove people to suicide: 'It is very certain that, as to all persons who have hanged themselves, or killed themselves in any other way, it is the devil who has put the cord round their necks, or the knife to their throats.'

The Devil, you see, had one aim: to get you into hell.

The Christian wanted to go to heaven. But that was tricky. Certain people – martyrs and saints – obviously got into heaven straight away. But what about the rest of us? What about if we died without confessing everything? Obviously, if you died with unconfessed *mortal* sins – murder for example – then that meant hell for all eternity. But what about lesser sins?

Well, for the rest of us, there was a safety net in place. It was called purgatory.

Purgatory was a place of cleansing, a place where you could be purged of the smaller sins. Generally it was imagined as a crowded place, where you had to spend a long time enduring a series of trials or punishments. A bit like going to IKEA.

Depictions of purgatory found in literature such as Dante's

Divine Comedy, or Catherine of Genoa's *Treatise on Purgatory*, show it as a place where souls are being punished, but in a good way. They are happy to accept the punishments being meted out because they know that a visit to purgatory will, in the end, bring rewards. Like IKEA.

But purgatory wasn't heaven. And most people looked to spend as little time there as possible . . . Like IKEA.

And so a whole purgatory-avoidance industry grew up. One of the chief purgatory-avoidance schemes was the saying of a Mass for the souls of the dead. People would leave money in their wills to pay for Masses to be said for them, and the reward was that you would get some time taken off your stay in purgatory. But that was expensive, and only really an option for the wealthy. So another scheme was created in which ordinary people could buy a voucher which would give them – or one of their relatives – time off from purgatory. These promo codes shortening your stay in purgatory were backed by the authority of none other than the Pope. And they were called indulgences.

The way they worked was that the Pope had a kind of bank of unused merit. You remember all those saints and martyrs who were fast tracked into heaven? Well, clearly they hadn't needed all the spiritual merit they'd accumulated on earth. So all their unused, spare merit, went into the Church's treasury, where it could be dished out by the Pope to any soul he deemed worthy. And, for a small fee, you could actually buy some of this merit in the form of an indulgence. Indulgences had originated as a special bonus gift for anyone who signed up to the First Crusade, but such was the popularity that they were soon made available to cash customers. And it was not just your own stay in purgatory that could be shortened: the papal bull *Salvator Noster* (1476) extended this insurance to cover not just the living but also the dead. It acted retroactively.*

* A papal bull is not a variety of Catholic livestock, but a decree authenticated by the stamp of the Pope's own *bulla*, or seal. After it was publicly proclaimed, the person reading it would say, 'This is a papal bull', and all the people would reply, 'Holy cow!' Or I could have made that last bit up.

A lot of people questioned the sale of indulgences; Luther was by no means the first, or the only person to object to this trade. Earlier in 1517, for example, magistrates in the German city of Rostock strenuously opposed a three-month indulgence sale that had just been launched. What particularly miffed them was that they were already supporting 204 monks and nuns in their city and 182 working altars.

But the Pope needed money. Building new cathedrals and financing crusades did not come cheap. For both sinners seeking heaven, and for popes seeking finance, every little helped.

Modern devotion

Most people happily accepted all of this, and enthusiastically went along with everything that was on offer. But at the same time a lot of them weren't content *just* to let the professionals get on with it; increasingly, they were finding ways to experience a bit of that beauty and glory for themselves.

One of the main ways in which people did this was to go on pilgrimage. Travelling to famous shrines like Santiago de Compostela, Rome, Jerusalem or Canterbury would not only show you the world; it would also get you time off in purgatory when you prayed to the saint and venerated his or her relics.*

Some people sought their own personal experiences. Mystics like Julian of Norwich, and the unknown author of the treatise called *The Cloud of Unknowing*, wrote hugely influential works that were all about a personal, unmediated revelation. Mysticism, by its nature, bypasses the ordinary routes, skips round all the sacraments and goes straight to the heart of the individual, which

---

* Curiously, Wittenberg was one of these centres of pilgrimage. Luther's patron and protector, Frederick the Wise, Elector of Saxony, was not only a supporter of reform; he was also the proud owner of one of the biggest collections of relics in the world. In fact, he had so many relics that he issued a printed catalogue of his collection with illustrations by Lucas Cranach.

is why the official church was always a bit ambivalent about it. They applauded the sentiment but rather regretted that the divine revelation hadn't been revealed through more official channels. But this kind of writing was widely read. In fact, Luther's first published work was an edition of the *Theologia Germanica*, a mystical treatise by an unknown priest living in Frankfurt. (Luther gave it the rather less mystical and more culinary-sounding name: *Der Franckforter* – the Frankfurter.)*

Another way in which ordinary people claimed their own stake in the spiritual life was by joining lay 'brotherhoods'. These offered a kind of monasticism for ordinary believers. The most significant of these was a movement called the New Devotion – *Devotio Moderna* – which emerged in the Netherlands and spread into Germany. Devotees of *Devotio* formed small groups known as 'the Brethren of the Common Life' who met together in 'congregations'. The groups included married couples and families, and their 'houses' were controlled by the local town corporations, not by abbots or bishops. The idea was that everyone could be an apprentice of Jesus, an imitator, as it was called in the movement's most famous work, *The Imitation of Christ*, traditionally ascribed to a certain Thomas à Kempis.† In particular they focused on nurturing a rich, inner devotional life, nourished by reading and imaginative meditation. They ran schools as well, teaching Latin,

---

* Luther produced an edition in 1516, and an expanded edition in 1518, when he was in the white-hot atmosphere of the early days of the Reformation. He said that, 'Next to the Bible and St Augustine, no book has ever come into my hands from which I have learned more of God and Christ, and man and all things that are.' Surprisingly, though, it's a thoroughly medieval work, which suggests that Christians could pursue perfection, as seen in the life of Christ, by renouncing sin and selfishness, and, in effect allowing God's will to replace human will. Which explains why Calvin hated it, saying that it was 'conceived by Satan's cunning . . . it contains a hidden poison which can poison the church'.

† Or Thomas from Kempen, which is a town in the Netherlands. Their books went on to have a massive effect in the other direction as well, having a noted influence on the Basque soldier Ignatius Loyola, creator of the *Spiritual Exercises* and founding father of the Jesuits.

grammar and rhetoric. In 1497 the young Martin Luther spent a year at one of their schools in Magdeburg.

The fact is that the pre-Luther days were not dry, arid, hopeless times of spiritual desolation. On the contrary, people were already nourishing their faith outside the official channels. And it's important to note that these were reform movements. Because, while everyone accepted that the Church was crucial to salvation, most people also realised that it was also awash with scandal and corruption. And they blamed the man at the top.

Hopeless popes

Sometime between 1490 and 1500, Bosch painted *The Haywain*. Its theme is drawn from a Flemish proverb: 'The world is a haystack and everyone snatches what he can from it.' The left-hand panel shows three scenes from the first chapters of Genesis: Adam and Eve in the Garden of Eden, tempted by a half-man, half-serpent and then expelled. The huge middle panel shows an enormous wagon of hay – the haywain of the title. On the hay, and surrounding the wagon, are a throng of people doing all the things of ordinary life. People are being tricked out of their goods, others are fighting, dancing, drinking. A couple snog in a tree. The wagon is being pulled, typically for Bosch, by bizarre creatures: fish with legs, or people with ape-like heads, or long, dagger-like beaks. These are demons, pulling the world and all those in love with it away from Eden and towards the panel on the right, where a scarlet-flamed hell is waiting, peopled – if that's the right word – with even-more-grotesque and surreal devils. All those on and around the haywain seem cheerfully oblivious to their fate. And among those enthusiastically following the cart are two significant figures: the Emperor and the Pope.

Yep, the Pope is heading in the wrong direction.

The idea that the reformers were the first who dared criticise the Pope is not true at all. Criticising the Pope was commonplace. And this was mainly due to the fact that the popes had a long history of appalling behaviour. One key factor was the so-called Great Schism of the fourteenth century. From 1378 there were two Popes, 'elected' by rival factions and backed by different European rulers. One of them was French and lived in Avignon; the other was Italian and lived in Rome. And for thirty years Avignon and Rome each elected their own popes. They tried to sort the problem out through a council at Pisa in 1409, which both the Popes refused to attend. So the council elected another Pope. Now there were *three* Popes. The situation wasn't resolved until 1419. But it severely damaged the idea that the Pope was in any way a responsible adult, let alone Christ's representative on earth.*

Everyone knew that fish rotted from the head down. And it is a fact that calls for reform feature in every major church summit between 1378 and 1514, though nothing ever happened. The real problem was that for those in power it was always the *other* part of the Church that needed reforming, not their bit. The cardinals were never going to give up any of their power. And the popes were having *way* too much fun.

In fact, the list of popes in the fifty years before Luther came to prominence contains some of the worst examples of papal misbehaviour in church history. I wouldn't dream of sullying this noble work with their behaviour.

Oh all right then. Here's a quick list:

Paul II (Pope from 1464 to 1471)
He considered himself so good looking that he originally tried to call himself Pope Formosus (the Handsome) until he was talked out of it by his cardinals. I'll be honest, his portraits don't really

---

* When Luther wrote his famously incendiary book *The Babylonian Captivity of the Church*, he was using language which had already been used about the Avignon Pope.

support his own estimation of his beauty. He wore rouge in public, organised carnivals and horse racing, and had a weakness for good-looking young men and for melons (probably not at the same time, but you never know). To be fair to him, he did repair a lot of Rome's ancient monuments, and he allowed two Germans to set up the first Roman printing press.

Sixtus IV (Pope from 1471 to 1484)

As a Franciscan monk, he was wedded to a life of poverty. As Pope he and poverty got a quickie divorce and he married extravagance instead. His coronation tiara alone cost more than a third of the papacy's annual income. To raise money, he sold indulgences and church jobs: he gave the archbishopric of Milan to an eleven-year-old and the archbishopric of Lisbon to a boy of eight. He also appointed many of his nephews cardinals.*
He did build some churches and hospitals as well, not to mention the chapel named after him – the Sistine Chapel – which he had decorated by famous artists like Botticelli, Ghirlandaio and Perugino. (Michelangelo did his bit of painting and decorating much later. He was only six at the time. Although I suppose he could have been made Archbishop of Florence or something like that.) In 1478, Sixtus issued a bull ordering an inquiry into the role of Jews in the Spanish court. Although nobody was expecting it, this was the beginning of the notorious Spanish Inquisition.

Innocent VIII (Pope from 1484 to 1492)

He was a hopeless nonentity, totally dominated by others who used him as their puppet. (Not literally, although I wouldn't have put it past them.) He did make several relatives cardinals, not

---

* The word 'nepotism' comes from this habit of popes and bishops, who would give places to their 'nephews'. The Italian word for nephew is *nipote*, hence 'nepotism'. The practice was only ended by Pope Innocent XII in 1692.

his nephews this time, but his children by a Neapolitan mistress. By the end, Innocent was waking up only to gorge himself on gargantuan meals. He grew so fat and so ill that the only nourishment he could take was 'no more than a few drops of milk from the breast of a young woman'. Well that was his excuse, anyway. Towards the end of his life, three young men died in an attempt to give him a blood transfusion.

Alexander VI (Pope from 1492 to 1503)

This was the Pope in charge when Bosch painted *The Haywain*. And you can see why Bosch has him heading in the other direction. Alexander was one of the notorious Borgia family. Though aged sixty-one, he had a nineteen-year-old mistress whose brother, Alessandro Farnese, the Pope made a cardinal. He commissioned work from both artists and assassins.* He staged sex shows in the Vatican and for the last few years of his life had to go out wearing a mask because his face was disfigured by syphilis.† Alexander VI, then, was that rare thing, a pope with an STI. It was alleged that he died when an attempt to poison one of his cardinals went wrong.

Given this list (and there are more to come), it's not surprising that people resented Rome for its extravagance, expense and general not-very-Christ-like behaviour. This was especially keenly felt in northern Europe, in Germany and the Netherlands, and other places where people lived far away from all that loose-living, olive-oil growing, melon-eating lifestyle. As well

---

* A lot of the assassinations were organised by his cruel and rapacious nephew, Duke Cesare (who was also a cardinal). According to a report from the Venetian ambassador, 'Every night, four or five men are discovered assassinated, bishops, prelates and others, so that all Rome trembles for fear of being murdered by the Duke.'

† The disease was new – it had arrived with the French soldiers when they invaded Italy in 1494. The Italians called it The French Pox – a name which, much to the irritation of the French, was quickly adopted throughout Europe.

as the popes, there was widespread criticism of priests and monks. It has been estimated that anything from between 30 to 70 per cent of the Catholic clergy – depending on the region – did not occupy their offices; instead they just took the money and employed a locum – a temporary vicar – to stand in for them. (One of those who benefited from this system was the young John Calvin.) Many priests lived with concubines and had children of their own, and the Church would levy a 'cradle tax' on each child. In Bamberg the bishop charged five gulden for every child, which one year brought him 1,500 gulden. In the much larger diocese of Constance a tax of four to five gulden brought in 7,500 gulden. (Which means that there were at least 1,500 clerical 'bastards' in the diocese.) This was a handy revenue stream, which is why the clerical authorities were reluctant to crack down on it. Sometimes the townsfolk got really annoyed at such behaviour. In Osnabrück, in Saxony, for example, the city council got so fed up they forced priests' 'wives' to wear plain clothes and a striped coat as a mark of shame. To be fair, many priests were ashamed as well. In a pamphlet by a reformer called Eberlin von Günzburg we find a priest eaten up with self-loathing about his own hypocrisy. He complains that the laity tolerate clerical concubines 'the way stable boys become accustomed to dung':

> on the one hand I cannot live without a wife, on the other I am not permitted to have a wife. So I am forced to live a publicly shameful life to the detriment of my soul and my honour . . . How shall I preach about chastity and promiscuity, adultery and knavish behaviour when my whore goes to church and is seen on the streets and my bastards sit before my eyes? How shall I read the Mass in such circumstances?

Not exactly PC language, but you get the point. And the fact is that, once the reformers suggested that clerical marriage was OK, many monks, nuns, priests, prelates and even the occasional ex-cardinal rushed to join in. Even one of Luther's most dedicated opponents, Duke George of Saxony, described the Church as not so much the Bride of Christ, more 'a stinking decayed corpse'. Critics of the Church called for *reformatio in capite et membris* – reform in head and members.

For all this, it was the Pope who was chiefly blamed. 'If the head is sick, the limbs also feel the pain. If reform is to be accomplished, it must begin with the pope and the Roman curia. It is the pope and the cardinals who daily commit the most fearful transgression and abuses . . .' said a German priest in 1451 to the papal representative Nicholas of Cusa.

But for all that, people didn't want to get rid of the Pope or the local priest – they wanted *better* popes and *better* priests. They wanted a clean-up, not a clear-out. They wanted to prune the tree, not chop it down. And this was not just talk: in the century before Luther there were some who had really wielded the secateurs with a vengeance.

Pre-Reformation reformers

At the Fifth Lateran Council in 1512, Gianfrancesco Pico della Mirandola, rather optimistically, given who was Pope at the time, urged the Pope to act: 'These diseases and wounds must be healed by you Holy Father,' he said, and then added, rather ominously: 'otherwise I fear that God himself, whose place on earth you take, will not apply a gentle cure, but with fire and sword will cut off those diseased members and destroy them, and I believe that he has already clearly given signs of his future remedy.'

What signs was he thinking of? Perhaps he was recalling what happened in Florence ten years earlier when a Dominican friar called Girolamo Savonarola had come to power. He was a fiery preacher who claimed direct communion with God and who hated the wealthy aristocracy that ruled the Italian states at the time, especially the Medici in Florence, the Duke of Milan and, most of all, Pope Alexander VI. Here's a taste of his rhetoric:

> Popes and prelates speak against worldly pride and ambition and are plunged in it up to their ears. They preach chastity and keep mistresses . . . They think only of the world and worldly things; for souls they care nothing . . . They have made of the Church a house of ill fame . . . a prostitute who sits upon the throne of Solomon and signals to the passers-by . . . O prostituted Church, you have unveiled your abuse before the eyes of the whole world, and your poisoned breath rises to the heavens.

Savonarola established a 'Christian and religious republic' in Florence. It was, in fact, the first truly modern republic, as in 'ruled by the whole people'. The new constitution granted every citizen in good standing the right to a vote in a new parliament: the Great Council. At the same time Savonarola enforced a strong moral code, banning same-sex relationships, adultery and public drunkenness, while self-appointed bands of young men acted as religious police, patrolling the streets and telling people off for their immodest dress. Savonarola also introduced regular 'bonfires of the vanities' during which citizens would come and chuck their mirrors, make-up, fancy clothing and paintings on the fires, along with worldly books, musical instruments and even games such as chess. (Sadly, the paintings burned included several by Michelangelo and Botticelli.)

It could not last, of course. The powers that be eventually got their act together and Savonarola was executed. But he established a model. Burning books, destroying art, policing morality, were all to become features of the Reformation. (Not to mention all-powerful city councils dominated by charismatic, and slightly unhinged, religious leaders.)

Savonarola was a reformer before the Reformation. But he was not alone. The most famous of the pre-Reformation reformers was the man called 'the morning star of the Reformation', John

Wycliffe.* Wycliffe – an academic and professional grumpy old man – was Doctor of Divinity at Oxford University. During the time of the two Popes, he began to put forward some radical ideas. He attacked many of the Church's most revered institutions including the papacy, church hierarchy, monastic orders and worship of saints.

Wycliffe grounded his ideas in the Bible, which he regarded as the ultimate authority – above the Church and its traditions, above the teaching of the Church Fathers, above the rulings of the Pope. Wycliffe thought that the idea of transubstantiation was ridiculous, a distortion of the original biblical story. He saw Communion as a moral and spiritual gift, not a conjuring trick played with substances and accidents and all that Aristotelian wiffle.

He claimed that, insofar as Christ intended to leave a 'church', it must have been a spiritual body with no earthly possessions. This was not an argument which was likely to convince churchmen, who quite liked their possessions. And if it was a spiritual institution, then the Church should have nothing to do with secular power and legal systems. The Pope was not some kind of secular ruler, he was the Bishop of Rome, no more, no less. The authority of the Pope – or of any church leader for that matter – did not rest with their political or military power, but came from their moral authority. Which, given how immoral many of them were, was something of a problem.

Ordinarily Wycliffe would have been swiftly encouraged to shut up, using a large axe. But he was protected (a) by his own reputation, (b) by the geographical distance between Oxford and Rome and (c) by the political situation in England where the ruling class saw some advantage to themselves in weakening the power of the Church.

* Aka Wyclif, Wycliff, Wicliffe, Wiclef, Wicliffe, Wickliffe. Medieval autocorrect was rubbish.

TOP REFORMERS

John Wycliffe

Born: Yorkshire, England, c.1325
Died: Lutterworth, England, 1384

AKA: Wyclif, Wycliff, Wicliffe, Wiclef, Wicliffe, Wickliffe, etc. 'The morning star of the Reformation'

This proto-reformer attacked many clerical institutions such as the Pope, monastic orders and transubstantiation. He inspired the translation of the Bible into English. Although declared a heretic, he died peacefully. However, 44 years later, his bones were exhumed and burned just to make sure.

Fun Fact: Wycliffe's patron, John of Gaunt, was also the patron of Geoffrey Chaucer.

INFLUENCE	50
THEOLOGICAL IMPORTANCE	88
FACIAL HAIR	85
GENERAL GLOOMINESS	355
ABUSIVENESS	12
HAT QUALITY	12
PROPENSITY TO VIOLENCE	5

He wasn't executed, therefore, but was condemned at a synod in 1382, sacked by the university and sent into oblivion. Or Leicestershire as it's known. He retired to the small town of Lutterworth, from where he continued to chunter his denunciations of the Church, until he died of clinical grumpiness two years later.

(But that in itself was a message: Wycliffe died in his bed – the Pope was powerless, if the state did not want to do something.)

To Wycliffe, scripture was key. He wanted everyone to read it in their own language, so some of his followers made the first translation of the Bible into English. The so-called 'Wycliffe' Bible was probably the work of two men: Nicholas of Hereford who did a rather wooden version of the Old Testament, and John Purvey, who revised the Old Testament and completed the work. The translation was condemned as heretical but it proved amazingly popular. It was particularly associated with a group of Wycliffite followers who became known as the Lollards – a word which was supposed to imitate the muttering, mumbling sound of a group of lay people stumbling their way through the Bible.

The English nobility were all in favour of power moving from the Pope towards them, but they didn't want it going any further than that, thanks very much. And when the peasants revolted in 1381, they blamed the Wycliffe Bible for filling the peasant heads with a load of revolutionary ideas. In 1407, Thomas Arundel, Archbishop of Canterbury, banned the making and reading of Wycliffite Bibles, without the approval of the Church, and in England translating the Bible was to remain illegal for another one hundred and fifty years.

Lollardy was driven underground, but it survived, mainly among traders and merchants and the emerging professional middle classes. Small groups of Lollards continued to meet in secret. Each group appointed their own leaders, they allowed lay people to preach and to officiate at the Eucharist, and they read from their Bibles. We will see similar radical, underground splinter groups emerge at the fringes of the Reformation.

Wycliffe's ideas were taken up by a load of Bohemians. Although part of the Holy Roman Empire, Bohemia (roughly the western part of what today we call the Czech Republic) had a strong independent streak, and that was embodied in Jan Hus, Dean of the Philosophical Faculty in Prague's newly established university. Radically, Hus offered communicants both the bread and the wine, something which had not been done for centuries. He denied the power of popes to issue indulgences and expressed doubts about the existence of purgatory. Like Wycliffe, he relied on the Bible for his inspiration. In 1414 Hus was eventually ordered to present his radical ideas before a council – the same council that had been called to sort out the embarrassing multi-Pope situation. He was given a promise of safe conduct by the Holy Roman Emperor, Sigismund, but the council decided that promises didn't count if they were given to a heretic, so they had Hus arrested. After six months in prison he was hauled before a show court, sentenced to death and then burned at the stake.

This duplicitous stupidity turned Hus into a martyr. His betrayal and death sparked off an armed revolt in Bohemia, a revolt which the troops of the Holy Roman Empire were unable to suppress. The result was that Bohemia was allowed to establish an independent Hussite church, free from papal control, in the middle of Catholic Europe. The Hussites continued to receive both bread and wine in Communion. And in the future, Bohemia was to prove a staunch ally of the Reformation cause.

In 1415, shortly before he died, Hus was reported to have made a punning prophecy. 'You may roast this goose,' he said – and here, it helps to know that 'Hus' means 'goose' in Czech – 'but a hundred years from now a swan will arise whose singing you will not be able to silence.' Swans, of course, don't sing, but leaving Hus's lamentable ornithological knowledge aside, it was almost exactly a hundred years later that Martin Luther launched his Theses on the world. Whether or not Hus ever said anything of the sort, Luther certainly believed that he was the swan. And after his death, Lutheran churches used the symbol, putting swan-shaped weather vanes on their churches while their paintings and engravings often portrayed Luther with a swan.*

---

* Slightly unfortunate, perhaps, given what we've learned about swans elsewhere. See p. 15. And, while we're on the subject of swans, while they don't sing as such, they grunt, whistle, honk and hiss. Which is not a bad description of *some* of Luther's writings, at least.

TOP REFORMERS

John Hus

Born: Husinec, Bohemia, c.1372
Died: Constance, Germany, 1415

AKA: Jan Hus, John Huss

The reformer before the reformers, he took Wycliffe's ideas and established Bohemia as the first reformed kingdom. His reforms of the church and Eucharist were an example to many later reformers. He was accused of heresy, tricked into attending the Council of Constance and burned at the stake.

Fun Fact: In 1929 Benito Mussolini published a biography of Hus.

INFLUENCE	55
THEOLOGICAL IMPORTANCE	35
FACIAL HAIR	25
GENERAL GLOOMINESS	18
ABUSIVENESS	2
HAT QUALITY	54
PROPENSITY TO VIOLENCE	10

This, then, was the medieval world. It was a world of hierarchy and authority, where the Church controlled access to heaven, but also where individuals were beginning to make their own claims on holiness and spirituality. It was a world where a great many people recognised the need for reform, but where too much radicalism was clamped down upon. It was not that people didn't have radical ideas, or see the need for reform, but their ability to spread those ideas was extremely limited.

But some forty years after the death of Hus, everything changed.

2 The escape of knowledge

Mr Gooseflesh and his marvellous machine

In 1454 a man called Mr Gooseflesh changed the world.

His full name – his *very* full name – is: Johannes Gensfleisch zur Laden zum Gutenberg. We know him better as Johannes Gutenberg. And he invented a device called a printing press.

The usual production method for a book in the Middle Ages was a monk. Books were copied by hand, which, even for simple, straightforward designs, made book production a laborious and eye-wateringly expensive affair.*

Monks were unreliable. Richard of Bury complained that the monks cared 'more about drinking beer than writing books', but then again, don't we all. But, sober or not, human error inevitably led to mistakes creeping in. Because they were handwritten they were slow to produce. Because they were slow to produce they were scarce. And because they were scarce they were expensive. So people simply didn't encounter books in any great quantities. In 1424 the library at the University of Cambridge had just 122 books in it. The Vatican Library – at that time the largest library in the world – had about 1,100 books in it.

---

* In 1309 the nuns of Wasserler in the diocese of Halberstadt sold a complete Bible they had for sixteen pieces of silver. Three years later they used the money to buy 180 acres of land, two farmhouses and a farm with two acres of woodland and another wood. Well, I say 'used the money'. Used *some* of the money. They still had eleven pieces of silver left over.

What Gutenberg did was to replace the old printing technology (i.e. a grumpy monk with a pen) with three crucial elements which were to survive pretty much unchanged for the next six centuries: metal type, an oil-based ink (which was needed to ensure the ink adhered to the metal type) and a top-down press based on the olive and wine-press.* When a whole page of type had been 'set', it was inked up and a piece of paper put on top. The paper would then be pressed down onto the type and a printed page would emerge. Repeat the process and you have a number of identical pages. And when the whole thing was done, you could then simply redistribute the type and reuse it to make another page of another book. It was a radical new way of working, and it was to change everything.†

Gutenberg's revolution changed the world. For the first time, books could be mass-produced in huge quantities. They became cheaper and more widely available. But like many inventors, Gutenberg never actually grasped the true potential of his invention. His first book – an edition of the Bible – used the same design as a handwritten manuscript and was printed on parchment.‡ The production process took him two years, only produced 150 copies and virtually bankrupted him. In fact, the only full-sized books Gutenberg ever printed were two editions of the Bible. Instead, he used his invention to print smaller items: some

---

* Although Gutenberg is credited with the invention, there are other claimants such as Waldvogel of Prague. He lived in Avignon from 1444 to 1446 and it was claimed he invented a system of 'artificial writing' which involved single letters cast in metal. However, he left us no actual examples of his work so, sadly, Waldvogel is relegated to a footnote in history. Like this one.

† Not everyone abandoned the old ways. The Abbot of Sponheim argued that, despite the arrival of printing, hand-copying books was still a worthy occupation for a monk, as it would keep him from being idle, encourage diligence and knowledge of scripture, keep him off the streets and away from drugs, etc. He claimed that the written word on parchment would last a thousand years, while the printed word would be gone in a jiffy. Strangely, though, when it came to his own books, he had them all done at the printing office.

‡ He even left a space so that the first letter of each chapter and the headings could be added by an illuminator.

calendars, a very short Latin grammar and, ironically, given the impact of printing on the Reformation, papal indulgences. What he was trying to do was to show that printing could produce the same high-quality work as before. But he failed to realise that the world didn't want that kind of work. They wanted cheap. They wanted available. They wanted to read.

It was others who really grasped the revolutionary power of print and made money from it. They published smaller, cheaper, more-readable books, and instead of expensive parchment they used paper. Printing presses spread quickly: by 1500 around one thousand presses were operating in 250 European towns and cities. Writing in 1470, an Italian bishop observed that three men working at a single press for three months could produce three hundred copies of a book. It would take three scribes a lifetime to achieve the same number. Assuming they didn't die of severe writer's cramp.

The figures are staggering. It has been estimated that in the fifty years following Gutenberg, some twenty-seven thousand titles appeared from presses across Europe. By the mid-sixteenth century, a reader would have been able to choose from some eight million books, more, probably, than had been produced in all of history before then. A lot of these were Bibles. In 1466, Mentelin in Strasbourg printed a one-volume German Bible, which was much smaller and cheaper than Gutenberg's version. In the years leading up to the Reformation, over 70,000 Bibles were printed in Central Europe, not to mention some 100,000 New Testaments. As well as the Latin Vulgate version there were translations galore. Bibles appeared in High German, Low German, and every German in between, Dutch, Catalan, Portuguese, Polish, Czech, French, Italian, Russian and even Ethiopian. (But not, of course, English. That was still banned.)

But there were other kinds of books as well. The most widely circulated printed works were pamphlets, small booklets of anything up to thirty-two pages which were cheap to buy and easy and quick to consume. The Germans called them *Flugschrift*, from which we get our word flysheet or flier. The name implies the speed with which these little booklets would fly about to a wide audience. They were quick to produce; where a book might take weeks or months to typeset, a pamphlet could be printed in a few days.

Democratising knowledge

What the printing press did was to democratise knowledge. Information and ideas spread further and faster than ever before. The early fifteenth century saw the foundation of many schools and universities (so along with the invention of printing we also got the invention of the student. It's not all good news, you see). With printing, scholars could now pursue their ideas in larger libraries, without the need to travel to consult a book chained somewhere else. Printing also cut out the middleman. A bright, well-read student might reach beyond their teacher's knowledge. It was no longer necessary to sit at the feet of the master and wait for the pearls of wisdom to drop from his lips. 'Why should old men be preferred to their juniors now that it is possible for the young by diligent study to acquire the same knowledge?' asked an author with the lovely name of Giacomo Fillipo Foresti di Bergamo in 1483.*

Previously, books had been a conspicuous sign of wealth, but now they were a sign of a different kind of wealth: an intellectual richness. There was a new class of person in the world: an intellectual aristocrat, someone who understood things better than anyone else. Or, perhaps, people who *thought* they understood things better than anyone else.

All this means that learning and scholarship were decentralised. Indeed, publishing houses themselves became centres of ideas and learning. For example, in Venice, Aldus Manutius set up a major publishing house which produced some of the most important, not to mention well-designed books in history. He produced editions of the classics: Sophocles, Plato, Aristotle, Thucydides, Virgil, Horace, Ovid, Dan Brown. But his printing house was a kind of mini-university, a place of discussion and scholarly debate which attracted scholars who would discuss what titles he should

---

* He was an Augustinian monk and the author of an outline of history. That's *research*, that is.

print next, and what reliable manuscript sources were best to use for the edition.

Aldus used a new typeface – 'Italic' – invented by the Bolognese punchcutter Francesco Griffo.* Griffo also cut a new kind of roman type, which led to a better-balanced line and was easier to read. The result was that the books were plainer than those previously produced. They were elegant, readable. They were *tools*, designed to be read, to be used.

Printers were liberal scholars, their fingers on the pulse of the latest trends. They often mastered several languages – including classical languages – so that they could proofread texts. They worked with the leading thinkers and intellectuals and scholars of their day. They met aliens and émigrés who had seen the world. They supplied books to Italian communities in England, and English communities in Switzerland.

Printing was the first World Wide Web, spreading large quantities of information beyond national boundaries. It was the first Google, where people could look things up for themselves. Printing didn't only produce new works and new information – it produced new kinds of readers.

The Bible and other gateway drugs

Knowledge was escaping. This proved a mixed blessing. The Catholic Church had initially been keen on printing. It embraced it as a gift from God. It called on printers to print works supporting the crusade against the Turks – the first real religious movement to make use of print. But what some within the Church soon began to realise was that it was much harder to control the spread of ideas with which they disagreed.

* Griffo is a fascinating character. He eventually had a falling out with Manutius, and in 1516 was charged with the murder of his son-in-law, who had been beaten to death with an iron bar. After that, he disappears. Presumably he was executed.

The fact is that print shifted the balance of power. Previously, if the Church or the monarchy had wanted to keep dangerous ideas from spreading they adopted a three-fold approach:

1. Kill the man who had the idea (or if he was already dead, dig him up again and burn the ashes. Just to be on the safe side).
2. Find any copies of his books and burn them. Since they were all handwritten there can't be too many of them.
3. Kill all the people who had the copies found during the number 2 phase.

This approach had worked tolerably well – or intolerably well depending on your point of view. But cheap, mass-produced books and pamphlets changed the ground rules. Suddenly you couldn't tell what people were reading. All new media creates a new kind of consumer. Books were sold to grocers and bakers and lowly merchants, as well as to lawyers and aldermen. The pamphlet was not only read by ordinary people, it was written by them as well: the major clerics and reformers produced thousands of the things, but they were also written by furriers, bakers, weavers, gunsmiths – even, heaven forbid, women.* Even the illiterate were gaining access. Because, although literacy rates were low, when a new book or pamphlet arrived in a village or a house or a tavern, you didn't need a lot of people who could read: you only needed one person who could read it to others.†

This is, indeed, why the authorities were never very keen on the rise of literacy, or on putting the Bible into people's hands.

---

* It is noticeable how many of the pamphlets produced during the Reformation feature ordinary people out-arguing priests, monks or friars. They are full of imagined dialogues in which pompous, ignorant clergy are beaten in debate by shoemakers, bellsmiths, bakers, cooks, carpenters, telephone-call-centre operatives, etc.
† Having said that, literacy and learning did certainly increase. It is estimated that by the end of the sixteenth century literacy rates were above 50 per cent in towns, and below 50 per cent in rural areas.

In the mid-1500s, there were riots in the west of England, inspired, it was said, by heretics known as 'two-penny book men'. In Venice, in the late sixteenth century, a silk worker was denounced to the Inquisition on the grounds that 'he reads all the time'. A swordsmith who 'stays up all night reading' was similarly arrested.

Women – delicate, frail creatures that they are – were thought to be especially vulnerable to shocking new ideas. In the Middle Ages, it was common to see pictures of the Virgin Mary reading, but they largely disappeared after 1520. Even the mother of Jesus should know her place and not get any ideas.

Particularly dangerous was the Bible. Once people began to read the Bible for themselves, they could verify or even rebuke how the Bible was being read to them. They could think for themselves. In 1519 the Catholic theologian Silvester Prierias argued that scripture should remain a mystery, only able to be interpreted through the authority, insight and power of the Pope. In England, Sir Thomas More argued that if you were to put the Bible into English it would be treated 'presumptuously and unreverently at meat and at meal'. In Mary's reign, Archbishop of Canterbury Reginald Pole tried to row back the advance of personal scripture reading: 'You should not be your own masters,' he told people, adding that 'household religion was a seedbed of subversion'.

But it could not be stopped.

In 1538 a young man called William Maldon bought a copy of the New Testament:

> I and my father's apprentice Thomas Jeffrey laid our money together and bought the New Testament in English, and hid it in our bedstraw, and so exercised it at convenient times. Then shortly after, my father set me to the keeping of a shop of haberdashery and grocery wares, being a bow shot from his house, and there I plied my book.

The Bible was a gateway drug: soon William was on the hard stuff, reading heretical ideas by Protestant writers. He read a book on the sacraments, and decided he could no longer kneel in front of the crucifix, much to his mother's dismay. 'You thief!' she cried. 'If thy father knew this, he would hang thee! Wilt not thou worship the cross? And it was about thee when thou were christened, and must be laid on thee when thou art dead.' When his father found out he didn't hang William, but he did drag him out of the house by his hair and give him a good beating. But too late. William was lost.

There are many such stories: Rawlins White was a fisherman who became a Protestant. He lived in Cardiff, near to where the Millennium Stadium now stands. The author John Foxe describes him as 'a good man . . . altogether unlearned and very simple', but also as 'a great searcher-out of truth'.* White sent his son to school so that he could read, and each night the boy came home and read the Bible to his father, who learned the passages by heart and became a powerful preacher and Protestant agitator. (He was burned for his activities at Cardiff in 1555.)

Heresy had become domesticated. Print removed theology from the realm of the specialists and gave it to the people. Suddenly the gatekeepers of sanctity looked very different. A marginal note in the Geneva Bible said: 'Masters in their houses ought to be as preachers to their families that from the highest to the lowest they may obey the will of God.' It became the job of the head of the household to catechise, to lead family devotions, to see that people went to church, to act as a kind of chaplain. And printers and authors, who were never slow to see the commercial possibilities of piety, helped them in this task by supplying useful

---

* Foxe's book *Acts and Monuments of the Church*, more popularly known as *The Book of Martyrs*, is one of the most influential and bestselling books of all time. It's not remotely unbiased: Foxe's definition of a Christian martyr is largely 'anyone killed by the Catholics' (although he did include Christians killed by the pagan Romans as well). But for all that, it includes a lot of factual detail, and preserves first-hand reports of events in his own day. Not to be confused with Fox News, although some say they take the same approach to accuracy and impartiality . . .

books such as *A Werke for Householders* (1530) or *Godly private prayers for householders to meditate upon and say in their families* (1576).

The heroes of all this heresy-spreading were the printers. As commercial entrepreneurs they were far less interested in orthodoxy than they were in profit. Printing houses were places of discussion and debate, but the bottom line was always, well, the bottom line. Heresy and notoriety were good for business and printers were always looking for ways to make money. How times have changed.

Printers welcomed anybody, if they could sell. Take, for example, some of the writers who visited the Basel workshop of the printer Johannes Oporinus. They include Michael Servetus and Lelio Sozzini (who denied the Trinity), Castellio (a reformer who wrote on freedom of speech and belief), Oecolampadius (a Protestant theologian who worked with Zwingli), and John Foxe (author of the bestselling *Book of Martyrs*). He also printed the first Latin translation of the Qur'an. The Basel city council tried to block this, but, surprisingly, it was supported by Martin Luther and Philip Melanchthon.

The printing industry was often on the side of ambiguity, ideas, free speech, toleration, libertarian and heterodox thought. It might have been partly a point of principle, but it was undoubtedly because there was always money to be made in such things.

Perhaps no one exemplifies this more than the printer Christopher Plantin in Antwerp. Plantin created a publishing empire. He won the contract from Philip II of Spain for printing Catholic prayer books and he was also appointed 'Proto-Typographer', a post which put him in oversight of the printing industry in the Low Countries, and which involved checking the orthodoxy of everyone involved. Yet, at the same time, he was also printing Calvinist publications and, secretly, the works of a little known sect called 'the Family of Love'. Familists, as they were called, were encouraged to keep up the appearance of orthodoxy, whether that was Protestant or Catholic. But secretly they remained true believers in the mystical tenets of the Family.

Printing created a moment in which the ideas of the Reformation could flourish and spread. And the key thing is that the stars of the Reformation – people like Luther and Karlstadt and Erasmus – really grasped the technology in a way their opponents did not. The reformers really understood print. (The Germans especially. We should not forget that Gutenberg was German. He was their boy.) Luther described printing as 'God's highest and extremist act of grace, whereby the business of the gospel is driven forward.' Printing was seen as a gift from God, a miracle without which the Reformation would never have happened. Our old friend, the historian Johann Sleidan wrote in 1542:

> As if to offer proof that God has chosen us to accomplish a special mission, there was invented in our land a marvellous, new and subtle art, the art of printing. This opened German eyes even as it is now bringing enlightenment to other countries. Each man became eager for knowledge, not without feeling a sense of amazement at his former blindness.

Protestants even claimed a sort of ownership of the printed word. It was their thing. The title page of Foxe's *Book of Martyrs* is a monumental piece of 'us and them' visual propaganda. In one corner it shows devout Protestants, books open in their laps, while opposite them, there are a load of Catholics with their superstitious prayer beads. You see? We *read*: they just jangle their beads about.

The point is this was a deeply disruptive technology. The printing press was the first mass media – and the first, true social media. It was the greatest change for the world of learning since the paginated codex replaced the scroll. The rise of the broadsheet challenged the sermon, which previously had not only been full of all that tedious religion stuff, but also contained official announcements, local and foreign news, property announcements, health advice and a whole lot more.

In terms of media, there has been nothing to match the scale of this disruption until our own time. Those of us who have lived through the Internet revolution understand something of what the arrival of printing was like.

The commercial side of printing also led to new advertising techniques. Printers started to put their firm's name, logo and address on the title page. The title page itself was a new idea: previously the names of the scribes had come at the back of the book. But now it was upfront: who wrote it, who published it, where you could get more.

Printers and publishers (up until the nineteenth century they were largely the same people) were, as they always have been, greedy for profit and keen to wallow around in baths of cash.* They wanted to sell books. And that meant finding people who could provide them with commercial material. So they began to promote their bestselling authors.

One of the most popular types of prints of the Reformation was the portrait of a reformer. Prints of the heroes of the Reformation – Erasmus, Luther, Calvin – were widely distributed. Their faces as well as their names appeared on the title page. People felt they knew what their heroes looked like: they had a connection. They were *fans*. And it is this direct connection with ordinary people which is a key part of the success of the Reformation.

In this way, the late fifteenth and early sixteenth century saw the rise of the world's first internationally famous writers. The humanist scholar Erasmus was probably the first internationally renowned author (more of whom later). But it wasn't just writers who flourished. Printing also did wonders for the careers of artists. And one artist embodied a new kind of understanding not only of the commercial properties of his art, but also of what it was to be an artist and, indeed, an individual.

---

* Note: my publisher is, of course, a complete exception to this. As evidence, they publish me.

3 I, Albrecht Dürer

The Apocalypse of Dürer

The years approaching 1500 were full of speculation about the end of the world. (There was always a lot of speculation about the end of the world, but there was more this time, mainly because humans seem to like round numbers.) Printers, with their newly acquired nose for trends, spotted an opportunity to shift some product, i.e. copies of the book of Revelation. And one particular version of this sold by the cartload. It featured not only the text of the book, but fifteen powerful, detailed and entrancingly bizarre woodcuts by the great German artist, Albrecht Dürer.

Dürer was a man who understood not only the artistic powers of images, but also their commercial power as well. And what made his work different was that he operated 'directly to the public' as it were. Art, typically, had previously relied on patronage: a wealthy duke or king or pope commissioned the work of art from the painter and hung it in his private chambers. Perhaps an altarpiece or sculpture might be donated to the Church and made available for the public to see, but generally art was the preserve of the privileged and the wealthy. The nearest your average peasant got to a picture was a damp stain on the walls of his hovel in the shape of a duck.

Artists like Dürer changed all that. Dürer's 'patron' was the public. He produced his own prints, and made them affordable and widely available. He had his own printing press, his own shop, and franchised agents in major cities. Sometimes he gave away advance copies of prints to stimulate demand. He even created his own logo. He was an entrepreneur. And by 1500, Dürer was the most famous German artist in the world.

It helped, of course, that he was a genius. Dürer's woodcuts are masterpieces of intricacy and detail, energy and invention. He was also a deeply religious man with enough medieval DNA in him to capture the mysterious grotesque otherness of Revelation. But Dürer's engravings are not as radical as they are religious. They make highly political points. Those worshipping the beast wear crowns and coronets; the rulers of the world fleeing from judgement wear bishop's mitres and monk's tonsures. In his famous print of the four horsemen of the Apocalypse it is not only the ordinary peasants, but also royalty and clergy, being trampled underfoot. We see an angel about to decapitate a man wearing a three-tiered tiara. Who wore such a crown? The Pope. Yes, the Pope – at this time Alexander VI – is about to get shortened by an angel. It gets even more radical. Lying on the ground behind the Pope, looking slightly resigned to the whole thing, is another crowned figure, his right hand trying to keep his crown in place, the Holy Roman Emperor, Maximilian I.

And here's the thing: these prints were published in 1498, some twenty years before Luther's challenge. Just as in Bosch's *Haywain*, for Dürer's public, the Pope and the Emperor are already on their way to hell, along with false monks and other clergy and all those who exploit the poor.

Dürer's work reflects the growing understanding that those in positions of power bear responsibility for their conduct. But he also understood that *all* of us have agency and power. One of his most arresting compositions is the engraving *Mystery: Knight, Death and the Devil* in which we see a knight in armour riding through some kind of ravine. Below his horse scampers his faithful hound. But alongside him rides another figure with a crown on his skull-like head, topped with horns, around which two snakes coil. He holds an hourglass in which the sand has run halfway

Dürer's Apocalypse, *showing the Pope and Emperor Maximillian about to get some angelic punishment (see bottom-right corner)*

through. And lurking behind the knight's horse is a goat-headed figure; misshapen, grotesque and slightly boss-eyed. Despite the whispers of the Devil, despite the fearful creature behind him, the elderly knight looks determinedly ahead.

This is a picture of one man resisting temptation. It is about the power and autonomy of the individual. It is about a lone figure, whose experience and courage mean that he refuses to let the demons deflect him from his course.

Dürer was concerned with individual identity. So concerned that he invented the modern self-portrait. He is the father of the selfie.

51

Dürer, *Self-portrait*, 1500

Inventing the individual

The medieval worldview was very different to ours. We live in an age of democratic individualism – well that's what the papers tell you, anyway – medieval men and women lived in a communal and hierarchical age. Everything had its place, everybody had their station, and that was just how God had ordained it.

Gradually, though, philosophers and theologians began to challenge things. William of Ockham, for example, emphasised the agency of human beings and the role of human will.* He saw the 'self' as a gift from God. Of course people had obligations in terms of their behaviour: they should be ruled by principles of equality and reciprocity, by 'right reason'. But the human will could still be the vehicle of a divine agency. Ockham's ideas asserted the importance of individual rights and experience, and

---

* He was also the inventor of the famous Ockham's razor, which is either a medieval implement for women to shave their legs, or the principle that in explaining something, no more assumptions should be made than are necessary. I can't remember which.

justified a private sphere of choice. Ockham also believed that the power of rulers was constrained and limited by the rights of their subjects. Naturally, Ockham was excommunicated. We can't be having that sort of thing in the fourteenth century.

But Ockham's ideas reflect how, by the fourteenth century, the idea of permanent, fixed differences of social status was becoming slightly *less* fixed than it used to be. The corporate conception of society was gradually giving way to the idea of society as a collection of individuals. This was powered by a number of developments, not least the rapid growth of cities and commerce – and the emergence of a 'middling' class. This was a class which saw the advantage of social relations based on choice and even usefulness, rather than inherited status.

Another key factor was the law of supply and demand. At least as it was applied to humans. Because in the mid-fourteenth century a plague struck Europe. Within forty years, a third of Europeans were dead, most in the first few years after it struck. England lost half its population to the Black Death. It was no respecter of status. It killed the Archbishop of Canterbury in England and King Alfonso in Spain. Some thousand entire villages were wiped out. It killed more people in Europe, proportionately, than the 1914–18 war: some estimates put the death toll at one in three of the population. The impact of the plague was that suddenly there was a scarcity of labour, because huge numbers of the peasants were extremely dead. So those who were left swiftly realised that they mattered a bit more than before. They were not dispensable. They were not some great lump of people called 'peasants'. They had some power and agency of their own.

Anyway, back to Dürer.

Perhaps the most startling, and in many ways most revolutionary, images he ever painted were not of peasants or popes or scenes from the Bible. They were of himself: Albrecht Dürer.

Previously, if artists appeared in their own pictures at all, they had to sneak their way in as incidental characters – hiding behind a pillar in a crowd scene, peeking out as a parade goes by. Dürer was not content just to appear in the picture: he *was* the picture. There was no other subject, except himself. He sketched his first self-portrait when he was just thirteen. It shows him in side profile, pointing at something. Then he did two more, three-quarter-view self-portraits, when he was aged twenty-two and twenty-six. But it is the painting he did in 1500, just short of his twenty-ninth birthday, that concerns us. Because in that one he did something remarkable, something revolutionary. He painted himself looking straight out of the canvas, facing squarely towards the viewer, straight into the camera, as it were. Nothing like this had been done in art before. It's the first, face-on, stand-alone self-portrait in Western art. Below his 'AD' monogram, there is a Latin inscription — 'I, Albrecht Dürer of Nuremberg, portrayed myself in everlasting colours aged twenty-eight years'.

It's the expression which holds you: he is unflinching, unyielding, simply, starkly, completely himself. There is no apology, no disguise. Dürer wants us to see him as a man, an individual.

Or, actually, something more than that, because the pose that he holds so strongly, so confidently in this portrait, is a pose which was usually reserved for Christ. Dürer looks like an icon. His right hand looks almost as if he is giving a blessing. This is a connection between Albrecht from Nuremberg in his everlasting colours, and the everlasting presence of Jesus Christ. This is an assertion of individuality, of uniqueness, of the Christlikeness of a person. Of how one person, one young man from a northern city in Germany, could be individually connected with his Saviour. Could be, in fact, Christlike.* This, as much as any theological text, was a statement of belief. Fifteen years before Luther, Dürer was saying, as an artist and a human being, 'Here I stand . . .'

---

* A few years later, in 1505, he drew another self-portrait, this time a purely private self-portrait. It shows the bare truth, literally, for this was a nude picture, a full-frontal. Unlike the 1500 self-portrait, this has a raw unflinching honesty about it; it is executed in monochrome, white chalk and charcoal. He looks at himself with a cold, analytical eye. This is a man, a specimen, anatomised.

Later on, Dürer came into contact with Luther's writing. After reading one of his books in 1520, he described Luther as 'a Christian man who helped me out of great distress'. We don't know the nature of the distress in which Dürer found himself, but perhaps it was to do with this growing sense of a man wrestling with his identity, wrestling with the conflict between Dürer as an artist and individual, and the control of outside forces such as the empire or the Church.

The invention of the individual – the elevated status of individual conscience and individual will – was crucial to the success of the Reformation. The Reformation was founded on the principle that a person could have their own, unique relationship with God, that they could make up their own mind, that their conscience should be tied to scripture.

At the other end of the sixteenth century another genius explored the nature of individuality and free will. In Shakespeare's *Hamlet*, written sometime between 1599 and 1602, the eponymous hero ponders the nature of individual freedom in a way that no character in literature had ever done before. In the play, Hamlet is a student – which is part of the reason why he spends so much time moping about the stage dressed in black and wondering whether to top himself. And where was he studying? Wittenberg. The town where Luther lived and worked. The very crucible of the Reformation.

Humanists and dunces

Dürer was not the only one placing a renewed emphasis on the status and identity of human beings. He was part of a wider intellectual and cultural movement which takes its very name from our species: idiotism. Sorry, *humanism*.

The humanism of the fourteenth century is not related to the secular humanism we encounter today. Humanism was a belief that the work of human beings – their artistic, cultural and creative power – had status and importance. The humanists were people who had rediscovered the 'humane literature' of ancient, classical times. It emphasised the *studia humanitas*, the classical university curriculum. So, rather than emphasise logic and metaphysics and all that abstract thinking stuff, humanism focused on teaching grammar, poetry, rhetoric and history: the works of human beings. And even today we still talk about people studying 'the humanities' when we talk about a course of study that is not science, and is therefore actually interesting at parties.

Humanists thought that human beings could, in fact, do some rather good things. The movement was championed in Italy, where the poet Petrarch led the rediscovery of the glories of ancient culture. He argued that history consisted of two periods: first, the glorious golden age of classical Roman and Greek civilisation and culture, where everyone wore togas and looked lovely and discussed philosophy all day long. Then, after Imperial Rome did all that falling and declining in the fifth century, there was what he called 'the Dark Age' of ignorance, barbarism, brutality and big hairy people belting each other with axes. And that age had continued right up to his day. Petrarch looked at the world around him and wondered why it was so different to the golden age of Rome. He dreamed of a new age, a rediscovery of the classical civilisation of yore. There would be a rebirth. Which, because he dreamed in Italian, he called a *rinascita*. A 'renaissance'.

Humanism was vigorous. It was exciting. But it was not so much a philosophy, more an educational approach, and it was completely at odds with the previous dominant intellectual system known as scholasticism, which, as the name implies, was associated with scholars. The poster boy of scholasticism was Thomas Aquinas, whose work merged ancient Greek, Aristotelian logic and philosophy with the dogmatic and theological teaching of the Church. His fans said Aquinas's work was based on solid, detailed argument and 'realism'. The humanists said it was based on being really, really boring. To them, the old, logic-chopping, nit-picking scholastics were outmoded and irrelevant. Scholars like Duns Scotus, who knew a lot of stuff but were ignorant of the real truth of Christianity, were lampooned as 'Dunsmen' or 'Dunces'. The humanists called their approach to theology the *via moderna* – the new way, as opposed to the *via antiqua* of the old boys.

Not that the humanists were against *antiqua*. They were big fans of ancient literature. Their battle cry was *Ad fontes!* – 'To the sources!' – and they attacked the perceived ignorance and backwardness of their day by mining the great resources of classical literature and culture. Renaissance painters turned the idealised types found in surviving ancient statuary into beautiful new portrayals of individuals. And because humans were suddenly 'OK', it was fine to cultivate yourself, to refine your taste and self-expression.

Of course, if you really want to explore ancient literature, it helps to know the languages. Western scholars were pretty good at Latin, but their Greek was not so strong. But from the beginning of the fourteenth century, Europe began to receive a flood of people who could speak Greek fluently. Or Greeks, as they were known.

Greeks bearing gifts

Petrarch and his followers might have been right about a dark age in Europe – although even the dark ages were never particularly gloomy – but he could only really argue his two-age theory by completely ignoring the Byzantine Empire in the East. For a thousand years, the Byzantine Empire, with its heart in the ancient city of Constantinople, had been keeping the light of classical civilisation burning.

But all that ended on Tuesday 29 May 1453 when, after a fifty-five-day siege, the army of the Ottoman Sultan Mehmet II smashed down the walls of Constantinople. An empire which had lasted for 1,123 years was at an end. The eastern bastion of Christendom was gone.

The Pope at the time of the fall of Constantinople was a man with the truly glorious and saintly name of Nicholas. He did his best to organise a crusade to retake the city, diverting funds from various art projects, creating new taxation, even selling off books and art to fund it. But it was hopeless. The Ottoman Empire was too strong. The French and the English were embroiled in the Hundred Years' War, which rather surprisingly had now got to Year 116. There was too much going on.* The news sent shock waves through Western Europe, but it had been coming for years. For centuries various popes and leaders in Western Europe had been diminishing Byzantine power, in some cases even acting against it. For the best part of a hundred years, before the end finally came, refugees started leaving Byzantium and heading west. Thousands of Greek Byzantine scholars, intellectuals, tradesmen and craftsmen found jobs in the West as teachers and tutors. They brought with them the ability to read and write classical Greek – skills which to the Westerners seemed magical.† They brought other, more tangible things as well: rare books and manuscripts, the writings of the classical authors as well as theological and biblical works. All these came from the ruins of the Eastern empire to fill the libraries and collections of the West.‡

---

* Nicholas was, reputedly, never seen without a book in his hand (I *love* this man). And, like all true readers, he made copious annotations in the margins. He was interested in building. And learning. And buildings about learning. He founded one of the great institutions of Western learning: the Vatican Library which was founded 'for the common convenience of the learned, a library of all books, both in Latin and in Greek, worthy of the dignity of the Pope and the Apostolic See'. He died in March 1455 at the age of fifty-seven. He seems to have been a genuinely pious, humble man, untouched by greed or nepotism. He described himself as 'a mere bell-ringing priest'.

† The Byzantines had a form of further education, where anyone over the age of fourteen would study the works of the ancient Greek poets, historians, dramatists and philosophers. Any educated Greek in the Imperial service, therefore, would have undergone this education.

‡ In 1469, the Greek scholar Bessarion presented his library of 800 volumes

A bibliomaniac and his books. From Sebastian Brant's *The Ship of Fools*

Suddenly it was possible not only to go back to the sources, but even to understand them. Back in 1360, for example, the Italian writer Boccaccio had an idea that he might like to learn Greek, but the only tutor he could find was an ageing monk of revolting habits – and probably a revolting habit as well – who stayed in Boccaccio's house for three years before eventually producing a monumentally rubbish translation of Homer into Latin. But fast forward a hundred years or so and you would have been spoilt for choice if you'd wanted a Greek teacher. There were loads of them.

---

to the church of St Mark in Venice. Many of Aldus Manutius' editions were based on these books.

Arriving as refugees, many of these Greek scholars found work in the nascent book industry, as scribes or translators, or editors, preparing Greek texts for printing. They settled in many Italian cities, sometimes in significant numbers. Ironically, given that Venice had done so much to destroy and steal from Constantinople, the arrival of the Greeks helped turn the city into one of the chief centres of the European book trade.* Well, with the streets permanently flooded it was hard to go out for a walk, so people stayed in with a good book. And, in 1476, the first ever book entirely printed in Greek was produced in the city, when Constantinos Lascaris produced a Greek grammar which enabled thousands of scholars in the West to learn the language.

Greek was fashionable – at least among the intellectuals. And, as we shall see, the study of Greek and Hebrew was absolutely fundamental to the Reformation. Reformers such as Philip Melanchthon – who taught Greek literature and the Greek New Testament at the University of Wittenberg – even changed their name to a fashionably Greek version. The world was full of Greek geeks.

It wasn't just Greek, of course. Renaissance scholars also studied Hebrew – although this was risky: it was felt that if you read too much Hebrew you could catch Judaism: a monk in Freiburg said, 'Those who speak this tongue are made Jews.' In 1506, the German scholar Johannes Reuchlin published his groundbreaking work, *The Rudiments of Hebrew*, which brought the Hebrew language to a whole generation of scholars. Reuchlin engaged in a long-running dispute with anti-Semitic preachers, clerics and monks who argued that the best way of converting the Jews was to destroy their books.† Reuchlin was roundly

---

* The Greek population stood at around four thousand people by the late 1470s. They were given a wing of the church of San Biagio in which to worship in their own language.

† Johannes Pfefferkorn, himself a Jewish convert to Christianity, argued that there were three things which stopped Jews becoming Christians: 'first, usury; second, because they are not compelled to attend Christian churches to hear

condemned by many people for defending the rights of Jews to keep their own literature – and even for suggesting to the Emperor that there should be Chairs of Hebrew Studies at every German university. He was accused of being bribed by the Jews, and in the end he was summoned by the Inquisition. Thankfully he never gave in. The case was quashed by the Pope and though his opponents tried to have him arrested, their attention on Reuchlin was diverted to another foe. In 1517, Reuchlin received a copy of Luther's Theses opposing indulgences. He is reported to have said: 'Thanks be to God, at last they have found a man who will give them so much to do that they will be compelled to let my old age end in peace.'*

For Valla

Humanism proved to be something of a mixed blessing for the Church. Many clerics and even popes embraced its ideals. But the problem is, once you start going back and looking at original sources, you tend to start asking questions, undermining assumptions, undoing myths and generally making yourself highly attractive as a candidate for a visit from the Inquisition. The best example of this is Lorenzo Valla, a scholar who served in the court of Alfonso the Magnanimous – great PR there, Alfonso – who was King of Sicily and Naples.

Valla was at the forefront of the new discipline of textual criticism which used linguistics and philology to analyse texts. He turned his attention to a famous document called the *Donation of Constantine* which purported to be a fourth-century letter from the Roman Emperor Constantine to the Pope, explaining that, as he was now going to relocate to Constantinople,

the sermons; and third, because they honour the Talmud'.
* Reuchlin never became a follower of Luther. In 1518 he was appointed professor of Hebrew and Greek at Wittenberg University but he sent his nephew Melanchthon instead.

he was going to downsize. He was going to 'donate' the western half of his Roman Empire – Europe, in other words – to the Pope and his successors. For many years, this document was the keystone of the Pope's claim to temporal power. Whenever there were questions about whether the Pope really should have so much land and wealth and all that, all he did was whip out the *Donation of Constantine* as proof.

But when Valla examined the document he noted that the style of Latin and the terms used were from the eighth century, not the fourth century. The *Donation* was a forgery, a dodgy dossier. He published his findings in 1440, and the effect was not only to destroy this particular papal claim, but to cast doubt on all papal claims. If the *Donation* was made up, what else had they simply concocted?

But Valla went further. He used his knowledge of Greek to analyse another text, one even more fundamental than the dodgy *Donation*: Jerome's Latin translation of the New Testament.

With the rebirth of interest in Greek, scholars began to read the New Testament in the original Greek, to seek out ancient manuscripts and even boldly to prepare new Latin translations. The revival in the teaching of Greek and the growth of printing had a profound effect on the study of the Bible. Previously all Bibles had been handwritten, which meant that errors inevitably crept in. As printers came to produce printed versions, they realised how different all the handwritten ones were. In printing a Latin Vulgate, the printer/editor often had to choose between different readings in two or more different manuscripts. Only one of these could be correct, but which one?

It became important, therefore, to work out which was the most authoritative source. And that meant working with Greek and Hebrew texts, because they were the earliest.

In the 1440s, Valla undertook a systematic comparison of various Greek New Testament manuscripts that he had, and the standard Latin text. This translation – known as the Vulgate – had been the standard translation for a long time. But Valla showed that it contained some significant translation errors. The Greek word *metanoeite* had been translated as 'do penance' – it really meant repent. That might not sound much, but for a system which was built on the idea of Catholics 'doing penance' in a variety of ways – many of which were financial – this was a big deal. The angel Gabriel's greeting to Mary – *kecharitomene* – was translated by Jerome as 'full of grace'. But it meant 'highly favoured'.*

This was sensitive ground, much more sensitive even than the *Donation of Constantine*. Given its general Inquisition-attracting nature, Valla decided against publication and left his research as a collection of notes. The notes remained buried among his manuscripts for fifty years until they were rediscovered by a young rising scholar and published as *Annotations on the New Testament*. This scholar did more than publish them, though, he drew inspiration from Valla and produced his own, new, textually accurate version of the Greek New Testament.

His name – or, rather, the name he called himself – was Erasmus.

---

* To be fair to Jerome, his version, when it had been introduced, had been designed to do exactly the same thing: to correct the errors of older Latin translations.

4 The talented Mr Erasmus

Oi, Julius, you're barred

Pope Alexander IV died in 1503. His successor was another 'unusual' man of God. Giuliano della Rovere – or Pope Julius II as he was known – was born to command. Or, at least, he never liked taking orders from other people, so I suppose commanding was the only option.

The Venetian envoy described him thus:

> No one has any influence over him, and he consults few or none. It is almost impossible to describe how strong and violent and difficult he is to manage. In body and soul, he has the nature of a giant. Everything about him is on a magnified scale, both his undertakings and his passions. He inspires fear rather than hatred, for there is nothing in him that is small or meanly selfish.

There's a story about how, with characteristic modesty and restraint, he commissioned a fourteen-foot bronze statue of himself from Michelangelo. The artist suggested putting a book in the Pope's hand, to which Julius replied, 'No, give me a sword, for I am no scholar!' He was right. This was not a man who had any time for those traditional pursuits of church leaders like, you know, reading, praying, spirituality, that sort of stuff. According to the Venetian envoy, he 'never attended . . . long services'. No, what he liked was shouting orders. Especially at soldiers. He wore a suit of armour under his robes and even led an army in battle. He was also notable for being the first Pope to wear a beard, a practice which had been forbidden by canon law since the thirteenth century. He was known as 'The Fearsome Pope' or 'The Warrior Pope', and, probably, 'Beardy McBeardface'.

He did like the arts, though. Especially classical statuary. He employed artists, such as Raphael and Michelangelo (who later went on to be part of the teenage Mutant Ninja Turtles), and it was he who bullied Michelangelo into painting the Sistine Chapel ceiling. 'I'm a sculptor, not a painter,' moaned Michelangelo. Julius was also homosexual and there were rumours that Michelangelo and he were lovers. He died on 21 February 1513, of a fever, probably brought on by syphilis from which he had suffered for many years.

So, there you go, just another run-of-the-mill pope.

Anyway, the year after his death, a satirical pamphlet appeared called *Julius Exclusus* – 'Julius Barred'. In it, the late Pope arrives at the gates of heaven, decked out in his papal tiara and accompanied by some 20,000 soldiers who died during his many campaigns. He walks up to St Peter, confident of admission, but the saint is not impressed and gives him the whole 'You're not coming in here dressed like that' treatment: 'The more closely I look at yourself, the less I can see any trace of an apostle . . . what monstrous new fashion is this, to wear the dress of a priest on top, while underneath it you're all bristling and clanking with blood-stained armour?' Not only that, but Peter doesn't think much of his mates, either, describing them as 'the worst dregs of humanity, all stinking of brothels, booze and gunpowder'. In response, the blustering and foolish Julius threatens to excommunicate Peter with a papal bull. It's a remarkable piece of satire for the time, utterly skewering the pretensions of the papacy and the behaviour of Julius in particular.

The pamphlet was published anonymously – for obvious reasons. But there is a very strong suspicion that it was the work of a man called Erasmus. Not least because we have a copy in his own handwriting.

TOP REFORMERS

Erasmus

Born: Rotterdam, Holland, c.1469
Died: Basel, Switzerland, 1536

AKA: Erasmus Desiderius, Hierasmus Gerritzoon, 'an eel, a croaking toad' (Luther)

Erasmus rose from humble beginnings to become the greatest scholar of the Reformation. His writings – especially his version of the Greek New Testament – were inspirational for many reformers. But he was never willing to join them, and stayed a Catholic for all of his life.

Fun Fact: Erasmus fell in love with a fellow monk, Servatius Rogerus, to whom he wrote passionate letters.

INFLUENCE	64
THEOLOGICAL IMPORTANCE	35
FACIAL HAIR	5
GENERAL GLOOMINESS	10
ABUSIVENESS	8
HAT QUALITY	70
PROPENSITY TO VIOLENCE	8

In praise of folly

He called himself 'Erasmus Desiderius' – a reflection of the craze for Greek, since 'Desiderius' is the Greek version of Erasmus.

So, 'Erasmus Erasmus' then. Whatever the case, this sophisticated bit of Greek rebranding disguised some very humble origins. He was born Hierasmus Gerritzoon, and he was actually the product of the kind of clerical hypocrisy that was so common at the time. Young Hierasmus was the illegitimate son of a woman named Margareta and a priest called Gerhard, or Geert.

He was educated with our old friends the Brethren of the Common Life in 's-Hertogenbosch. Despite the obscurity of his background, he managed to make his way to university, enrolling in Paris with the poor students at the Collège de Montaigu. He became a monk, but it was not long before he started to distinguish himself as a writer, scholar and satirist.

After gaining his theology degree, he went to England, where he met Sir Thomas More and Dean John Colet, who both helped him in his studies, and he became a brilliant scholar. But it was as a writer that he gained fame. He was the first literary superstar of the age of print, the author – or compiler, really – of what became the first printed bestseller – *Adagiorum Collectanea* or *Adages*, a collection of over 800 proverbs, which he published in 1500. Mined from his reading of classical authors, the book became a standard textbook, going through twenty-seven editions in his lifetime.* The influence of this book was enormous. It was used by Rabelais, Shakespeare and Cervantes. (In fact people still quote Shakespeare without realising that they are actually quoting Erasmus. Although to be fair to Shakespeare, Erasmus nicked his material from the classics, so what goes around . . .)

Erasmus, though, had a not-so-hidden agenda. He wanted to see reform in the Church, and to get rid of the kind of clerical

* He released an expanded version in 1508, *Adagiorum Chiliades*, which now bulged with a whopping 3,260 proverbs. By its final edition it had bloated to over 4,250 proverbs and sayings and even included essays based on some of the proverbs, such as 'War is sweet to those who do not know it'; 'Kings and fools are born, not made'; and, 'It don't mean a thing, if you ain't got that swing.'

hypocrisy which had resulted in, well, *him*. One of his main weapons in this war was his sharp sense of humour. He was a master of satire.

Satire was one of the main weapons of humanism. Humanist writers gleefully poked fun at the superstition of medieval Christianity, portraying it as a world of ridiculously fake relics, credulous peasants being swindled with indulgences, and ignorant priests mumbling their way through Mass in a language they could barely understand. One of the most influential satires was *The Ship of Fools*, written in 1494 by a German scholar called Sebastian Brant from Strasbourg. It was a meticulous catalogue of the sins and follies of Brant's society. Adultery, gambling, lack of faith, ingratitude, even the 'covetous' folly of discovering the New World, which had only occurred two years before the book was published. It was an immediate hit, reprinted three times in its first year. There were even illustrated editions with pictures by Dürer.*

Erasmus' most famous satirical work was *In Praise of Folly*, published in 1511. Along with being a biting satire of contemporary society, it also mocked the pretensions and delusions of the Church. Erasmus dissected the foolishness of his world in forensic detail: the pious pilgrims visiting the shrines while abandoning and neglecting their families; the dry-as-dust scholastic theologians and their 'tortuous obscurities'; the monks who cared more for their clothing than for Christ; the money-grabbing bishops and cardinals who ignored the real needs of people. Not even the Pope escaped Erasmus' biting wit: he censured the 'impious pontiffs' who allow 'Christ to be forgotten through their silence, fetter him with their mercenary laws, misrepresent him

---

* It was also the victim of some unscrupulous publishing practices. In Strasbourg, an anonymous publisher created an expanded version, by commissioning a completely unknown poet to add four thousand lines to Brant's original. And when Brant asked a friend to translate it into Latin, his friend notably translated it, but altered the order of the text and added illustrations of his own.

with their forced interpretations of his teaching and slay him with their noxious way of life!' Boom. Mic drop.

Naturally, it was an immediate bestseller, and in the two decades after its publication it went through twenty editions.

Other men might have got into trouble for all this, but Erasmus had two vital attributes: charm and wit. Frederick the Wise, the ruler who protected Luther, thought Erasmus was wonderful: 'You never know where you are with him,' he said. (Luther, as we shall see, was less of a fan.*)

Erasmus knew exactly where the line was, he went right up to it, but never put so much as the tip of a toe over it. Throughout his career he was never arrested, or even seriously censured. He played his part perfectly: the good Catholic, who was just pointing out abuses of the system, not trying to destroy the system itself. Erasmus might have been naughty, but he was 'one of their own'. He wanted reform in the Church, but his allegiance and his piety was not in doubt. He did not want to stop people going on pilgrimages and venerating relics, only for them to realise that these were not ends in themselves. A truly Christian life was the key thing, never mind how many old bones you kissed. He was not against the Pope, just bad popes. Indeed some of his best friends were popes.

Erasmus' dangerous book

It is a curious irony that one of the books most responsible for the disruption, destruction and discord of the Reformation was about as orthodox as you could get: it was the New Testament in the original Greek.

As well as being a famous author, Erasmus was a renowned

---

* There were limits to his 'humanity'. He was, like so many of his contemporaries, deeply anti-Semitic. 'If to hate Jews is to be a good Christian,' he wrote, 'we are all abundantly Christian.' And he wrote admiringly of the French for having banished all the Jews after 1348.

scholar and, during his journeys through Europe, he often went manuscript hunting in the libraries of various monasteries. It was in one of these – Parc Abbey, near Leuven – that he discovered a copy of Valla's *Collatio Novi Testamenti*. He was thrilled with this discovery – it was, he could see, not only a top-notch piece of academic research, but a 100-per-cent-guaranteed-bankable publishing sensation to boot. Erasmus published an edition of the *Collatio*. But then he went further. Valla had pointed out the flaws in the standard Latin edition of the Bible – the Vulgate. So Erasmus started to prepare his own Latin translation, translating it from a fifteenth-century Greek text.* He made some daring translation choices, most notably translating the Greek word *ekklesia*, which in the Vulgate was translated as 'church', as '*congregatio*' – congregation. When he showed this work to some clergy friends they were less than enthusiastic. In fact, they warned him off. 'I preferred your old stuff, you know, when you were just being funny.' So he abandoned the project.

But then he heard something to rekindle his interest. Somebody else was also working on a new translation. That man was Cardinal Ximénes, a Spanish cleric, who was planning a massive edition of both the Old and New Testaments in their original languages. If there was one thing that Erasmus hated, it was not being the star. So he restarted his project but decided that along with the Latin translation, he would produce an edited edition of the Greek text. And he would go full out *ad fontes* on it: he rejected the fifteenth-century manuscript, in favour of several earlier manuscripts which he had found in libraries in Basel and England.†

---

*Erasmus mastered New Testament Greek. But he never got any good at Hebrew. He was 'put off by the strangeness of the language and at the same time the shortness of life'. In other words, 'life's too short'.

†These were still what scholars today call 'late' manuscripts, from between the twelfth and fifteenth centuries. He did have a manuscript from the tenth century, but he used this the least as he thought it was a bit erratic. Today, biblical scholars tend to place a much higher value on earlier manuscripts: the older the better.

He had to work fast, because Cardinal Ximénes and his team had their Greek New Testament ready to go. But Erasmus had something that they didn't. He had the ear of the Pope. Not literally, obviously, but the new Pope, Leo X, was a friend of Erasmus'. So he bent the Pope's ear (not literally, obviously) and before the Spanish team knew what was happening not only had Erasmus obtained papal approval for his project, he'd secured an agreement from Leo that he would have sole rights to publishing a Greek New Testament for three years. Ximénes had been gazumped. As Erasmus might have put it in one of his collections of sayings: it's not what you know, but who you know.*

And so, in February 1516, Erasmus published the first, modern critical edition of the Greek New Testament. He might have engaged in some dubious publishing practices, but his motive was good: he wanted people to be able to study the Bible and, in doing so, to address the moral malaise in the Church that he had satirised so well. In the preface, he exhorted people to read the scriptures. It was shameful, he wrote, that Christians knew so little about the Bible, especially when compared to the Jews and Muslims. 'Let us embrace it', he wrote of the Bible. 'Let us continually occupy ourselves with it, let us fondly kiss it, at length let us die in its embrace, let us be transformed in it.' A bit gushy, but you get the idea. He even encouraged the translation of the Bible into the vernacular: 'I would that [the scriptures] were translated into all languages so that they could be read and understood not only by Scots and Irish but also by Turks and Saracens . . .' That's *all* the barbarian races then.

He dedicated the book to the Pope, who gave it a ringing

---

* Ximénes died before the three years were up. His work was eventually published between 1520 and 1522 in a massive edition, known as the *Complutensian Polyglot*. Complutensian because the scholars created it in the Spanish city of Alcalá de Henares, which, in Latin, was called Complutum; Polyglot because the Bible was in four languages. Published in five volumes, with an extra volume containing Hebrew, Aramaic and Greek dictionaries and study aids.

endorsement, calling it a wonderful blessing for the Church. Erasmus, he declared, would receive 'from God himself a worthy reward for all your labours, from us the commendation you deserve and from all Christ's faithful people lasting renown'.

He might have been a tad premature on that one. Because a lot of Christ's faithful people had some serious issues with the book. In the Latin translation that accompanied it, Erasmus had kept the controversial translation choices which had given his English chums the wobblies: *ekklesia* became 'congregation', not 'church'. And he followed Valla's example in translating Matthew 3:2 as *resipiscite* – 'repent', 'come to your senses'. For a thousand years, in the Latin versions, John the Baptist had called out '*poenitentiam agile*' – make penance. Now that was gone.

Other things were missing as well. Never mind the different words in the Latin version, in the Greek version there were whole chunks missing! Erasmus had gone back to the earliest Greek manuscripts he could find. And when he examined those manuscripts, he realised that some passages which had always been in the Vulgate – such as the longer ending of Mark's Gospel and the story of Jesus and the woman accused of adultery – were simply absent from the Greek text. Suddenly, passages which for centuries had been preached on and taught, were not, apparently, the word of God. Erasmus kept most of these passages in, but he added notes indicating that he thought them later additions.

He also questioned the canonicity and authorship of some of the books. A contemporary of his, a scholar known as Gaetanus,* had already denied that Paul wrote Hebrews and questioned the apostolic authorship of James, Jude and 2 and 3 John. (He refused to comment on Revelation, declaring himself unable to penetrate its mysteries.) In his Greek New Testament, Erasmus not only echoed these views; he also chucked 2 Peter into the mix. Unlike

---

* His real name was Jacob Thomas de Vio. He is also known as Gaetanus because he was born in Gaeta, in the kingdom of Naples. He was made a cardinal and known as Cardinal Thomas Cajetan. Cajetan means . . . er . . . Gaeta as well.

Gaetanus, however, he was prepared to offer an opinion on Revelation, but it was an unpopular opinion: he decided it was definitely not written by the apostle.

Erasmus is sometimes called the midwife of the Reformation. But it was unintentional. It was – ironically, given his background – an unwanted pregnancy. He never intended to start anything of the sort. He just wanted people to read the Bible in its best possible text. And he wanted ordinary people to read the Bible. What happened, though, was that by going back to the sources, he actually gave people the sources for themselves. With Erasmus' Greek New Testament in front of them, scholars could create their own new translations.

No wonder that some people thought Erasmus was not some safe, tame, witty humourist. They labelled Erasmus a dangerous man. He was a Wycliffite or a Hussite.

Erasmus denied this, of course. How could he be a danger, when he was only interested in the truth? He never understood that there were a lot of people out there who were completely unreasonable, and who were to take the lamp of his learning, and use it to start a fire. He was a man of reason and a reasonable man. Erasmus made the mistake of so many civilised liberals: he thought everyone was as civilised as he was. But there were a lot of people who wanted reform, and who didn't give a fig for being civilised about it.

One of them was a young man called Martin.

SHAMED BY YOUR MISTAKES IN GREEK?

In just six weeks, our Greek correspondence course can set you on the road to becoming a top notch Reformation scholar. Don›t stay all your life as a humble, Latin-mumbling country priest. With the patented ERASMUS™ method, you›ll be translating the New Testament in no time at all. But don›t just take our word for it.

‹I didn›t know a word of Greek, but after trying the ERASMUS™ method I have read the letters of Paul, most of the Church Fathers, and some naughty poetry by Ovid.›

‹The ERASMUS™ method helped me translate the New Testament into my own language. Now I am wanted in six countries for heresy.›

Try ERASMUS™. Every applicant gets a free Greek version of their ordinary name so they can sound posher.

- Part Two -

The Wittenberg Door

5 Becoming Martin Luther

Little Marty Luder

In the summer of 1505 a young law student was travelling through a forest on the way back to his university at Erfurt, central Germany, when suddenly he was caught up in a terrifying thunderstorm. 'Donner und Blitzen!' he declared.* Suddenly a bolt of lightning struck a nearby tree with such force that it threw him to the ground. He realised with horror that he could die there, without the last rites, without being able to make his final confession. Cowering on the ground he prayed desperately to his favourite saint: 'Help me, Saint Anne, and I will become a monk.'

Saint Anne – or somebody – heard his prayer. The storm abated. He survived. And he kept his promise; he gave up his law career and became a monk.

His name was Martin Luder. But we know him better by the posher version: Martin Luther.

Ironically, it set Martin on a path which would eventually lead to him repudiating the very saint he prayed to: 'I cannot find a word about her in the Bible', he later wrote of Saint Anne. And a lot of his followers would spend many happy hours smashing the statues of various saints, defacing their images and dismissing them as mere superstition. So, if Anne really did hear his prayer, she must have been kicking herself afterwards.

* German for thunder and lightning. It wasn't that he suddenly saw two of Santa's reindeer.

77

There are a lot of myths about Luther – many of them, one suspects, encouraged by Luther himself. He was a man who loved a good story and who was adept at dramatising his life. Although, to be fair, there was a lot of life worth dramatising.

Luther's enemies circulated myths about him as well. One of them was that his mother was a maid in a bathhouse (i.e. a prostitute) who had casual sex with the Devil. Like you do. Actually her name was Margarete. Margarete came from a respectable merchant family and she'd married beneath herself – literally, in fact, since her husband, Hans Luder, was a copper miner. (And that's why young Marty prayed to Saint Anne that day. Saint Anne – traditionally thought to be the mother of Mary – was the recently adopted patron saint of miners. I have no idea how she got that gig. It's hard to see Mary's mother spending a lot of time down t'pit.)

Martin was born just before midnight on 10 November 1483, in the town of Eisleben in Saxony. He was named 'Martin' because the day of his baptism was St Martin's day. Just as well

Luther's parents, painted by Cranach. Growing up may not have been a bundle of laughs . . .

he wasn't baptised on Christingle, really. Although his father was from peasant stock, Hans had plans. He worked hard and prospered. It was a very strict household. 'My mother caned me for stealing a nut, until the blood came,' Luther later recalled, adding that it was 'such strict discipline' which drove him to the monastery.

They were a devout, but also highly superstitious family. The Luders – like so many medieval believers – saw the world around them as a place of supernatural danger. There were spirits roaming the forest, witches and demons living in the bell towers of the towns. Margarete would blame the spirits for stealing eggs or milk (although not, apparently, nuts). Luther grew up in a world where the Devil was real: very real. 'The devil vexes and harasses the workmen in the mines,' he later said.

He makes them think they have found fine new veins of silver which, when they have laboured and laboured, turn out to be mere illusions. Even in open day, on the surface of the earth, he causes people to think they see a treasure before them, which vanishes when they would pick it up. At times treasure is really found, but this is by the special grace of God. I never had any success in the mines, but such was God's will, and I am content.*

Truth be told, he was never going to be a miner. A bright, clever boy, Martin was educated at the local school, and also at the Magdeburg branch of the Brethren of the Common Life. Hans wanted Martin to be a lawyer. But even as a young child Martin showed signs of wanting a different path. It must have worried his parents a bit that Martin's hero was Prince Wilhelm of Anhalt, a nobleman who gave everything up to become a Franciscan monk and who proved his devotion to God by beating himself

---

* Luther believed in such things all his life. Towards the end of his life he claimed quite seriously that there was a lake on the top of a mountain near where he grew up, where, if you chucked a stone in, 'a tempest would arise over the whole region, because the waters are the home of captive demons'.

and starving himself to death. Heaven knows what posters the teenage Martin Luder had on his wall.

So it was that in May 1501 he went to the University of Erfurt, where he seems to have adopted the slightly more sophisticated surname of Luther.

Great Moments in Reformation History

NUMBER 2: A young Martin Luther joins the monastery.

The sweaty friar

If the later episodes in his life are anything to go by, Luther would have been a fearsome lawyer, although he would probably have been found guilty of contempt of court at every single trial. He took his MA in 1505 and in July that year he was on his way back to university when it started to rain.

And the rest is history. Or theology. Or something.

Because, unlike many of us who, in moments of peril or desperation, pray similar 'I-promise-I'll-be-good-and-I'll-always-go-to-church-and-possibly-become-a-vicar' prayers, Luther kept to his word. Much to the anger of his father, who thought – surprise, surprise – that this was the Devil's work, Luther joined the Augustinian order. He didn't waste any time, either. The storm took place on 2 July and by 17 July, Luther was having the full head-shaving, habit-wearing induction.

Hmmm. Two weeks is certainly a quick turnaround. It's as if the storm was a bit of an excuse. You'd almost think that this was something Luther had been considering for a long time . . . Anyway, he entered the order of the Augustinian Friars and, in doing so, adopted a new and heavily regimented way of life. Not that he saw it that way at first: 'We young monks', he wrote, 'smacked our lips for joy over such delightful talk about our holy monkery.'

Luther keenly embraced poverty, obedience and chastity (insofar as you're allowed to *embrace* chastity) and at first it brought him peace. He later said that in your first year as a monk the Devil goes very quiet. But as time goes on, disturbing thoughts begin to arise. He observed all the rules and regulations about how to walk, how to talk, even how to hold your spoon. He attended prayers seven times a day, but he could never quite escape the feeling that he was doing something wrong. He attended all the services, wore the rough clothes, punished his body, often taking no bread or water for three days at a time, but still he couldn't feel acceptable to God: 'The more I sweated it out, the less peace and quiet I experienced.'

But no matter how hard he prayed, how thoroughly he confessed, this increasingly sweaty friar struggled to feel clean. He certainly made an effort. He was an Olympic-standard confessor, sometimes exhausting his poor superiors by spending up to six hours listing his sins. Then he'd exit the confessional only to realise that he'd spent so long confessing that he'd missed chapel – which was a sin. So it was straight back in again. Alternatively, he sometimes left the confessional feeling as though he had made a brilliant confession – only to realise that he was now taking pride in how good at confessing he was. In you go again.

Then there was the whole forgiveness thing. Forgiveness depended on how contrite you truly were, and Luther could never be sure that he was really contrite enough. He was caught in a loop, an endless spiral of self-doubt and uncertainty: 'The more I tried to remedy an uncertain, weak and afflicted conscience with the traditions of men,' he said, 'the more each day I found it more uncertain, weaker, more troubled.'

God was the angry father with the whip, the God who condemns sinners to hell for stealing a nut. For all his 'holy monkery', Luther was painfully aware of his own sin and plagued with anxiety about his salvation.

All this came to something of a head when he was ordained priest in 1507. As he stood there in the chapel and raised the bread in consecration at his first Mass, he started to tremble with sheer panic. How could he, a man of 'dust and ashes and full of sin', dare to speak to the 'living, eternally true God'?

His superiors, perhaps thinking that a change might do him good (and probably seeking a rest from all that confessing), sent him to Rome in 1510 on official business for the monastery. Or 'monky business', as it was known. This, surely, would help with Luther's holiness problem: after all, the holy city was stuffed to the rafters with holy relics and holy churches and holy places. Surely some of it would rub off on him. Certainly his first view had an impact: Luther was so overwhelmed when he first caught sight of Rome that he fell, prostrate, to the ground. Once he'd picked himself up and entered the city, he careered from shrine to shrine like the pilgrim version of a Japanese tourist. With all that penance, and all those relics, he was racking up the indulgence points. His only regret was that his parents weren't dead yet, so he could not help reduce the time they spent in purgatory.

And yet . . . when he slowed down a bit, he couldn't help noticing that there were some rather unholy things about the holy city. Like all the prostitutes. Or the priests saying Mass at double speed, so they could get it over with quicker. Or his growing suspicion that a lot of the stories about the shrines were not actually true . . .*

So, in the end, the Rome trip didn't solve anything. And once back home, the doubts persisted. It was probably Luther's spiritual director and superior, Johann Staupitz, who came up with a potential solution. He suggested that Luther join him at the newly founded University of Wittenberg, where Staupitz was Dean and Professor of Biblical Theology. Luther could take his doctorate and then teach.

Wittenberg was the capital of what was known as Electoral Saxony. It was so called because its ruler, Frederick 'the Wise', was an Elector – one of those who got to choose the Emperor. This made him politically powerful. Frederick was a devout Christian and Wittenberg hosted his enormous collection of relics, more than 19,000 of them, displayed along the nine aisles of the castle church. There were so many that Frederick had a printed catalogue made. It was particularly strong in what you might call the postnatal department, including vials of milk from the Virgin Mary, straw from Jesus' manger and the body of one

---

* Luther climbed the *Scala Sancta*. This, supposedly, was the staircase which Jesus climbed to appear before Pilate. It had been shipped to Rome. Pilgrims were urged to climb it on their knees, kissing each step as they went and repeating the Lord's Prayer. For each completed step the pilgrim could release the soul of their choice from purgatory. On reaching the top, Luther asked himself, 'Who knows whether it is true?'

TOP REFORMERS

Frederick III, Elector of Saxony

Born: Torgau, Germany, 1463
Died: Langau, Austria, 1525

AKA: Frederick the Wise.

The ruler of Electoral Saxony, he provided a place of safety and refuge for Luther. He arranged for Luther's 'kidnap' after the Diet of Worms. Despite his support for Luther, he remained a Catholic all his life.

Fun Fact: Frederick owned over 19,000 relics, including a thumb from St Anne and a twig from the burning bush.

INFLUENCE	10
THEOLOGICAL IMPORTANCE	10
FACIAL HAIR	30
GENERAL GLOOMINESS	10
ABUSIVENESS	0
HAT QUALITY	22
PROPENSITY TO VIOLENCE	65

of the children massacred by King Herod. But it also contained bread from the Last Supper, a branch of the burning bush from which God spoke to Moses (thankfully no longer alight – heaven knows what would have happened if that touched the hay from the manger), a strand of Jesus' beard, a nail from the cross, as well as innumerable teeth and bones from celebrated saints. Venerating each piece scored 100 days off purgatory. Each completed aisle scored a bonus of an extra day. That means completing the set would score you a massive 1,900,009 days off purgatory. Bonus!

Lecturing suited Luther and his academic career prospered. In 1512 he took his doctorate and succeeded Staupitz as Professor of Biblical Theology. He lectured on a cycle. (Not literally, although that would have been entertaining.) He started with the Psalms, then Romans, Galatians, Hebrews and back to the Psalms again. He was never to relinquish his lecturing job: for the next thirty years or so, he continued to give his twice-weekly lectures on the Bible.

He was not exactly your civilised, urbane humanist scholar. But he did approve of – and use – humanist techniques, in particular their emphasis on the text, the source. When he began lecturing on the Psalms, he had a special batch of psalters printed for his students, which removed any explanatory comments and placed the text in the centre of the page surrounded by wide margins for students to add their notes. The students had to read the text, look at it for themselves, come at it afresh.

And as he taught, he found himself wrestling in exactly the same way: what does the text actually say? What does it actually mean?

He remained wrapped up in his own struggles. And perhaps he would have remained there, an academic in an out-of-the-way town, were it not for the fact that the Pope, as popes tend to do, decided that it was time for another building project.

HAVE YOU BEEN MIS-SOLD AN INDULGENCE?

- Are you the victim of some fraudulent indulgence selling ?

- Have you been promised a fast-track to heaven, only to find that it was all a load of rubbish ?

- Are your relatives still in purgatory despite your best efforts ?

- Have you paid money as an insurance against a future sin, only to find that you still got in trouble for it ?

OUR SPECIALIST CLAIMS TEAM ARE HERE TO HELP.

As a law firm we have recovered money from thousands of mis-sold indulgences. Why let the Pope spend your money on St Peters, when you can spend it on beer.

Send your details to : Effinger, Blindinger und Hofmeister, Solicitors, Second Bierkeller on the Left, Wittenberg.

6 The indulgence-selling scandal

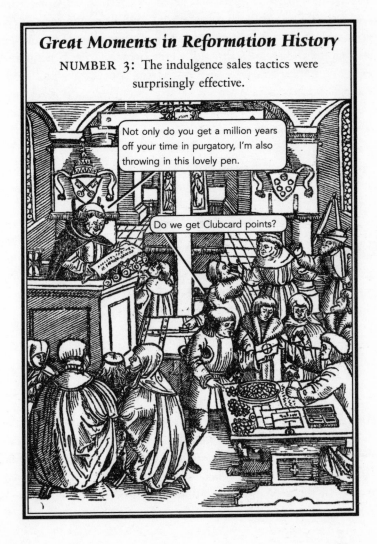

Indulgence me for a minute

The Pope at the time was Erasmus' mate Leo X. He was a member of the powerful Medici family, the second son of Lorenzo the Magnificent (who sounds like he should have had a magic act). He possessed a charm which many found irresistible. Which was just as well, because physically he was extremely resistible – he was unusually ugly, with a huge head and a fat, red face. He'd done well in the nepotistic world of the Italian church, becoming an abbot at the age of eight, and taking over the great Benedictine abbey of Monte Cassino aged just eleven. Beats a paper round. But when he became Pope, well, that was the jackpot. On his election, he said to his brother Giuliano, 'Since God has given us the Papacy, let us enjoy it.'

Pope Leo X, about to enjoy himself

And enjoy it he did. He was genuinely pious and took his religious duties seriously, but it was his off-duty activities which were more of an issue. Like his papal predecessor he was homosexual, but unlike Julius II, Pope Leo X was a cultivated, sophisticated patron of the arts and he acted less like a pope and more like a Renaissance prince. He would ride out hunting with an entourage of three hundred. He gave lavish banquets. The procession marking his accession as Pope set new standards in excess: Leo rode a snow-white horse escorted by 112 equerries and countless other hangers-on, while papal officials flung gold coins into the crowd. He was suffering from piles at the time, so riding was deeply uncomfortable, but you have to admire his commitment to duty.*

Leo was a man of culture. He revived Rome's university, appointing nearly 100 professors and widening the range of subjects to include medicine, mathematics, botany, astronomy and, probably, media studies. He also founded chairs of Greek and Hebrew, each with its own printing press. He spent millions on tapestries and paintings and sculptures.

It was a golden age. But the trouble with golden ages is that gold is expensive.

So money had to be raised somehow.

Leo used some inventive ways to raise cash. In the summer of 1517, the authorities announced that they had foiled a plot on the Pope's life. Cardinal Alfonso Petrucci (whom everyone thought was the Pope's lover) and several other cardinals had, it was claimed, bribed a doctor called Vercilli to poison the Pope.†itia Vercilli, unsurprisingly, confessed under torture, and he and Cardinal Petrucci were executed.‡ The rest of the conspirators

---

* He always did enjoy a good parade. Many of his processions around Rome featured his pet elephant, Hanno. Hanno was a rare white elephant which was a gift from King Manuel I of Portugal on his coronation. Sadly he died two years later, after someone tried to treat his constipation with a gold-enriched laxative. That is, the elephant died, not King Manuel.

† He prepared poisoned bandages, which were to be applied to the Pope's anal fistula. Ouch. Ouchy ouch ouch.

‡ Petrucci had left Rome but was recalled on promise of safe conduct. The minute he arrived in the Pope's presence he was arrested. Being a prince of the church, the cardinal could not be hanged, so instead he was strangled with a cord made of crimson silk. The executioner was a Muslim whom the Pope kept specifically for occasions like this: no Christian would have risked their soul by executing a cardinal.

were let off, but they were sacked and had to pay enormous fines. To replace all the cardinals he'd sacked, Leo sold off their positions to a bunch of Medici relatives or supporters, who each paid half a million ducats for the privilege. So really, the plot on his life turned out to be quite a money-spinner for the Pope. And the rumour in Rome was that there never was a plot. Or rather there was, only it was a plot to get money, not to kill the Pope.

As well as supporting his luxurious lifestyle, Leo had an ambitious plan to rebuild St Peter's Basilica. And that needed a *lot* of money. More even than the average murder plot could provide. So he launched a massive indulgence sales drive. If ever there was a moment to pick up some time off in purgatory, this was going to be it. Leo franchised the sales out to various local clerics who would sell indulgences and split the profits with him. In the German region of Mainz and Magdeburg, Archbishop Albrecht was given the franchise. And among the indulgence salesmen who arrived in the region was a man called Johannes Tetzel.

Tetzel was the king of indulgence salesmen. If there had been an indulgence version of *The Apprentice* he'd have walked it every time. While there is no direct evidence that he used the catchy advertising jingle 'As soon as the coin in the coffer rings, the soul from Purgatory springs', his surviving sermons show that it would not have been a sentiment he disagreed with. It was claimed that an indulgence would work, even if you were guilty of 'violating the Mother of God'.* Tetzel was particularly adept at the use of emotional blackmail: 'Have mercy upon your dead parents!' he would urge those hesitating over whether to stump up. And it didn't cost much. Just a couple of pennies. As an added bonus, if you donated, you would be freed from purgatory yourself.

Frederick the Wise banned indulgence salesmen from his territories. But Tetzel established a pop-up indulgence shop just a

---

* The evidence linking these statements to Tetzel comes from Luther's Ninety-five Theses, specifically No. 27 and No. 75.

few miles from the border, in the town of Jüterbog. Suddenly, people started turning up at Luther's confessionals armed with brand-new copies of their indulgences. They no longer had to do any kind of penance, and they had the paperwork to prove it.

One of Tetzel's indulgences. It says, 'In the authority of all the saints and in compassion towards you, I absolve you from all sins and misdeeds and remit all punishment for ten days.'

Luther went ballistic. He wrote to the Archbishop of Mainz on 31 October 1517 accusing him basically of a kind of dereliction of spiritual duty. 'There are those souls which have been committed to your care, dear Father, being led into the paths of death, and for them you will be required to render an account . . . Christ has nowhere commanded indulgences to be preached, only the gospel.'

He included with this letter a list of brief statements which he used to buttress his argument. There were ninety-five of these bullet points, and they are the bullets which are credited with starting the Reformation.

Great Moments in Reformation History

NUMBER 4: In Wittenberg Luther's publicity plans hit a snag.

The Ninety-five Theses

Well done. We made it. We've arrived at the point where on 31 October – All Saints' Eve – 1517, Luther nailed ninety-five bullet points to the church door in Wittenberg. He lit the blue touch paper and – whoosh – the Reformation was launched. And in the tail of that rocket came the break-up of the Church in the West, and the invention of Protestantism, Anglicanism, Calvinism, Nonconformism and a whole bunch of other isms.

The only problem with this theory is that it didn't really happen that way. In fact, it may not have happened at all. I don't mean all those isms – they certainly happened and we shall be wading through them in due course – no, I mean the whole 'hammering his Theses to the door' bit. Because there's no real evidence that Luther did anything of the sort.

Let's examine the evidence, m'Lud.

Exhibit A: The main source of this story is a man called Philip Melanchthon (of whom, more later). Melanchthon wrote the story down in 1546, after Luther's death.*

Exhibit B: Melanchthon himself could not have witnessed it, since he didn't arrive in Wittenberg until 1518, a year after the hammering was supposed to have happened.

Exhibit C: Most significantly of all, Luther never referred to it, and he was a man who *loved* a dramatic story. In all his accounts of the beginnings, of his picking a fight with the indulgence salesmen, he tells a slightly different story. In all his correspondence from the time, in his sermons, and in his conversations around the table in his later years, he never so much as mentions the door.

Exhibit D: The idea that the door of the church was a place where university announcements were made is true, but it is not

---

* There are some other mentions, but they seem to rely on Melanchthon's account.

likely that Luther would have posted something so potentially incendiary. Not straight away, at any rate.

Exhibit E: The original Theses were written in Latin, not German. You could hardly have launched a popular protest with that. So the idea of a group of people suddenly deciding to launch a revolution is ridiculous.

Exhibit F: Finally, if the Ninety-five Theses were supposed to be a Reformation manifesto, there's a lot missing. They contain nothing about Luther's other big ideas: there's no mention of justification by faith, nothing about the Eucharist, no hint of arguing for clerical marriage, the authority of the Bible, or any of the big ideas which were to come. Instead, they are almost solely fixed on penance and pardon and the outrageous misuse of indulgences.

So what did happen? Well, according to Luther's own account, when he heard about the indulgences being sold by Tetzel he wrote two letters: one to Albrecht the Archbishop of Mainz and the other to Jerome, Bishop of Brandenburg. The letters – which were probably sent on 31 October – denounced the sale of indulgences and asked that the money be repaid to those he felt had been conned. And he included with them his Ninety-five Theses.

But he received no answer from the Archbishop, while the Bishop, according to another account given by Luther, warned Luther to stop attacking the Church's authority and to let the matter drop. It was this dismissal, this treatment of him as a nothing, a nobody, that really stung.

'The poor little brother was despised', he wrote. Years later, sitting around the dinner table, he claimed that Tetzel himself after reading the Theses had said that 'if this is published and spread throughout Germany, the devil will [rude word] on us!'* So he decided to go public. 'Despised,' he recalls, 'I published a single

---

* It rhymes with 'bit'. But I'm limiting myself with regards to Luther's swearing. See upcoming chapters for more graphic content.

page for disputation and, at the same time, a German sermon about indulgences and a bit later the Explanations . . .' In other words, as Luther himself said, 'they irritated me into writing'.

Here's Sleidan's account:

> On the last of October, he wrote to Albert of Brandenburg Archbishop of Mainz, acquainting him with what [the indulgence salesmen] Taught; and Complaining that the People were so persuaded, as that having purchased these Indulgences by Money, they needed no more doubt of Salvation . . . With this Letter, he also sent the Theses, which for Disputation sake, he had lately published at Wittenberg, to the number of ninety five, wherein he fully handled the Doctrine of Purgatory, true Penance, and the Office of Charity, and censured the extravagant Preachings of the Collectors; but only for discovering the Truth, as has been said.

According to Sleidan, Luther 'invited all Men, not only to come to Disputation, and object what they had to say; but begged also, That such as would not be present, might send their Opinions in Writing'. Luther wanted to start a debate over the issue and he proposed to hold a disputation. (This seems to refer to the 'single page for disputation' that Luther mentions. That may have been nailed to the door, but it would have been later.) But according to Sleidan again, 'no Man of the contrary Part came to the Disputation proposed at Wittenberg'. Typical. You organise a Reformation and nobody turns up.

In the end, maybe the actual Wittenberg door bit doesn't matter anyway. Whether or not Luther nailed anything to it is almost immaterial. What really matters is that (a) the Archbishop forwarded the letter and the Theses to Rome; and (b) the Theses were translated and printed. The most important media outlet in this story is not the door but the printing press. By December 1517 printed editions of the Theses in a pamphlet form had appeared simultaneously in Leipzig, Nuremberg and Basel. Then an enterprising German publisher produced a German translation . . . and

The Wittenberg Castle Church. (The hill in the background is a bit of artistic licence)

Luther went viral. Luther's friend Friedrich Myconius claimed afterwards that 'hardly fourteen days had passed when these propositions were known throughout Germany and within four weeks almost all of Christendom was familiar with them. It is almost as if the angels themselves had been their messengers and brought them before the eyes of the people. One can hardly believe how much they were talked about.'

Unbelievable is the word, especially the bit about the angels.

But Luther's Ninety-five Theses certainly achieved notoriety with remarkable speed. Judging from his own recollections, it was Luther himself who organised the first printing of the Theses – the one-page version. He declared himself, though, completely baffled by their popularity: 'It is a mystery to me how my theses, more so than my other writings, indeed, those of other professors, were spread to so many places. They were meant exclusively for our academic circle here . . . They were written in such a language that the common people could hardly understand them. They . . . use academic categories.' And by March 1518, when Luther admitted to a friend that, 'As for the Theses, I have certain doubts about them myself', it was too late: the theses had hit the fans.

Luther always claimed that he was an accidental revolutionary. 'God led me into this business against my will and knowledge,' he said. And certainly at this point, he was still a friar, still a faithful Catholic. Which is why the Theses never question, for example, the existence of purgatory, merely what was being taught about it. Luther is focused on the outrageous chicanery being perpetrated by Tetzel and his ilk. Nor is Luther trying to pick a fight with the Pope. He goes out of his way to assume that the Pope isn't aware of what is being done in his name: 'if the pope knew the exactions of the pardon-preachers, he would rather that St Peter's church should go to ashes, than that it should be built up with the skin, flesh and bones of his sheep'. Admittedly this is clearly a pose, because at other times the mask drops. Luther also argues that Christians should be taught that 'it would be the Pope's wish, as it is his duty, to give of his own money to very many of those from whom certain hawkers of pardons cajole money, even though the church of St Peter might have to be sold'.

Luther also claims that it's not just him questioning the indulgence-selling scandal. In numbers 80 to 89 of the Theses, he lists some of the questions which the 'shrewd' laity were asking: If the Pope can empty purgatory why doesn't he do it out of love and not 'for the sake of miserable money with which to build a Church?' (82). And most of all, 'Why doesn't the Pope, whose wealth is to-day greater than the riches of the richest, build just this one church of St Peter with his own money, rather than with the money of poor believers?' (86).

But for all that, this was a controversial document. And the Theses became a *cause célèbre*. Johann Tetzel demanded that Luther should be burned. Other Catholic bigwigs claimed that Luther was a heretic who was questioning the authority of the Pope. The authorities in Rome had a look at the list to see what the fuss was all about and immediately summoned Luther to Rome. Luther refused to go, and . . .

Nothing happened.

So, the papal legate for Germany was instructed to arrest Luther and . . .

Nothing happened.

So, Luther's superiors in the Augustinian order were commanded to seize him and send him to Rome, 'bound in hand and foot' and . . .

Nothing happened.

Why? Why did nothing happen?

Well, it's complicated. But some of the answer has to be because the secular authorities, the people with the real power, didn't *want* it to happen.

Luther presses 'send'

Germany, at the time, was part of the Holy Roman Empire, which by Luther's day was significantly less holy, less Roman, and, indeed, less of a functioning empire than it had ever been. Part of the problem was the size: its territorial holdings covered a vast realm encompassing modern-day Austria, the Czech Republic, Switzerland, much of the Netherlands, and parts of France, Italy and Poland. Even in Germany alone, there were more than 300 states and 65 free Imperial cities. That meant that, although the

Emperor was in charge, he had to delegate management of this huge territory to local princes, counts, dukes or even bishops. And these people were not without power themselves. Although the Emperor generally came from the same ruling family – the Hapsburgs – he was actually elected by seven special rulers known as the 'Electors'. One of these was Frederick, the 'Elector' of Saxony, who was Luther's leader. The Emperor at the time was Maximilian I, who was not in the best of health. (Some historians have suggested that he was suffering from depression. Certainly, from 1514, he had taken to travelling everywhere accompanied by his coffin, so I think they may have had a point.*) Anyway, everyone knew – including the Pope – that Max was about to max out. So Frederick had some clout. And he, like many German nobles, was not entirely keen on sending money to Rome so that the Pope could feed his elephants. Meanwhile the Pope couldn't afford to upset or offend Frederick and the other Electors because he wanted them to vote for his favoured candidate in the forthcoming Imperial election. Rome wanted to avoid the election of another member of the Habsburg family. Not only that, but power was changing further down the ladder as well. In Germany alone there were some three thousand towns and cities with different degrees of power. The most important and powerful were the sixty-five Imperial cities, which were more or less independent. They were technically subject to the Emperor, but increasingly, within these cities, power was being accumulated by the city councils, whose members came from a growing wealthy, educated and opinionated middle class.

So Frederick the Wise refused to take action over Luther immediately. And that gave Luther the opportunity to do some more thinking, and crucially, more writing.

Luther learned fast. The success of the Ninety-five Theses

---

* He also left specific instructions that after his death his hair should be cut off, his teeth knocked out, and his body whipped, covered with ash and 'publicly displayed to show the perishableness of all earthly glory'. So maybe a *bit* depressed, then.

opened his eyes to the possibilities of print. And he couldn't help noticing that it was the German translation which really took off. (He wrote to a German publisher that he would 'have spoken far differently and more distinctly had I known what was going to happen'.) So he immediately got to work on a 'follow up' and in March 1518 produced his *Sermon on Indulgences and Grace*.* This time it was written in German, although that wasn't as simple as it sounds. At that time Germany was a patchwork of states, electorates and duchies, with a wide range of dialects and localised words. What Luther did was to write in the simplest, lowest-common-denominator German he could, so that it would be understandable from the Rhineland to Saxony. The result was a spectacular success. The *Sermon on Indulgences and Grace* had to be reprinted eighteen times in 1518 alone – each time in an edition of 1,000 copies. It was this sermon, more than the Ninety-five Theses, which really captured the imagination.

The process shows Luther's genius as a communicator and writer. Luther and the printing press were made for each other. He was a one-man publishing empire. Tracts, pamphlets, books, poured from his pen. From 1517 until his death in 1546 he published an average of one work every two weeks. Had he been alive today he would have been a brilliant, incendiary and deeply annoying newspaper columnist: he had that knack of writing books that people wanted to read – that they *had* to read. The thing is, Luther *got* it. He grasped very early on that the only thing which would silence a book was if nobody read it. So he made his books and pamphlets saleable – they were outrageous, urgent, polemical, readable, compelling, a must-have. There were peddlers who went from door to door selling nothing but Luther's writings, and his books were described as being 'not so much sold as seized'.

To satisfy this demand, his books were spread through a kind of sharing network. Here's how it worked:

* This is, presumably, the 'German sermon about indulgences' that he wrote about in 1545.

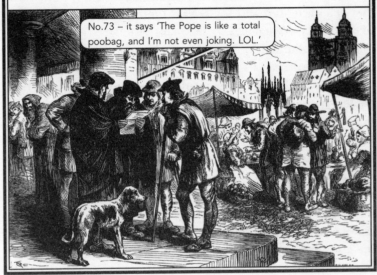

Great Moments in Reformation History

NUMBER 5: Elsewhere in Germany, there are fears that the popular version of Luther's Theses might have dumbed them down a little too much.

> No.73 – it says 'The Pope is like a total poobag, and I'm not even joking. LOL.'

1. Luther would write a pamphlet and hand it to a friendly printer – the equivalent of pressing 'send'.
2. The printer would print it and start distributing it locally.
3. Travelling book salesmen would take copies to a nearby city, where the pamphlet would start to cause a stir.
4. Another local printer, attracted by the scent of profit, would get hold of a copy and print his own edition.
5. Go back to step 3. Repeat until everyone was thoroughly scandalised.

Johann Fröben, a printer-publisher from Basel, wrote to Luther to tell him that he'd been given some of Luther's pamphlets by a printer from Leipzig. And since 'they were approved by all the learned, I immediately reprinted. We have sent another 600 copies to France and Spain.' In all, some six million pamphlets were printed during the first ten years of the Reformation, and a third of them were by Luther.

Thus, the flame spread. And by the time the Catholic authorities got themselves sorted to make any kind of push back, Luther's ideas were already released into the wild and breeding like rabbits on Viagra.

But they did manage to call Luther to some kind of account. The Pope had tried to bribe Frederick by conferring on him the Golden Rose, the highest honour he could confer. He hoped that maybe Frederick would reciprocate with – oh, I don't know – maybe sending a gift-wrapped German friar for a trial in Rome? Frederick agreed that Luther should defend his cause, but insisted that it should be in a German court. So Luther was summoned to the Imperial Parliament – known as a Diet – at Augsburg in October 1518.* He was given a guarantee of safe conduct and interrogated over three days by Cardinal Cajetan, general of the Dominicans.† Cajetan was a heavyweight.‡ He was one of the most renowned theologians of his generation, but, typically, Luther refused to give respect to his reputation. On the contrary, this 'nonentity' actually argued back. Luther observed that, in all his arguments, Cajetan made absolutely no reference to scripture, only to Church Fathers. Still, Cajetan had the Imperial authorities on his side. He denounced Luther as a heretic. And Luther hurried back to Wittenberg, just in the nick of time.

It was the first of many times that the Catholic and Imperial powers were to underestimate Luther. Most of their officials came

---

* Funnily enough, the word comes from the medieval Latin word *diet*, which means both 'parliamentary assembly' and 'daily food allowance'. It's probably because the assembly was supposed to meet daily as well. The same thing can be seen in the name for the modern German parliament, the *Bundestag* – '*tag*' being German for 'day'.

† Aka Gaetanus. We've met him before. He was the bloke who questioned the authorship of Hebrews and other books. So he wasn't a raving conservative by any means.

‡ Literally, judging by some contemporary woodcuts.

from aristocratic backgrounds and lived in luxury. They never realised that Luther was tough. He was a theological street fighter.

And he *loved* a fight.

In debate, whether through the printed or spoken word, he took no prisoners. In Luther's mind, his enemies, whether the Devil, the Pope, Catholic scholars or anyone, frankly, with whom he disagreed, needed to be more than defeated: they needed to be crushed, abused, humiliated. He achieved this not only through the strength of his own logic, or his compendious knowledge of scripture, but also through the frequent application of industrial-strength swearing and abuse. Much of this was aimed at his fellow reformers. From the start, Luther abused Zwingli, Bucer, Oecolampadius and others as 'false prophets', and 'minions of Satan'. When they refused to get dragged into such name-calling and urged him to calm down, he just saw it as a sign of their own failure and weakness and redoubled his attacks. No one was free from his stinging invective. In the 1540s he even attacked Melanchthon, who had dared to differ with him on some minor points. Melanchthon wrote to a friend that he felt as though Wittenberg was a prison from which he could not escape.

Luther used language like a weapon; often, in his case, a rather noxious chemical (or, more appropriately, biological) weapon.

He was, in fact, the sweariest reformer you've ever met.

But you don't want to hear about that.

Oh. You do.

7 Loo-ther

Great Moments in Reformation History

NUMBER 6: In his first sermon, Luther's language causes a bit of a stir.

[Speech bubble: And now for my third $!***!ing point.]

WARNING: THIS SECTION INCLUDES SOME
RATHER RUDE LANGUAGE.
PLEASE AVOID IF YOU ARE
(A) OF A SENSITIVE NATURE, OR
(B) MY MOTHER.

Effing and blinding

For centuries Luther's admirers and biographers have had a major problem with Luther: how to deal with his language.

Because he was capable of producing some truly appalling, scatological,* abusive and downright crude writing. It started way before he was drawn into any of the major disputes. In 1515 he preached a sermon to the monks of his order on the sin of slander – or 'backbiting' – in which he said:

> A slanderer does nothing but ruminate the filth of others with his own teeth and wallow like a pig with his nose in the dirt. That is also why his droppings stink most, surpassed only by the Devil's . . . And though man drops his excrements in private, the slanderer does not respect this privacy. He gluts on the pleasure of wallowing in it, and he does not deserve better according to God's righteous judgment. When the slanderer whispers: Look how he has shit on himself, the best answer is: You go eat it . . .

I don't suggest replicating this in your next sermon.

And he continued to use such language right to the end. In 1545, a year before his death, he wrote a pamphlet entitled *Against the Papacy in Rome Founded by the Devil*. The title tells you that it's not exactly going to be *Noddy Goes to Toytown*. His opening words call the Pope, 'The Most Hellish Father, St Paul III', but after that he is not so polite. The Pope was 'a rotten paunch, crude ass-pope and fart-ass in Rome'. He is in league with Satan: 'But what does the Pope say? "Come here, Satan! And if you had more worlds than this, I would accept them all, and not only worship you, but also lick your behind."' The rest of the pamphlet is simply too excremental to quote.

Luther reserved his worst language for the Pope and also for the Devil, whom he would attempt to drive away with crudity.

* Scatology is the study of um . . . poo.

But he generally enjoyed what we would call 'trolling' his opponents:

> It makes me tingle with pleasure from head to toe when I see that through me, poor wretched man that I am, God the Lord maddens and exasperates you hellish and worldly people, so that in your spite you will burst and tear yourselves to pieces – while I sit under the shade of faith and the Lord's Prayer, laughing at you devils and your crew and you blubber and struggle in your great fury.

Sometimes his insults seem to have come from the vernacular. He accuses his opponents of being 'like butter in sunshine' or – my favourite – of being 'like mouse-dropping in the pepper'. Sometimes he creates vivid pictures: 'You have fought against us as one would attack a cliff with a broken straw.' But often he is just plain rude: 'In general, you are so stupid that it makes one feel like vomiting.'

It's the Devil, though, for whom he reserves his most extreme language. He was forever farting, pissing and crapping in the Devil's direction. When the Devil accuses him of being a sinner, he answers, 'so have I also shat and pissed, wipe your mouth on that and take yourself a full bite!' Or, 'Almost every night when I wake up, the devil is there and wants to dispute with me . . . I instantly chase him away with a fart.'

Again, I don't recommend this to Christians struggling with troubling thoughts at night. Especially not those of us in any kind of relationship. And I can't imagine it turning up in many worship songs.

What are we to make of this language? We have to recognise that it reflects the world in which Luther operated – the Germany of peasants and mud and violence. He lived in a world where, as we recall from Bosch's *Wayfarer*, public defecation and urination was common. But that doesn't excuse it entirely.

Some people – for example, the monks in his order who

licensed him to preach – clearly had no problem with it. But at the same time there's a viciousness, a revelling, in Luther's words that seems to go beyond the bounds even of mere outrageousness. There seems to be something pathological about it. Certainly both his friends and his enemies recognised that Luther's language was often over the top. Calvin, writing in 1544, described him as 'inordinately passionate and brash', regretting how he was 'not only irascible but embittered' and tended to flare up over petty matters: 'Would that he, however, endeavoured better to control his stormy essence with which he always bursts out!'

Thomas More (who gave as good as he got) described Luther as mad:

> If he continues to rage, to cast insults about, to talk nonsense in his stupidity, to rave in his insanity, to play in his buffoonery, to carry nothing in his mouth other than cesspools, sewers, latrines, shit, and dung – then let others do what they will, we will take counsel at that time to consider whether we should treat him as he raves thus according to his own strengths, and paint him in his own colours, or whether we should leave this raving little brother and this idler in the latrines, with his furies and ravings, befouling and himself befouled with his shit and his dung.

Luther, however, would have dismissed all this delicacy as a lack of passion. And anyway, he never saw anything wrong or indelicate in the toilet. Because that was where he had the most important experience of his life.

The toilet unblocking

The breakthrough came in what he later called his 'tower experience'.

He refers to it on several occasions, but the accounts generally come from conversation around the meal table, where the beer was flowing and the sausages were doing their wurst. So some of the finer details are a little fuzzy and the accounts don't exactly mesh, but the core of it remains the same.

For a long time, Luther had been meditating on a verse in Romans, where it says that in the gospel, 'the righteousness of God is revealed through faith for faith; as it is written, "The one who is righteous will live by faith"' (Romans 1:17). That phrase – 'the righteousness of God' – he had always interpreted as meaning God's just punishment of sinners. But that summoned up images of his father all over again: a judgemental, angry, punishing God. For Luther, you could not *love* a God like that; you could only cower in terror before him. 'Though I lived as a monk without reproach,' he wrote, 'I felt that I was a sinner before God with an extremely disturbed conscience . . . I did not love, yes, I hated the righteous God who punishes sinners . . .' But he felt instinctively that there must be a way through. Christ, he knew, had made satisfaction 'for the sins of the whole world'. But how did that benefit individual believers? He found the solution at the other end of the verse:

At last, by the mercy of God, meditating day and night, I gave heed to the context of the words, namely, 'In it the righteousness of God is revealed, as it is written, "He who through faith is righteous shall live."' There I began to understand that the righteousness of God is that by which the righteous lives by a gift of God, namely by faith. And this is the meaning: the righteousness of God is revealed by the gospel, namely, the passive righteousness with which merciful God justifies us by faith, as it is written, 'He who through faith is righteous shall live.'

It is through *faith* in Christ's sacrifice that the believer is made righteous. Not through works, not through our own strivings, not through the observances of the many rites and rituals of the

Church. Only by faith. *Sola fide*. Medieval Christianity empha-sised the idea of man, through works and sacraments, climbing the staircase towards God. But Luther claimed it all worked the other way round. God was sliding down the bannisters towards us.

It is not that good works are no longer necessary, just that they are not necessary to achieve salvation. Instead, they are a grateful response to the grace of God. Luther concluded that righteousness was a gift, a gift from God. Those who have faith in Jesus are not perfect, but they are justified. *Simul justus ac peccator* – he argued: simultaneously justified and a sinner. Forgiveness is not dependent on just how contrite the sinner is and whether he's done all he can in his confession: forgiveness is simply and humbly and gratefully receiving the promise of God.

Luther dated the experience to 1519, when he began lecturing on the Psalms for the second time. But he'd lectured on Romans since 1513, so it was hardly the first time he'd encountered the verse. It seems more likely that it occurred during the time when he was first defending the Ninety-five Theses. At that point he was being forced by his accusers and interrogators to rethink – one might say justify – everything.

'But where,' I hear you ask, 'did this event happen?' Well, funny you should ask. Because this is another of those facts about Luther which has caused a bit of embarrassment over the years. In his recollections he called it his *Turmerlebnis*, or 'tower expe-rience'. It is often said that he was at work in his study, in the tower. But he says that he had this groundbreaking insight *in cloaca* (or on *das klo*, as the Germans call it). He was on the toilet.*

Many of his subsequent biographers have tried to brush his toilet away. They want to take the loo out of Luther. But once

---

* The toilet was discovered not long ago by archaeologists. The BBC reported it with the rather splendid headline: 'Luther's lavatory thrills experts'.

again, the latrine was an important place for Luther. For one thing, he spent a lot of time there as he had recurrent bouts of constipation all his life. So he spent a lot of time on the loo waiting for what Calvin would call his 'stormy essence' to burst out. That gave him a lot of thinking time. But spiritually, the latrine was where the Devil was supposed to loiter. Writing in 1531, Luther recorded a typically scatological 'conversation' he had with the Devil while he was using the facilities:

Devil: You monk on the latrine, you may not read the matins here!

Monk: I am cleansing my bowels and worshipping God Almighty; you deserve what descends and God what ascends.

For Luther there was no shame here. For him there was no part of life which was not open to God, no place where God could not challenge him, no human activity too low to be outside of God's control.

Sitting there, contemplating his end in every sense, Luther became convinced that believers are justified by faith alone. This was to become the bedrock of all his teaching. In Latin, the word *justitia* or *justus* literally means making someone righteous. But Luther understood it rather as a declaration of righteousness. The person was not righteous in themselves: they were still a sinner. But God, through his grace, gives them – in Luther's term, he 'imputes' to them – the righteousness of the crucified and risen Jesus Christ.

Not everyone saw it quite this way, even among the reformers. Other reformers had a different understanding of justification, or differing views on its relative importance. But, generally, the issue of justification and quite what it meant became the major point of difference between the Catholic Church and the reformers. It was, for Luther, *the* crucial sticking point. 'Nothing in this article can be given up or compromised,' he wrote, 'even

Great Moments in Reformation History

NUMBER 7: Luther introduces his students to the Letter to Romans.

if heaven and earth and things temporal should be destroyed.' On this belief, he argued, 'the church stands or falls'.*

In terms of historical significance, this moment, more than the nailing of the Theses, was the moment which jump-started

---

* Later, during a debate with a cardinal, Calvin called it 'the first and keenest subject of controversy between us'.

things; this was the defibrillating shock which reanimated the corpse of Luther's faith.

'I felt that I was altogether born again', Luther wrote later. 'I had entered paradise itself through open gates.'

Not many people have had those kinds of feelings on a toilet. I imagine it came as a bit of a relief.

8 Diets and disputations

Oh, Eck

Meanwhile, there were powerful forces hammering on the toilet door.

Attention had drifted a bit from Luther and the Ninety-five Theses, because there had been an election. Kaiser Max had died, and his nephew, the twenty-one-year-old Charles, was elected as the new Emperor. Charles was the King of Spain, although most of his territories were in Austria, and he himself was Flemish. Welcome to the confusing world of the Holy Roman Empire. Anyway, his election meant that in 1519 the Pope could once again turn his attention to this annoying monk and, in 1519, Luther was summoned to a debate at Leipzig.

This time they sent the formidable Doctor Johann Eck, an academic from Ingolstadt. Eck had written an anti-Luther book – an attack on the Ninety-five Theses – which Luther complained was filled with 'nothing but the foulest abuse . . . nothing less than the malice and envy of a maniac'. Herr Pot, meet Dr Kettle.*
Actually the debate wasn't initially between Luther and Eck, but between Eck and one of Luther's colleagues, Andreas von Karlstadt. (Of whom more later . . .) Luther went along simply to act as Karlstadt's adviser. But you couldn't keep Luther out of centre stage for long and soon he took the limelight.

---

* What really hurt Luther was that he thought Eck was a friend: 'What cuts me most is that we had recently formed a great friendship,' he wrote.

Doctor Johann Eck of Ingolstadt

Eck focused on the authority of the Pope. Was it a human or a divinely ordained authority? Luther responded that the early church in the East had never given such blanket allegiance to the Bishop of Rome. So clearly, historically, it was entirely possible to be a Christian and do the same. Eck countered with another question: which had the final say – the Bible or the Pope? Luther plumped for scripture and said that he didn't need the Pope to understand the Bible. Eck called Luther a disciple of the 'damned and pestiferous' heretics John Wycliffe and Jan Hus.

Luther denied any heresy. But then he did something strange. Brave, even. During a break in proceedings he went away and actually read some of the things that Hus had taught. And he realised that actually he *was* in agreement with Hus. But that wasn't the really brave thing. The *really* brave thing was that

115

Luther returned to the debating chamber and said that he had found in Hus's teachings 'many which are truly Christian and evangelical, and which the Church Universal cannot condemn'.

This was about much more, now, than mere indulgences. This was bigger, much bigger. Hus had been condemned and executed as a heretic by the council. To ally yourself publicly with his teaching was to cross a line. So what made Luther take this step? Perhaps it was the tower/toilet experience, or maybe the fact that by now Luther had significant public support and therefore felt that he was not alone. Whatever the case, for Luther it was a turning point. From now on he was absolutely clear that his real enemy – along with the Devil and his irritable bowels – was the Pope. If the Pope claimed superiority to scripture, then how could the Church ever be reformed on the basis of scripture?

Eck was delighted. This was the smoking gun. Luther had condemned himself. Eck wrote to the Pope urging him to take immediate action against Luther. The universities of Cologne and Leuven declared themselves opposed to Luther's ideas and began to burn his books.

Book burning – or biblioclasm to give it its proper name – is one of the most characteristic activities of the Reformation. It was the Reformation's major contribution to global warming. Both sides did it,* but it was always a symbolic rather than practical act. The printed book could not effectively be silenced. Burn an edition of a book and someone would print another edition elsewhere; close down a printing press in one place and another would spring up somewhere else.

Erasmus wrote, 'The burning of his books will perhaps banish Luther from our libraries; whether he can be plucked out of men's hearts I am not so sure.'

---

* The first major book burning following the publication of the Ninety-five Theses took place in Wittenberg. Students managed to buy up, or steal, 800 copies of a response to Luther written by Tetzel and burned them, much to Luther's embarrassment.

TOP REFORMERS

Martin Luther

Born: Eisleben, Germany, 1483
Died: Wittenberg, Germany, 1541

AKA: Martin Luder, The Wittenberg Nightingale

The one who started it all! After picking a fight over the indulgences in 1517, his theories of justification by faith and the supreme authority of scripture became core Reformation doctrine. A prolific and powerful author, his rude, crude, passionate sermons and writing changed the course of history.

Fun Fact: Luther loved music and was proficient at playing the lute. Making him, of course, Martin luter.

INFLUENCE	95
THEOLOGICAL IMPORTANCE	80
FACIAL HAIR	0
GENERAL GLOOMINESS	30
ABUSIVENESS	86
HAT QUALITY	20
PROPENSITY TO VIOLENCE	10

The year of writing dangerously

Clearly Luther's books were already seen as dangerous. But it was in 1520, after the dispute with Eck, that he really got into

117

gear. In that year he published three of his most influential books, books which show just how far and how fast Luther had travelled intellectually. Just over two years before, Luther had posted his objections to indulgences; in these books he took his hammer to the entire edifice of the Catholic Church.

The first of this incendiary trilogy was addressed to the German princes: *To the Christian Nobility of the German Nation*. Luther argued that, since the Pope was obviously not going to do anything, it was up to the German princes to reform the Church of what he called 'the Romanists'. So he called on the German princes to abolish a few things. Nothing major. Just paying tribute money to Rome. Oh, and clerical celibacy. That as well. And maybe a few more things, such as Masses for the dead, indulgences, obligatory fasting, the canonisation of saints, pilgrimages and all religious orders. The book sold out of its initial print run of four thousand copies in five days, and rapidly went into sixteen further editions.

Luther's writing fizzes with outrage. Perhaps his most radical argument in the book, though, was to deny any real distinction between laity and clergy: 'All are truly priests, bishops, and popes', he wrote. 'A cobbler, a smith, a peasant, each has the work and office of his trade, and yet they are all alike consecrated priests and bishops . . . For all Christians whatsoever really and truly belong to the religious class, and there is no difference among them except insofar as they do different work.' This idea was to have far-reaching consequences. It was to inspire all manner of people to become their own religious leaders, to set up their own churches.

Later in the year he published *The Babylonian Captivity of the Church*, which compared the 'spiritual' captivity of the laity to the Babylonian exile of the Jews. This was nothing less than a full-scale assault on the sacraments. Luther described the sacramental system as 'miserable servitude'. He dismissed the system of penances as 'a factory of money and power' and argued that only two things made something a sacrament: a divinely instituted visible symbol (which meant, in practice, water, bread and wine) and the gospel promise of the forgiveness of sins. So the only real sacraments were baptism and the Eucharist. Out went confirmation, penance, ordination, marriage and extreme unction. Luther attacked transubstantiation ('a monstrous word and a monstrous idea') and he called for the laity actively to participate in Communion by receiving both the bread and wine. Apart from that, the book was entirely uncontroversial . . .

Not that Luther didn't believe that the bread and the wine were, in some way, the body and blood of Jesus. He believed they were; he just didn't hold with all that accidents and substance gubbins. He simply had faith in the fact that it happened. This was, as we shall see, something which was to bring him into conflict with other reformers.

It is a sign of how far his influence was being felt that the major rejoinder to this book came all the way from England, from the lofty pen of King Henry VIII himself. Sort of. *Assertion of the Seven Sacraments* was credited to Henry but was largely ghostwritten by Henry's secretary, Sir Thomas More. (Of whom Sir Thomas More later.) And it contains some rather un-regal language. Luther is mocked as 'a knavish little friar' who 'spews out viper's venom' and 'belches out of the filthy mouth of the hellish wolf those frightful barks which the ears of the whole flock detest, disdain and abhor'. Given that a lot of the 'whole' flock had responded quite positively to Luther, one has to question Henry's research. Pope Leo was so pleased, he gave Henry the title of *Fidei defensor* – 'Defender of the Faith'. Given what happened later, this has to go down as a bit of an own goal.

Luther of course, responded with respect, calling the king a pig, a dolt, and a liar who deserved to be covered in excrement.

The final book in Luther's year of writing dangerously was *The Freedom of a Christian Man*. Luther actually dedicated it to the Pope 'as a token of peace and good hope', which has to go down as one of the most optimistic dedications ever, not least because in the book he described the Pope as a 'man of sin and the son of perdition' who 'increases the sin of the Church and the destruction of souls'. Not exactly an attempt to win the Holy Father over, there. In an open letter accompanying the book, Luther was a little more moderate, portraying the Pope as an innocent surrounded by villains:

> The Roman church, once the holiest of all, has become the most licentious den of thieves, the most shameless of all brothels, the kingdom of sin, death and hell . . . Meanwhile, you, Leo, sit as a

lamb in the midst of wolves and like Daniel in the midst of lions . . .
How can you oppose these monsters?

It was a good try, but Luther could never keep the niceness up.
'I have truly despised your see, the Roman Curia,' he continued,
'which . . . neither you nor anyone else can deny is more corrupt
than any Babylon or Sodom ever was.'

Diplomacy at its best.

This book is Luther's declaration of independence. The
Christian has been liberated by faith, freeing him from the obli-
gation to do good works. 'For faith alone and the efficaciousness
of the Word of God, bring salvation', he wrote. And he called
on the rulers of Europe to cleanse the Church of corruption. The
papacy should be stripped of its riches and its lands. Oh, and
clergy should be able to marry. And monks should be able to
stop being monks. 'It is time for the glorious Teutonic people to
stop being the puppet of the Roman pontiff!' he urged.

These books must have been astonishing to read in the sixteenth
century. This is medieval punk theology, agitprop protest writing
four hundred years ahead of its time. It was all powerful, incendiary, intoxicating stuff. Luther dipped his pen in pure outrage
and let rip. Small wonder that Luther's writings scorched across
Europe. The speed with which they arrived, the everyday, engaging
language, the enthusiasm with which ordinary people devoured
this material, all gave people a sense of involvement and connection. Small wonder that one-third of all books sold in Germany
in the early 1520s were by Martin Luther.

But you have to wonder whether he really grasped the impli-
cations. In *Freedom of a Christian Man* he wrote the famous
line that, 'A Christian is a perfectly free lord of all, subject to
none. A Christian is a perfectly dutiful servant of all, subject to
all.' It sounds good, it sounds as though he's making some sort
of balance, but the reality is that it's the first half of that sentence
that people notice. You write stuff like that and all sorts of people
will run with it.

Luther understood the reading public, but he also understood the non-reading public. He wrote hymns so that people who could not read could still learn scriptures and participate in the church service. He may have been the author of the immensely popular ditty which runs:

> Now we drive out the Pope
> From Christ's church and God's house.
> Therein he has reigned in a deadly fashion
> And has seduced uncountably many souls.

Luther was also turned into a folk hero in song: Hans Sachs, a shoemaker from Nuremberg, wrote a series of ballads about him. He called Luther the Wittenberg Nightingale. It's not very accurate: I've heard a nightingale sing and not one of them has actually tweeted swear words and abuse.

As well as words, Luther also understood the visual image. In his books he used drawings – often sharp, satirical cartoons. Unlike some of the other reformers, Luther understood the potency of pictures. (He even had a picture of Mary in his study.) He knew how to propagandise theology. So to accompany his books he commissioned his friend Cranach to create heavily politicised prints, contrasting scenes from the Bible with scenes from modern life. In one scene Christ is shown fleeing from the Jews because they are trying to make him king, while the Pope is shown wielding a sword to protect his earthly domain. Get the message?*

And the Church didn't know how to respond. Like so many authoritarian regimes since, it was caught in what has been called

---

* Cranach was the court painter in Wittenberg for Frederick the Wise and produced many of the most powerful images of the Reformation. He was a close friend of Luther, both of them standing as godparent to a child of the other. Like Dürer, he used the power of print to great effect, becoming very wealthy through his painting. He had one of the biggest houses in Wittenberg and he and his son, Lucas Cranach the Younger, produced many portraits of the famous reformers.

the conservative dilemma: 'If we don't reply to Luther then people might think he is right. But if we do reply to him they'll compare the two arguments and make their own minds up.' Most of all, it didn't know how to use this new technology of the book, which Luther had mastered so thoroughly. Most of the writers who defended the Pope and the traditional teaching did so in Latin.* This was their problem: they spoke theology, but Luther spoke German.

Great Moments in Reformation History

NUMBER 9: Luther's supporters realise that burning a papal bull is not what they thought.

So the Church tried to do things the old way. As well as encouraging the bonfires, the Pope, from his hunting lodge where he was chasing wild boar (which sort of proved Luther's point,

---

* One critic actually translated one of Luther's pamphlets from German, into Latin, so that he could write about it!

really), sent out a papal bull. This one was titled *Exsurge Domine*, and forty-one of Luther's ideas were condemned in it as heretical. Luther was given sixty days to recant. If he didn't he would be excommunicated and placed under the ban – which meant that nobody would be allowed to offer him shelter, but had to hand him over. Luther responded in typical fashion: he knocked out a little tract entitled *Against the Execrable Bull of Antichrist.** And at the end of the sixty days Luther's followers in Wittenberg organised their own little bonfire. They threw onto it volumes of canon law, Catholic theology and books by Eck and other critics. Then, when the fire was good and hot, Luther stepped forward and threw the papal bull into the flames.

'You have condemned the truth of God,' he said. 'He also condemns you to the fire.'

Damn, that man was great at PR.

The Worm Diet

It was a declaration of war. The Pope responded with a second bull on 3 January 1521, *Decet Romanum Pontificum* – 'It befits the Roman Pontiff'– which excommunicated Luther and threw all his followers in for good measure.

And now the new Emperor got involved. Luther was summoned to appear at the next Imperial Diet – at Worms (pronounced Vurms) and there he would have to present his case to Charles V (pronounced Charles W).

The Diet of Worms sounds like the worst Hollywood slimming plan ever. Certainly Luther went to the city of Worms in fear and trepidation. He had been given a guarantee of safe conduct, but those were slippery promises at the best of times – Jan Hus

---

* This is probably the first time that a pope was called the Antichrist in print. The identification would often be repeated in anti-Catholic books, sermons and art.

had been promised safe conduct and he ended up barbecued – so Luther knew the risks. But he went: 'Christ lives,' he said, 'and we shall enter Worms in spite of all the gates of hell.'

When it came to it, though, the gates themselves weren't particularly hellish. Luther entered the city on the evening of 16 April 1521, to a hero's welcome: thousands lined the streets, craned out of windows, gathered on rooftops to see him. (Still, Luther had read his Bible. He knew that a hero's welcome didn't necessarily guarantee a happy ending.)

What it showed both Luther, and the authorities, however, was that the case had caught the popular imagination. The Emperor's secretary reported in Worms that there were pictures of Luther which sold out so quickly he couldn't even get hold of a copy. Mind you, in Augsburg it was even worse: there they were selling the same kind of pictures, only this time Luther had a halo.

The next day the crowds were so dense that Luther had to be sneaked into the court through a back alley. So it was that, at four in the afternoon, Martin Luder, the miner's son from Saxony, came face to face with Charles V, Holy Roman Emperor, King of Germany, King of Italy, King of Spain, Archduke of Austria, Duke of Burgundy, Top of The Pops, Best of Breed and Leader of the Pack.* The Emperor was not impressed at Luther's appearance. 'He will not make a heretic out of me,' he muttered.

---

* His full title was Charles V, by the grace of God, Holy Roman Emperor, forever August, King of Germany, King of Italy, King of all Spains, of Castile, Aragon, León, Navarra, Grenada, Toledo, Valencia, Galicia, Majorca, Sevilla, Cordova, Murcia, Jaén, Algarves, Algeciras, Gibraltar, the Canary Islands, King of Two Sicilies, of Sardinia, Corsica, King of Jerusalem, King of the Western and Eastern Indies, Lord of the Islands and Main Ocean Sea, Archduke of Austria, Duke of Burgundy, Brabant, Lorraine, Styria, Carinthia, Carniola, Limburg, Luxembourg, Gelderland, Neopatria, Württemberg, Landgrave of Alsace, Prince of Swabia, Asturia and Catalonia, Count of Flanders, Habsburg, Tyrol, Gorizia, Barcelona, Artois, Burgundy Palatine, Hainaut, Holland, Seeland, Ferrette, Kyburg, Namur, Roussillon, Cerdagne, Zutphen, Margrave of the Holy Roman Empire, Burgau, Oristano and Gociano, Lord of Frisia, the Wendish March, Pordenone, Biscay, Molin, Salins, Tripoli and Mechelen. But you can call him Chuck.

*Charles V, Holy Roman Emperor, King of Spain,
Lord of Misrule, Top of the Morning, etc.*

It was not a debate, but a hearing. Or a stitch-up, to use the technical term, since a deal had been worked out between the Emperor and the papal nuncio, Aleander, that Luther would be denied the opportunity to mount a defence. Instead, Luther was to be presented with a pile of his books (a pile so high that the Emperor was reluctant to believe that one man could have written them all) and asked two questions: 'Are these your books?' and 'Do you recant?'

To question one he said 'yes'. To question two he said, 'Er, hang on.' Surprisingly, Luther asked for time to think. Even more surprisingly, the Emperor granted it. Luther was given a day to think things through and warned what would happen if he didn't give the right answer.

First mistake. Never give Luther time to prepare a speech, or a moment.

'The fool entered smiling,' Aleander said, 'but when he left he did not seem so cheerful.'

Second mistake. Never underestimate Luther.

Luther was not so much downhearted as preoccupied. He had expected to be questioned on specific issues, but now he was being asked to repudiate everything that he had written. They wanted a wholesale rejection. So he went away to do some serious thinking. I don't know if quality time on the toilet was involved, but I wouldn't rule it out.

Great Moments in Reformation History

NUMBER 10: Luther makes his famous statement at Worms.

He returned the next day, 18 April, at six o'clock in the evening. And in a crowded, stiflingly hot room, in which only the Emperor was allowed to sit, Luther made the speech of his life.*

---

* Luther gave accounts of this event to some of his disciples much later in Wittenberg. There was a contemporary report which seems to have drawn on Luther's own account as well. The report starts in the third person, a bit like a newspaper report, but in the end has Luther's own words describing

The hall was dim, smoky and packed to the rafters with people.

'High on the walls were many torches, since it was dark,' Luther recalled. 'I was not accustomed to such turmoil and activity.' Nevertheless, he spoke with confidence. He started with his books. He didn't deny that the books were his, but he classed them in three categories: first, 'textbooks interpreting sacred scripture' in which there was nothing bad or wrong; second, 'polemical writings in which I quarrelled with the Pope and my opponents' – and he said that if anything bad was found in them that could be changed; and finally 'books in which I deal with Christian teachings', which he described merely as 'propositions for debate'. And although he admitted that some of the books got a bit angry and vitriolic, he didn't see that was a reason for withdrawing them. Instead he challenged the court to show that anything in his books was contrary to scripture. Come and have a go, if you think you're holy enough. And that went for the Emperor as well: 'The Holy Scriptures and my conscience are my Emperor,' he said. 'I cannot, and will not, withdraw what I have said.'

His statement is quite rambling at times and hard to follow, which may be why Eck, in the end, got annoyed with him and demanded a plain answer: would he, or would he not, revoke what he had said?

Luther gave him a reply which has gone down in history:

Since your Imperial Majesty and Lordships demand a simple answer I will do so . . . Unless I am convicted by the testimony of Scripture or by evident reason (for I trust neither in Popes nor in councils alone, since it is obvious that they have often erred and contradicted themselves) I am convicted by the Scripture which I have mentioned and my conscience is captive to the

the events. It is contained in *Die gantz Handlung, so mit dem hochgelehrten Doctor Martin Luther*. That's German, that is.

Word of God. Therefore I cannot and will not recant, since it is difficult, unprofitable and dangerous indeed to do anything against one's conscience. God help me! Amen.

Luther never said the famous phrase 'Here I stand.' Even though he was there. And he was standing.* He was standing not only against the Catholic authorities, but also against the Emperor. (Not literally, obviously, although he did feel a bit faint.) Now he, and all those who abetted him, were effectively outlaws.

As he left the room there were angry cries of 'To the pyre with him!' But any precipitate action was unlikely: those inside the room cannot have been unaware of the support of the crowds in Worms. Later, Cardinal Aleander suggested that 90 per cent of Germany supported Luther. He was probably overstating it, but in the city of Worms, with all those crowds, it must have seemed that way. Certainly Luther didn't hesitate to play to the crowd, shouting, 'I've come through! I've come through!' as he emerged.

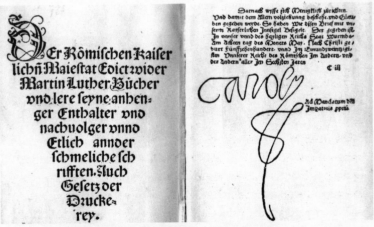

The Edict of Worms, with the signature of Charles V

* This phrase was made up by a printer who wanted a bit more drama.

Charles delivered his verdict the next day. One monk defying all Christendom had to be wrong. As far as the Emperor was concerned, Luther should be 'held in detestation . . . a limb severed from the church of God'.

Nevertheless, he would honour the guarantee of safe conduct. Luther could go. Later, when that detested limb started giving the empire a right good kicking, he rather regretted this decision.

Luther made the most of this break and hurried away before things in Worms turned. But as he was making his way through the forest on his way home his carriage was suddenly surrounded by armed soldiers. Luther was hauled from the carriage and taken away. If not the Emperor, then someone, it seemed, had decided that Luther should not get home safely.

News of his kidnap and disappearance spread quickly. Dürer spoke for many when he heard the news: 'O God, if Luther be dead who will proclaim the holy gospel so clearly to us?'

Great Moments in Reformation History

NUMBER 11: In the forest outside Worms, Luther is confused by the arrival of armed guards.

Want to lose weight fast ?

Try

DIET OF WORMS

- the healthy dieting plan that is taking the Holy Roman Empire by storm. This ground-breaking diet - literally, in fact - leads to guaranteed weight loss.

‹I›ve lost pounds through the Diet of Worms method. Largely because the things taste so repulsive I›d rather starve to death.› Mrs Z.

‹I had a nasty outbreak of heresy in my Empire. I was recommended to purge it using Diet of Worms and I›m delighted to say that the parasite has completely disappeared!› Charles V, Germany

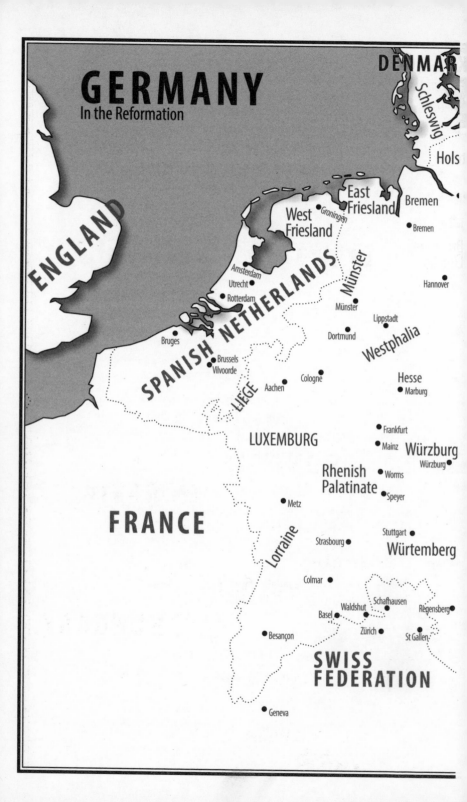

- Part Three -

Here Comes Mr Everybody

❖

9 The word on the street

Anfechtung

Meanwhile, miles away, in the city of Eisenach, a strange, bearded gentleman moved into a room in the castle of the Wartburg. He was known to those who saw him as Junker Jörg – Sir George – and he spent hours in the room, scratching away, writing. Health-wise, though, he was not in a good way. He was having visions. Bouts of depression. Insomnia. And stomach problems, or as he phrased it charmingly in a letter to a friend, 'My arse is bad.'

Hang on. That's a clue. Who's the most arsey person we know?

Yes, Junker Jörg was none other than Luther. He hadn't so much been kidnapped as taken into protective custody by Frederick the Wise who, in his wisdom, worried that the Emperor might have second thoughts about the whole 'safe conduct' thing. So, much to Luther's surprise, he was ambushed and taken by a roundabout way to the Wartburg. There he grew his hair long to cover his monk's tonsure, and a beard to conceal as much of the rest of his face as was possible.

For a man as garrulous and naturally gregarious as Luther, being isolated and alone took its toll. His old anxieties resurfaced. 'My temptation is this, that I think I don't have a gracious God', he wrote to a friend. He was hardly sleeping. When he did sleep he suffered nightmares. When he lay awake he had encounters with the Devil, who would taunt him with his sin and his failure.

Was it psychosis? Paranoia? Spiritual warfare?

Luther called his suffering his *Anfechtung*, a word which is hard to translate, but which contains overtones of temptation, trial, suffering, terror and even despair. It suggests an assault from without, an attack from a foe whom Luther met all his life: the Devil. 'I am a doctor of Holy Scripture, and for many years have preached Christ; yet, to this day, I am not able to put Satan off, or to drive him away from me, as I would', he would later write. To Luther, the Devil had always been real, tangible.*

It is not a unique, unheard of thing for the Devil to thump about and haunt houses. In our monastery in Wittenberg I heard him distinctly. For when I began to lecture on the book of Psalms and I was sitting in the refectory after we had sung matins, studying and writing my notes, the Devil came and thudded three times in the storage chamber [a cupboard or space behind the stove] as if dragging a bushel away. Finally, as it did not want to stop, I collected my books and went to bed. I still regret to this hour that I did not sit him out, to discover what else the Devil wanted to do. I also heard him once over the chamber in the monastery . . . But when I realised that it was Satan, I rolled over and went back to sleep again.

Luther's life was rarely calm and unperturbed. He was a man whose mind was always grinding away, and who faced all kinds of torments:

* The famous story about Luther throwing ink at the Devil comes from his time in the Wartburg. It was said that the Devil wanted to disturb him, but Luther drove him away by throwing an inkwell at him. Sadly the whole story appears to be a fake. It first appears towards the end of the sixteenth century, and in that version it's the Devil throwing ink at Luther. By 1650 the positions have been reversed and Luther is doing the ink chucking. After the Wartburg became a place of pilgrimage for Luther fans, they were shown the very ink stain on the wall and pious curators would touch up the stain every so often, in case it faded.

The human heart is like a millstone in a mill; when you put wheat under it, it turns and grinds and bruises the wheat to flour; if you put no wheat, it still grinds on, but then 'tis itself it grinds and wears away. So the human heart, unless it be occupied with some employment, leaves space for the devil, who wriggles himself in, and brings with him a whole host of evil thoughts, temptations, and tribulations, which grind out the heart.

His solution, later in life, was to get busy: 'When I am assailed with heavy tribulations, I rush out among my pigs, rather than remain alone by myself.'

He claimed that the Devil would roar and whistle in his ears, that his head would start spinning and his heart race so fast that he would actually fall out of his chair.*

He could deal with physical attacks. What really worried him was the Devil's most frequent accusation: that whatever Luther did, however hard he tried, whatever wonderful theological insights he might come up with, God had condemned him to hell.

This sense of an intense, hopeless dread and fear was not new to him. He had felt it during his first experience of taking Mass in 1515, when he suddenly seemed gripped by horror over the closeness of Christ. Sometimes when thinking about things like election and predestination, he had the overwhelming feeling of having been abandoned by God's grace and of being lost for ever. Writing in 1518 he described himself in terms echoing Paul in 2 Corinthians:

I myself 'knew a man' [2 Cor. 12:2] who claimed that he had often suffered these punishments, in fact over a very brief period of

---

* Some doctors think that maybe he had Menière's disease, a condition which attacks the middle ear and causes severe problems with equilibrium. This would also explain why, in 1541, he became rather deaf, after experiencing bad earaches and a discharge from his ears. He also appears to have had extremely high blood pressure, which eventually led to heart disease.

time. Yet they were so great and so much like hell that no tongue could adequately express them, no pen could describe them, and one who had not himself experienced them could not believe them. And so great were they that, if they had been sustained or had lasted for half an hour, even for one tenth of an hour, he would have perished completely and all of his bones would have been reduced to ashes. At such a time God seems terribly angry, and with him the whole creation. At such a time there is no flight, no comfort, within or without, but all things accuse . . . In this moment, it is strange to say, the soul cannot believe that it can ever be redeemed.

Over the years Luther's supporters have often denied that there was anything psychologically disturbed about him. They talk of his medieval mindset, of his spiritual battles, and point out, of course, that all this took place many years before Freud and Jung turned up to invent psychoanalysis. But for anyone who reads Luther's writings it doesn't take much to see that the man had issues. And those who deny Luther's psychological problems do so, I think, out of a misplaced sense of shame. They feel that to admit Luther had psychological issues would be to admit a weakness, a vulnerability. I would argue that it was absolutely crucial to Luther's make-up. He could not be himself without his problems. He could not have achieved what he did without these struggles, this sense of paranoia, even depression. Luther's *Anfechtung* was crucial to his theology: if he'd not felt those attacks, he would never have found the solace of justification through faith. He said this himself: 'I didn't learn my theology all at once. I had to ponder over it ever more deeply, and my [*Anfechtungen*] were of help to me in this, for one doesn't learn anything without practice.' The stress must have been immense. Luther believed that he would, in the end, be killed for the stance he had taken. By now the Emperor had published an official edict. The Edict of Worms declared Luther to be a heretic and warned of harsh punishments for anyone who was found to have aided and abetted him or given him shelter.

Anyway, he was so ill in the Wartburg that he could only manage to write twelve books.

Oh, and translate the New Testament into German.

A mean German

It wasn't that there weren't already German Bibles. Eight editions of the Bible in German had already been printed before Luther was even born. Indeed, the first vernacular Bible ever printed in Europe was German – the translation of Johannes Mentelin, printed at Strasbourg in 1466.

But Luther's experiences on trial had shown him that if he was to support his case using the Bible, it would help if there was one shared Bible on which everyone could consult. He had already seen the powerful effect of writing a tract in a kind of universal German: now he applied that approach to the New Testament. Luther decided that he would write the kind of Bible which ordinary people could understand. The thing that would set Luther's translation apart from the others was that it would use the language of the people. In doing so, Luther virtually invented a common German language – a 'mean German'.

So, in his small, sparsely furnished room, he set to work. He used the 1519 edition of Erasmus' Greek New Testament as well as a Latin version and a couple of earlier German translations. But his most valuable resource was the town marketplace outside the castle walls. There he could hear vernacular German in all its muscular simplicity. Reportedly, he would go out in disguise, into the marketplaces and the streets, listening to the way in which ordinary German people spoke. He wanted to hear the German of 'the mother in the home, the children on the street, the common man in the marketplace. We must be guided by their language, by the way they speak, and do our translating accordingly.'

Great Moments in Reformation History

NUMBER 12: In the Wartburg, Luther struggles with finding new words for his Bible translation.

What's German for zeitgeist?

Despite all the arguments with the Devil and the difficulties with his arse, he worked at a white-hot speed. By the end of February 1522, after only eleven weeks, he had completed the New Testament. After some revision and discussion, it was printed in conditions of the utmost secrecy. Luther's name was missing from the title page, which bore merely the words *Das Newe Testament Deutzsch* and the place: Wittenberg.

The first edition was published in September 1522, probably in an edition of 3,000 copies – a huge number for the time. It was followed by a second, amended edition in December, with some corrections and adjustments in the style of the German. It carried on being revised: over the course of his life, Luther oversaw a further fifteen corrected editions. But whenever it appeared, it flew off the shelves.

Its success so alarmed Luther's enemies that the ruler of Ducal Saxony, George the Bearded (I'll leave you to guess how he got that name), made purchasing the New Testament a criminal offence and offered to buy back the copies of anyone who had already purchased them. Only four people surrendered their copies. Luther, with typical politeness, called George 'the Dresden Hog'.

A man called Johannes Cochlaeus was given the job of trying to stop people buying the translation.* Cochlaeus made a career out of demonising Luther, spreading many lies and disinformation. He said that Luther 'lusted after wine and women'; that he was 'a liar, a hypocrite, a coward and a quarreller' – well, the latter has more than a grain of truth about it. He also was the first person to raise the 'birther' issue, claiming that Luther 'had not a drop of German blood in his veins'.

But Cochlaeus could do nothing to stop the success of Luther's New Testament: he lamented that 'even tailors and cobblers, even women and other simple folk who had only learnt to read a little German in their lives, were reading it with great enthusiasm as though it were the fount of all truth, while others carried it around, pressed to their bosom, and learned it by heart'.

Good lord. Common people treating the Bible like the fount of all truth. How very dare they?

It was understandable, it was cheap, it was mass-produced.

---

* His real name was Johann Dobneck or Dobeneck. The name Cochlæus is a nickname, from the Latin *cochlea* – a snail shell. It's because he came from a place called Wendelstein, and Wendel is German for spiral.

And it was well designed. In another example of Luther's mastery of print, he made sure that the layout was simple as well. Luther's New Testament was the first Bible printed in single columns. This enhanced the readability. It also allowed Luther to add many marginal notes as well as illustrations, specially commissioned from Lucas Cranach.*

Luther translated the New Testament because of his certainty of the fundamental importance of scripture. This lies behind one of the most crucial of Reformation ideas: *sola scriptura* – by scripture alone. Which is not to say that church tradition and teaching did not matter, but rather that scripture was the final authority in matters of faith and practice. As Luther said, 'The true rule is this: God's Word shall establish articles of faith, and no one else, not even an angel can do so.'

Not that *sola scriptura* was the only *sola*. There was also *sola fide* – only by faith. As in: we are justified by faith alone. And in Luther's translation he took a rather obvious step to make sure that this came out clearly. In his translation of Romans 3:23 he added an extra word to the text – the word 'alone' – to make it read 'we are justified by faith alone'. He clearly felt himself unable to leave *scriptura* quite *sola* enough. When critics pointed this addition out, Luther responded in typically measured fashion, calling them 'brazen idiots' or 'Dr Schmidt and Dr Snot-Nose'. He tried to justify his addition to the text on the grounds of it being a typically German way of expressing things. It's an unconvincing argument. In the end he was reduced to saying that, 'Luther will have it so, and he says that he is a doctor above all the doctors of the Pope'. Ner-ner-ner-ner-ner. It's my Bible and I'll do what I like, so there.

---

*These were typically polemical. In the picture of the fall of Babylon from Revelation, for example, the buildings look pretty identical to the city of Rome in the *Nuremberg Chronicle*. And the whore of Babylon wears the three-tiered papal crown. Actually, even Frederick the Wise felt that this was a bit too much, so the crown was removed in later editions. After Frederick's death, though, it came back fancier than ever.

'The world believes itself to be the expert in everything,' he moaned. 'Criticising everything and accomplishing nothing, that is the world's nature. It can do nothing else.' A good thing he never lived to hear radio phone-in programmes.

Interestingly, the book also reveals his doubts about some of the New Testament books. He had particular issues with Hebrews, James, Jude and Revelation, all of which he lumped together in a group at the back of the New Testament, changing the traditional order. He did this because he didn't think there was enough about Jesus in them – or, at least, not enough of the *right* stuff about Jesus. 'Whatever does not teach Christ is not apostolic, even though St Peter or St Paul does the teaching', he wrote. And it was Luther who decided what did, or didn't, teach Christ. So although he felt he had to include these books, he did so with a health warning.

Revelation he simply didn't understand at all (although he later became quite keen on it when he realised that the whole book of Revelation was really about the Catholic Church and the Pope was the Antichrist). Hebrews he disliked because it taught that there could be no repentance after baptism; Jude was just copying 2 Peter. The one that he *really* disliked, though, was James, because of its emphasis on works. He called it 'a right strawy epistle compared with the others'. One Sunday, when the set Bible passage was from the book of James, Luther read the passage, declared 'I don't want to preach on this', and went on to preach on something else.

Luther's New Testament was an international bestseller. Later, Luther went on to translate the Old Testament as well – although that took him much longer and he grew to hate the work. When Wittenberg printer Hans Luft retired in 1572, he reckoned he had printed some one hundred thousand copies of Luther's translations. Not only that, but Luther's work also formed the basis for translations into many other languages. There were Dutch, Danish, Swedish, Hungarian, Lithuanian, Polish, Romanian, Bohemian, Slovenian, even Icelandic translations.

In the Wartburg, Luther's dream was that people 'might seize and taste the clear, pure Word of God itself and hold to it'.

The problem was that, back in Wittenberg, people were doing just that.

Four portraits of Luther. Three by Cranach and one by Dürer (bottom right). Top right shows him with his Juncker Jörg beard.

10 The Martinians

Neighbour Andreas

When Luther debated with Eck in Leipzig in 1519, he was not supposed to be the centre of attention. He'd gone there as an adviser. The man who was supposed to be debating with Eck was Andreas Bodenstein von Karlstadt.

Karlstadt was a colleague of Luther's at the university and church of Wittenberg. He was actually Luther's senior, but in the theological revolution which broke out following the posting of the Theses, he'd become an ardent reformer. It was one of his publications which actually provoked the debate at Leipzig, a document containing a whopping 405 theses, outscoring Luther by a mere 310.

Karlstadt was a man of ideas and energy. In 1521, he went to Denmark to aid King Christian II in reforming his churches, but his efforts failed and he returned to Wittenberg to find Luther absent. With Luther being in the Wartburg, clearly someone had to take control at Wittenberg. So Karlstadt took the reins. It proved to be a wild ride.

He was aided and abetted by another of Luther's colleagues, a man called Philip Melanchthon. Melanchthon was, you will not be at all surprised to hear, not his real name. His real name was Philip Schwarzerd; Melanchthon was a Graecised version of the name. He arrived in Wittenberg in 1518 to teach Greek at the university. He had a brain the size of a planet – and if the engravings of him are accurate, his head bulged for all the world as though the brain was trying to burst out. Luther viewed him as a close friend; even, to some extent, an intellectual superior. Certainly Melanchthon was the figure who brought intellectual rigour to Lutheranism. It was Melanchthon who tried to make a systematic theology out of the very unsystematic Luther. He summarised the main tenets of 'Lutheranism' in a book called *Loci Communes* – 'Common Places'. Luther thought the book was brilliant. In a completely unbiased and self-deprecating way he described it as 'the best book next to the Bible'.

Philip Melanchthon by Dürer

Melanchthon was also a much more consensual and conciliatory figure than Luther. Which is not hard, I'll grant you. And probably it was this which got him into trouble, because Melanchthon was either unable, or unwilling, to stop Karlstadt instituting rapid, radical reform.* He published his reforms as *A New Order*

---

* Melanchthon described Karlstadt as 'a good person, of rare erudition and extraordinary culture, as recognised by his writings'. Not the words Luther would have used. Or, indeed, did use.

TOP REFORMERS

Andreas Karlstadt

Born: Karlstadt, Germany, c.1480
Died: Basel, Switzerland 1541

AKA: *Andreas Rudolph Bodenstein, Andreas Carlstadt, Andreas Karolostadt.*

One of the most radical of the reformers. While Luther was absent from Wittenberg, Karlstadt held services in the vernacular, got married and refused to wear clerical garb. Luther forced Karlstadt into exile, but his teaching remained highly influential.

Fun Fact: When he was exiled by the Lutherans, Zwingli found Karlstadt a job as a proofreader in Zürich.

INFLUENCE	55
THEOLOGICAL IMPORTANCE	65
FACIAL HAIR	32
GENERAL GLOOMINESS	14
ABUSIVENESS	22
HAT QUALITY	0
PROPENSITY TO VIOLENCE	15

for the City of Wittenberg. Monasteries were closed, religious funds were confiscated and distributed to the poor. Karlstadt made significant changes to the Mass. On Christmas Day 1521 he served the Mass wearing ordinary clothes, and not only did he 'shout' the words so that everyone could hear; he shouted them in German. He distributed both bread and wine to the participants. It was the original Mass participation.

The day after that, he showed his support for clerical marriage by announcing his engagement to a woman called Anna von Mochau. I say 'woman'; she was only fifteen. Although marrying at fifteen was not unusual in those days, there was a bit of an age gap: Karlstadt was forty-one.

Karlstadt was literally iconoclastic. He encouraged altars to be overturned, images to be smashed and burned. Later, he published the first Reformation condemnation of images, *On the abolishing of images*, in which he more or less argued that you have to kill the thing you love:

> My heart since childhood has been brought up in the veneration of images and a harmful fear has entered me which I gladly would rid myself of, and cannot . . . Forbidden fruit! The iconoclast is not colour-blind or tone-deaf when it comes to images. He loves them too much, so much that he needs to destroy them, and so to destroy the images in his mind and heart.

Then some 'prophets' arrived from nearby Zwickau. One of them, Nikolaus Storch, a weaver by trade, started to receive dreams and visions. Although Karlstadt decried violence, riots broke out in the fevered atmosphere.

This kind of behaviour alarmed everyone, including Luther's protector Frederick, who complained that 'the common man has been incited to folly'. Things were starting to get out of hand. Although he supported Karlstadt over things like icons, Melanchthon wrote to Luther to alert him. Luther was horrified. Yes, he had written all about people having liberty, but he never expected people to liberate themselves without him controlling them. So, as soon as it was safe, he returned from the Wartburg and took control. The Zwickau prophets were sent packing. Karlstadt was repudiated, and publicly humiliated. He was essentially forced out of his professorship and out of all leadership roles. He bought a farm near Wörlitz, and worked among the peasants. Then he went to the village of Orlamünde, where he persisted in his (to Luther's mind) dangerously radical behaviour, wearing peasant costume, asking to be called 'Neighbour Andreas' and buying everyone drinks in the pub.* Wittenberg was now Luther's city.

With regard to things like the removal of images and the Lord's Supper, Luther never agreed with Karlstadt – although many other reformers did. But in other matters, Luther followed Karlstadt. In time he too married, and introduced a German liturgy. What alarmed Luther with regard to Karlstadt was the speed, and the disorderliness of it all. Not to mention the unforgiveable nerve of Karlstadt for doing all of this without seeking Luther's approval.

Karlstadt was a threat to Luther's reputation, and not just because of what had happened in Wittenberg. He was an innovative theologian and thinker, and one of the most widely published and read of the reformers. Like Luther, he was a prolific author: he produced around seventy publications between 1517 and his death in 1541. Repeatedly, his ideas clashed with Luther's. Karlstadt defended the Letter of James, which he saw as an authentic, apostolic call to ethical living. In 1524 Karlstadt published a series of tracts which argued that the Lord's Supper was only a memorial commemoration of Jesus' death and which questioned the validity of infant baptism. For Luther this was outrageous and he responded with one of his most vitriolic works, *Against the Heavenly Prophets*.

'Doctor Andreas Karlstadt has deserted us,' it begins, 'and on top of that has become our worst enemy.' He rumbles on about the 'Karlstadtian abomination', and accuses Karlstadt of having

---

* In March 1523, Karlstadt published *The Manifold, Singular Will of God, The Nature of Sin*. On the title page he called himself 'a new layman'. He argued that faith should produce fruits in the form of changed behaviour: 'By our fruits we are able to know ourselves and others. Therefore, we must look to what we do.'

'a rebellious, murderous, seditious spirit'. If Karlstadt had his way and 'there were no more images, no churches remained, no one in the whole world held that the flesh and blood of Christ were in the sacrament and all went about in grey peasant garb, what would be accomplished thereby?'

Karlstadt's response called for people to embrace the spirit of Christ: 'We must, above all else, be like Christ in our inner being and have the likeness of Christ', he wrote. As to the matter of clerical garb, he said, 'Of what harm is my common dress since I do not give occasion with my grey garb for suspecting a false kind of holiness as Doctor Luther does with his monk's cowl.' He was critical of what he saw as Luther's increasing status:

> What do you think, Luther, would blisters on our hands not be more becoming than gold rings? . . . How do you like that, Luther, when you dare write, as I reported, that a preacher may demand and take two hundred guilders a year? . . . But Dr Luther not only lines his own bastard offspring with silver and gold, etc., but desires the poor man's sweat and blood and extracts it by force.

In August 1524, Luther and Karlstadt had a full and frank discussion about the issues in the Black Bear Inn in Jena, where Luther had gone to preach. Luther then made a visit to Orlamünde, which did not go well. He returned to Wittenberg and made a report to Duke John of Saxony, in whose territory Karlstadt was operating. A few weeks later, Karlstadt was banished from the district. You do the maths.

Luther never forgave Karlstadt (or 'Judas' as he sometimes called him). He persistently defamed him. Karlstadt, in return, called Luther the worst name he could think of: he said he was no better than the Pope.

Throughout his life, Luther appears to have been surprised and enraged when people took his ideas and acted on them. His reaction here reflects his essential social conservatism. He was a theologian, not a political radical. He didn't want dramatic social change: he believed social order was ordained from on high and reflected the order of the universe. Luther believed in reform but he also believed in princes. There had to be a hierarchy with the ordained leaders on top. Leaders like Frederick the Wise. And, well, Luther. He was fine with people challenging authority. What he wasn't prepared for was people challenging *his* authority.

Luther claimed that, despite Karlstadt publicly repudiating violence, in appealing to the common people, or 'Mr Everybody' as Luther called them, Karlstadt was playing with fire. He was arousing 'the masses . . . to boldness and arrogance'. 'My dear lords,' he wrote, 'Mr Everybody is not to be toyed with. Therefore God would have authorities so that there might be order in the world.'

There was a reason that he was writing this way. Because Mr Everybody was getting angry.

Damn the unbelievers!

Embarrassingly, Mr Everybody wasn't, in fact, inspired by Karlstadt. No, he was inspired by Luther.

In the early days of the Reformation many young disciples had embraced Luther's ideas. Among these 'Martinians', as they were called, was a young man called Thomas Müntzer. He had been in Wittenberg in the heady days of autumn 1517, when Luther wasn't nailing his Theses to the door, and had been 'brought to birth by the gospel' by Luther's teaching.

Luther approved of him and, in May 1520, appointed him pastor in a town called Zwickau – the same place that those troublesome prophets came from. There must have been something in the water in Zwickau, because Müntzer proved to be very outspoken. Argumentative by nature – one of the preachers in Zwickau called him a 'man born for heresies and schisms' – he absorbed not only Luther's teaching, but a mass of mystical and religious beliefs. (He had even read the Qur'an.) In 1521,

TOP REFORMERS

Thomas Müntzer

Born: Stolberg, Germany, c.1490
Died: Mühlhausen, Germany, 1525

AKA: Tomas Muncer, Munzer

Former priest, he was inspired by Luther but took his ideas in a violent, revolutionary direction. He moved to Allstedt, and then Mühlhausen, where he created worship services in German, embraced Anabaptism and demanded radical social reform. He led an armed uprising in the Peasants' War and was defeated, captured, tortured and executed.

Fun Fact: Müntzer was viewed as a revolutionary hero in Communist East Germany. He even featured on the five Mark banknote.

INFLUENCE	20
THEOLOGICAL IMPORTANCE	30
FACIAL HAIR	6
GENERAL GLOOMINESS	75
ABUSIVENESS	85
HAT QUALITY	75
PROPENSITY TO VIOLENCE	99

when Luther was in hiding and things were kicking off in Wittenberg, Müntzer fell in with the prophet-weaver Nikolaus Storch and started preaching a more extreme message. The Lutheran leaders grew alarmed at his outspoken nature and chastised him for preaching 'nothing but slaughter and blood'. He was expelled from Zwickau after less than a year.

He went to Prague, in Bohemia, the land of Hus – heresy-central – and from there he issued what is known as his *Prague Manifesto* in November 1521. It is full of Lutheresque denunciations of the clergy, or as he preferred to term them, 'pseudo-spiritual monks', 'donkey-fart doctors of theology' and 'hell-based parsons'. To me, that sounds like a brilliant movie trilogy. Müntzer claimed that God had a special purpose in store for him: 'God himself has appointed me for his harvest. I have made my sickle sharp, for my thoughts are zealous for the truth and my lips, skin, hands, hair, soul, body and my life all damn the unbelievers.'

He missed out his spleen, nose and lower intestine, but you get the point. Even for Prague this was too much. The authorities put him under house arrest and then evicted him in December 1521. He returned to Germany as an itinerant preacher. For a while he served as a chaplain at a Cistercian nunnery in Halles (the mind boggles . . .) but then he was chucked out of there as well.

Despite all this rejection – or maybe because of it – Müntzer was certain that something big was coming. He wrote that, 'the living God is sharpening his sickle in me so that I will later be able to cut down the red poppies and the little blue flowers'. (I don't know what it is with Müntzer and sickles. He was always banging on about harvesting.)

In 1523 Müntzer returned to Saxony, to the little town of Allstedt. With just 600 inhabitants, the town was under the protection of the reform-supporting Duke Johann of Thuringia, younger brother of Frederick the Wise. In Allstedt, Müntzer gathered around him a dedicated band of followers, a 'Christian League'. Five hundred people signed up straight away, including the entire town council. His preaching started to attract huge numbers: up to two thousand people came to hear him preach on Sundays. Unsurprisingly, things soon started to get out of hand. Again. A group of arsonists from Allstedt burned down a shrine to the Virgin Mary at nearby Mallerbach, and when Frederick the Wise called for punishment, Müntzer called him an 'old greybeard with as much wisdom in his head as I have in my backside'. I'm guessing this is an insult. Unless Müntzer had a surprisingly intelligent bottom.

Despite this, in a remarkable display of tolerance, Duke Johann determined to give him a fair hearing, and came himself to hear Müntzer preach. In an extraordinary sermon known as the *Fürstenpredigt*, Müntzer unleashed all barrels, comparing the rulers of Electoral Saxony to slimy eels, and the priests and all the clerics to snakes: the two groups, he claimed, were copulating together 'immorally in one great heap'. Amazingly, he wasn't arrested, or evicted, perhaps because at this time and in this atmosphere, the rulers simply weren't sure who was to be listened to and who wasn't. After all, what if Müntzer really *was* a prophet? Certainly Müntzer believed he had a direct line to God. He believed that true preachers were receptive to God's inner word received through the Holy Spirit and that anyone who did not have that was a waste of space, even though they 'devoured a hundred Bibles'.

Like Karlstadt, Müntzer had lost his faith in Luther. He launched a vicious attack on Luther, whom he called 'Brother Fattened-swine and Brother Soft-life', before, yes you've guessed it, more sickles: 'The tares must be pulled out of the vineyard of God at the time of the harvest . . . The angels who sharpen their sickles for the cutting are the earnest servants of God who fulfil the zeal of divine wisdom.' From Allstedt, Müntzer also wrote to Karlstadt, urging the people of Orlamünde to take up arms and join the struggle. They wrote back politely declining.*

Luther was not going to take all this sickling quietly, and he

---

* In *Against the Heavenly Prophets*, Luther – completely unfairly – accuses Karlstadt of secretly being in sympathy with what he calls the 'Allstedtians' and having 'a rebellious and murderous spirit, like the one at Allstedt'.

responded in a publication called, *A Letter to the Princes of Saxony concerning the Rebellious Spirit*. He urged the authorities to banish Müntzer, or the 'Satan of Allstedt' as Luther called him. However, Luther still didn't want to use violence: 'Our calling is to preach and suffer, not to strike and defend ourself with the fist. Christ and his apostles destroyed no churches and broke no images. They won hearts with the Word of God and then the churches and images fell of themselves.'

Luther's reply provoked Müntzer even further and he launched another tract called *A Highly Provoked Defence*, or to give it its full title: *Highly provoked defence and answer to the spiritless soft-living flesh in Wittenberg who has most lamentably befouled pitiable Christianity in a perverted way by his theft of holy Scripture*. Now *that* is a book title. And the text fairly scorches with insults: Luther was 'Doctor Liar', 'Father Pussyfoot', the 'ambassador of the devil', a 'venomous little worm'.

By now, Duke Johann had had enough. Müntzer was told to disband the Christian League and stop preaching provocations. In the end he chose to flee, climbing over the city walls in the dead of night, abandoning his poor wife and child and going to the much larger city of Mühlhausen. There he joined forces with an anticlerical ex-monk called Heinrich Pfeiffer. They started a programme of direct action: riots were started, altarpieces smashed, relics destroyed. When Müntzer, carrying a red cross and an unsheathed sword, led a march of 200 followers through the city, the Mayor and the city council fled *en masse*. In Mühlhausen Müntzer founded another band of true believers – the Eternal League of God – whose banner consisted of a rainbow with the motto 'The Word of the Lord Abides for Ever'. It claimed to be a spiritual organisation, but its ranks included captains, ensigns, sergeants, pipers and drummers. It was, literally, a salvation army.

And their time had come. Because in 1524 it wasn't just Mühlhausen and Allstedt that were up in arms. There was conflict all over the place.

The peasants were revolting.

11 Revolting peasants

The robbing and murdering hordes

There had been sporadic outbreaks of unrest throughout the fourteenth and fifteenth centuries, but in 1524 a mass uprising of peasants broke out in Germany. This was on a different scale. It was the largest popular revolution Europe had ever seen, with up to three hundred thousand rebels involved. It began quietly, with minor revolts that seemed more like industrial action than anything else. But it soon escalated and, in the end, much of Germany was engulfed, from Saxony to Swabia and the Tyrol.

'Peasants' is perhaps the wrong word. They were not quite the serf-like peasants that the word implies.* Nor was the war a purely rural affair. Miners and townspeople, too, were involved, and in some numbers. What they all had in common was that they were ordinary men, common people.

It wasn't a rebellion about religion, but religious ideas fuelled the flames. Significantly, given Luther's emphasis on the Bible, their protest was heavily informed by scripture. When they took to arms they gave themselves consciously religious names: 'Christian federation', 'Christian union', 'Evangelical brotherly league'. A manifesto produced in March 1525 – *The Twelve Articles of the Peasants* – called not only for the reform of rents,

* More like very, very low-level farmers. But 'The Very, Very, Low-Level Farmers War' was never going to catch on as a title.

159

taxes and servitude, but also for the reform of the Church, including the preaching of the 'pure' gospel, and the right to elect the parish priest. The manifesto was the work of Sebastian Lotzer, a tanner, and Christoph Schappeler, an evangelical pastor. The document is peppered with Bible references and, significantly, it also quotes Luther.

Luther certainly had some sympathy with the peasants' cause. The peasants, he believed, were being taxed 'out of their very skins'. He exhorted the princes to seek peace, and not to 'start a fire that no one can extinguish'. But he also rebuked the peasants for thinking they had a right to take up arms; that, Luther argued, was a right which only the secular authorities had.

It was too late. Violence erupted. Castles were plundered, hundreds of monasteries looted, churches ransacked. Sickles were wielded. And the rebels looked to Luther for support. In 1523, Luther had knocked out another treatise, *Secular Authority: To What Extent It Should Be Obeyed*, in which he claimed that under certain circumstances the nobility could be resisted. It called princes 'the greatest fools or the worst criminals on earth'. He was reacting to the fact that many rulers had ordered his books to be burned: 'God . . . has made our rulers mad; they actually think they can do what they please and order their subjects to follow them in it . . . It has now gone so far that the rulers order people to get rid of certain books and to believe and conform to whatever they prescribe . . .' In *The Babylonian Captivity*, he wrote further: 'No law, whether of men or of angels, may rightfully be imposed upon Christians without their consent, for we are free of all laws.' Most of all, at Worms, he had stood up to the Emperor himself. He demonstrated that it was possible – necessary, even – for an individual to put his conscience and his faith above secular authority.

Yet when it came to choosing between Prince Charming and Mr Everybody, Luther sided with royalty. To be fair, he was caught in an impossible situation. The Reformation was in its infancy; it needed protection. If rulers like Frederick the Wise came to equate reform with revolution then all would be lost. So one can understand why Luther decided on that course of action. But the issue, as ever with him, is the intemperate, extreme language he used. He wrote a tract – *Against the Robbing and Murdering Hordes of Peasants* – in which he called the peasants mad dogs and blasphemers. They were to be cut down like weeds, eradicated like vermin: 'Let everyone who can, smite, slay and stab, secretly or openly, remembering that nothing can be more poisonous, hurtful or devilish than a rebel.' He urged the soldiers to act: 'This is not a time to sleep. There is no place for patience or mercy. This is the time of the sword, not the day of grace.'

It's shocking reading. In language reminiscent of the Crusades, he declared that anyone who killed a rebellious peasant was doing God's will and that anyone who died fighting on the side of the princes would be a martyr in God's eyes, while each peasant who perished would become 'an eternal firebrand of hell'. And this from the man who had started his career by condemning indulgences.

Bad Frankenhausen

Meanwhile, back in Mühlhausen, Müntzer was happily getting his sickle out. For him, the peasants' revolt was serving a darker, apocalyptic vision. Initially Luther had sent a preacher to counteract Müntzer's teaching and, surprise surprise, Müntzer and Pfeiffer were expelled from the city. But this time the expulsion didn't stick. Pfeiffer was reinstated by popular demand, and Müntzer, who had gone on a preaching tour in Austria, rushed back in February 1525.

The old city council was toppled and a new, rather optimistically named 'Eternal council' was elected in its place. Müntzer reinstated the Christian League and this time some two thousand men enlisted. Now Müntzer was in full-on apocalyptic mode: 'The time has come, the evil-doers are running like scared dogs!' he proclaimed. The Day of the Lord was at hand. He urged the peasants to overthrow the tyrannical authorities.

He set out with some of his followers to help the peasant forces. In the end, only 300 from Mühlhausen joined Müntzer, but he assured his little Gideon's army that they were invincible. They joined with thousands of other peasants at a place called Bad Frankenhausen. Müntzer issued an appeal for more rebels to join them, wondering whether 'the Lutheran gruel-sloppers have softened you up with their grubby soft-heartedness'.

Against them were ranged the armies of Duke George of Saxony, and Philip, Landgrave of Hesse. Their troops were largely mercenaries: well trained and well equipped. Müntzer's forces were untrained and mostly had farming implements as weapons, including – yes you've guessed it – sickles and scythes.

The duke hinted that he might be merciful if the peasant army surrendered unconditionally. But he wanted Müntzer and the other leaders. Eventually his patience wore out. The canons opened fire, the cavalry thundered down, the peasants panicked and ran. Thousands were killed that afternoon, perhaps as many as ten thousand. Casualties for the duke's forces may have been as low as single figures. The site of the battlefield was known as 'Blood Alley' for centuries to come.*

Müntzer managed to escape from the battlefield. He was discovered during a house-to-house search, in an attic in Frankenhausen, hiding under bedclothes pretending to be an invalid. He was taken to Heldrungen Castle and, under torture, agreed to recant. Pfeiffer was also captured. The two men were taken to Duke George's army HQ at Görmar and beheaded on 27 May. Their heads were stuck on pikestaffs and displayed as a warning for everyone.

In all, over a hundred thousand peasants were slaughtered in 1525. Luther was widely criticised for showing no mercy to the now-defeated peasants and for producing a work which was 'unchristian and too hard'.

Luther denied that he was culpable for any of this. But he didn't deny that he had spoken out: 'My good friends, you who are praising mercy so highly because the peasants are beaten, why did you not praise it when the peasants were raging, smiting, robbing, burning, and plundering . . . No one spoke of mercy then. Everything was "rights"; nothing was said of mercy; it was nothing. "Rights, rights, rights!" they were everything.'

---

* The Battle of Frankenhausen is one of the historical scenes depicted on the world's largest oil painting, Werner Tübke's compellingly titled, *Early Bourgeois Revolution in Germany*. It is 400 feet (120 metres) long, 45 feet (14 metres) high, and is so big it can only be housed in its own specially built gallery. It was commissioned by the Communist leaders of East Germany, who saw Müntzer as a kind of early socialist revolutionary, instead of what he actually was, a delusional rabble-rouser with a thing for sickles.

He made a distinction between the 'ordinary evildoers' and all these smiting, robbing, burning kind of rebels. 'A rebel is not worth rational arguments . . .' he wrote. 'You have to answer people like that with a fist . . . their ears must now be unbuttoned with bullets till their heads jump off their shoulders.'

He was probably right, in *realpolitik* terms. If the Reformation was to succeed, to survive, it needed strong, politically and militarily powerful leaders. It's all very well having a big following among the peasants, but in reality you need a prince on your side. Even the Pope knew that religious authority only works in the world if it is backed up by a bloke with a huge sword.

To be fair to Luther, in the same letter where he defended his attitude to the peasants, he was also critical of those 'furious, raving, senseless tyrants, who even after the battle cannot get their fill of blood'. And yet there is something distasteful about the whole business. What Müntzer and other radical reformers recognised, which Luther could not or did not want to see, was the undercurrent of pain and injustice which characterised life for so many. There is, in Luther's self-defence, a concern with his own reputation. He found it hard to face up to the fact that many of the peasants were his 'children': they had fed on his ideas. His actions haunted him to some extent. Later in life he admitted the truth: 'In the rebellion I struck all the peasants. All their blood is on my neck. But I know it from our Lord God that he commanded me to speak.'

12 Relationships and other problems

Nuns on the run

It wasn't all blood and violence. There was room for some love as well.

In 1523, Luther received a message from some damsels in distress. In the light of his teaching, many monks and nuns were leaving their religious houses, and one group of nuns in a different German state wrote to ask Luther for advice: they wanted to leave, but the authorities where they lived had a tendency to execute runaway nuns. Luther – perhaps drawing on his own adventures as Junker Jörg – arranged an escape for them: they were smuggled out of the local convent in the back of a fish-monger's wagon, alongside barrels of herring.

Luther and his 'Katie'

Luther then took on the task of finding husbands for them – no easy task for a group of ex-nuns who smelt of herring. However, he succeeded for eight of them: and the ninth, he was persuaded to marry himself. He married her in June 1525. Her name was Katharina von Bora, and although he always said that he married her not out of love but out of duty, they seemed to make it work.

Luther's house in Wittenberg. It was a former Augustinian priory. Among other activities, Mr & Mrs Luther brewed beer on the premises

Luther's marriage was a hugely public event and he wrote extensively on both his wife and his children. (Not literally. He had paper.) They had six children of their own and four adopted orphans. He was very fond of his children, and was heartbroken when his daughter Magdalena died in her teens: 'The tenderness of the father's heart is so great that we cannot think of it without sobs and sighs, which tear asunder the heart . . .' he wrote.

Like his own father, he had married above his station. Katharina had in her pre-convent life been a *von* Bora.* Luther spoke fondly of her, calling her 'my Lord Katie' and 'my chain'. He said that he would 'rather have Katie than France or Venice'.

He loved his wife. And he also *loved* his wife, if you see what I mean. He talked about marital sex as being something more 'than is necessary for the begetting of children'. This was a genuine break with the view of sex being a necessary evil – a view which dated back to Augustine. He still viewed it as a bit sinful – 'intercourse is never without sin' – but that was all part of living in a fallen world. You couldn't escape that.†

Luther urged people to work at their marriage:

A wife is easily taken, but to have abiding love, that is the challenge. One who finds it in his marriage should thank the Lord for it. Therefore, approach marriage earnestly and ask God to give you a good, pious girl, with whom you can spend your life in mutual love. For sex [alone] establishes nothing in this regard: there must also be agreement in values and character.

The marriage became an image of the ideal Christian family. Martin and Katie sort of invented the ideal of the Protestant household. They showed how a home could be a place of worship, Bible study and prayer, as much as a monastery. Before the Reformation, men and women sat or stood separately in church, but when pews were introduced, they sat together as families.

---

* In German, the prefix *von* indicates a noble lineage. It's what is called a nobiliary particle, which sounds like something out of *Star Trek*. Anyway, basically, she was a bit posh.

† Calvin disagreed with the idea that sex was inherently sinful. Since marital sex stopped people committing adultery or fornication, it had to be OK. A remedy for a sin could not, in itself, be sinful. Bucer was even more liberal: he approved of divorce, if the whole thing wasn't working very well.

In the home, Luther knew his place: 'In domestic affairs I defer to Katie. Otherwise I am led by the Holy Spirit.' Indeed, the evidence seems to indicate that he was fairly liberated about women – at least in terms of the general misogyny of the sixteenth century. He even helped wash the nappies and look after the babies. And this was pretty radical for the time. In Luther's culture a man who washed nappies was not a real man: there are wood-cuts showing a man cleaning nappies while his wife looks on commandingly. It was a task which was beneath men, but Luther recommended it. 'These are truly golden and noble works,' he said. Doesn't sound like any baby I've ever dealt with.

They lived in the old monastery where Luther had been a monk. The Elector gave the building to Luther. Luther had a bowling alley built in the garden, and Katie ran their private brewery. They sold the beer to help make ends meet – they also drank a lot themselves. It was a place which welcomed many people, friends, students.

And even enemies. During the peasants' revolt, Luther also arranged sanctuary for Karlstadt and his family. Karlstadt had vehemently rejected Müntzer's invitation to join the revolt, but his detractors insisted on claiming that he was a part of the rebellion. So he found himself – again – a fugitive. He wrote to Luther, who arranged for him to be granted asylum in the environs of Wittenberg. Luther helped him out, although he did insist that Karlstadt retract his theological positions concerning the Lord's Supper. He made him publish a document titled, *Apology by Dr Andreas Karlstadt Regarding the False Charge of Insurrection Which has Unjustly Been Made Against Him*, to which Luther contributed a foreword.

In March 1525, Katharina even became godmother to one of Karlstadt's children. For the next four years or so, Karlstadt scratched a living in the environs of Wittenberg, first as a farmer and then as a peddler. Finally, by 1529 he'd had enough of the constant surveillance and control he felt under. He left Wittenberg, recanted his recantation and embarked on a peripatetic career of preaching and teaching until he eventually died of the plague in Basel in 1541.

Like dung in fancy vases

The relationship with Karlstadt is an extreme example, but Luther was always a man who, in the words of the Blessed Tom Waits, 'smoked his friends down to the filter'. His friendship with Erasmus also hit the rocks around this time – although, perhaps 'friendship' is putting it too strongly. Relationship. Acquaintance. Barely disguised disdain. Whatever.

Luther owed a massive debt to Erasmus: it was, after all, reading his Greek New Testament which converted him. And Erasmus wanted to reform the Church. But Erasmus rejected the extremes to which Luther was heading. Erasmus wanted to cleanse the Church from corruption, hypocrisy, greed and lust for power. When it came to medieval Catholicism, Erasmus wanted renovation and repair. Luther wanted demolition. Even early on, Luther had his reservations about Erasmus. He wrote in 1517: 'I am reading our Erasmus but daily I dislike him more and more . . . he does not advance the cause of Christ and the grace of God sufficiently . . . Human things weigh more with him than the divine.' Erasmus, for his part, grew increasingly alarmed by Luther's extremism, and, especially, his brutal, foul language.

Erasmus believed in courtesy and moderation. He could be friends with people who disagreed with him. Although he specialised in satire, he didn't like disagreeableness. He said, 'I think one gets further by courtesy and moderation than by clamour. That was how Christ brought the world under his sway.' It is a little bit of a stretch to recognise this as a picture of Christ. Whatever else he was, Christ was not a courteous urbane gentleman.

So Luther quickly gave up on him. Scornfully he told Erasmus that the cause of reform has 'long since outgrown your littleness'. He was right. Erasmus contributed to the debate, but he was never going to change anything.

In 1524 Erasmus wrote *On the Freedom of the Will*, an attack on Luther's Augustinian view of humanity: that the fallen human will is in bondage and cannot do anything good. Erasmus hated any idea that belittled or reduced the free will, responsibility and, indeed, abilities of humans. He believed in human potential and reason. And he argued that it was wrong to be so dogmatic on an issue like free will, about which there must be a lot of obscurity. This essentially challenged Luther's understanding of salvation by grace alone. Luther had gone too far: he was right, of course, to say that we can never earn our way to righteousness, but that didn't mean we couldn't do anything. God must reward our deeds somehow – after all, he is a loving father.

Erasmus actually was at home with ambiguity. He saw that the Bible was complicated and he distrusted attempts to simplify things. 'The sum of our religion is peace and unanimity,' he once said, 'but these can scarcely stand unless we define as little as possible.' Luther, on the other hand, loved to simplify things. His opinion was that if something in the Bible is complicated, then the right answer is: Whatever Luther Thinks. It was doctrine that mattered first and foremost – doctrine as established by Martin Luther.

Erasmus was, in his urbane, reasonable way, searching for a middle path, for compromise. Luther wasn't much interested in compromise. Or middle paths. Or being reasonable. Asking Luther not to be dogmatic on something was like, well, asking the Pope not to be Catholic. Or a bear not to have a tower experience in the woods. Luther was dogmatic about *everything*.

Luther's usual response to critical writings was to use them as toilet paper. But for Erasmus he made an exception and he actually read *On the Freedom of the Will*. He decided, though, that it wasn't so much toilet paper as the contents of the toilet itself. Luther dismissed Erasmus' clever arguments as nicely packaged dung: 'like refuse or ordure being carried in gold and silver vases'.

There was nothing urbane and civilised about Luther's response. *The Bondage of the Will* was grievous bodily theology. Luther argued that, 'for all we freely choose to do, we never naturally choose to please God, and therefore all our salvation must be God's doing, not ours'. He dismissed Erasmus' arguments as 'trivial, worthless and . . . so much dung'.

Around the table, to friends, Luther mocked Erasmus. He was 'an eel, a croaking toad'. 'I hate Erasmus from the bottom of my heart,' he declared. He even declared Erasmus to be 'the greatest enemy Christ has had these thousand years past'. It's typically ridiculous hyperbole. Erasmus was not the kind of reformer that Luther was, but he was never an enemy. Yet Luther could never distinguish between those who disagreed with some of what he stood for, and those who disagreed with everything he stood for. You had to be entirely for Luther, or you were against him. Such was his paranoia.

As for Erasmus, he remained his aloof, urbane self. When some monks in Cologne claimed that 'Erasmus laid the egg which Luther hatched', he denied it. 'I laid a poultry egg,' he murmured. 'Luther hatched a very different bird.'

date-a-protestant

✳ Recently left the monastery ? Looking for that special ex-nun with whom you can settle down ?

✳ Want to find that one person with whom you were predestined to find love ?

DATE-A-PROTESTANT is the service you need. With hundreds of ex-Priests, Monks and Nuns on our books, we can find just the right person for you to break your vows of celibacy with. Whether you're a Calvinist, a Lutheran, a Zwinglian, an Anabaptist or just pretending on the grounds that it's the only way you'll ever get a woman, find your lifelong partner with DATE-A-PROTESTANT.

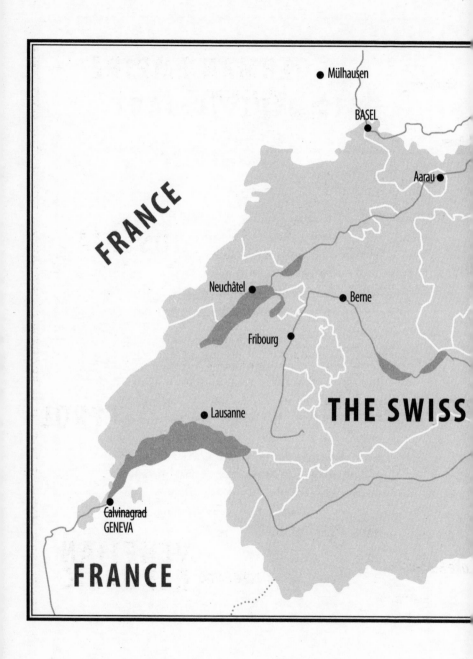

Mülhausen

BASEL

Aarau

FRANCE

Neuchâtel

Berne

Fribourg

THE SWISS

Lausanne

Calvinagrad
GENEVA

FRANCE

- Part Four -

The Swiss Role

❖

13 Zwinglin' in the rain

'An unknown ignoramus'

'But what,' I hear you ask, 'of Switzerland?'

What an excellent question. It's a good time to skip across the Alps to the land of snow, skiing, cuckoo clocks, dubious banking practices and major reformers.

Yes, the Reformation wasn't just a German phenomenon. Much to Luther's irritation, there were other leaders. Let's meet Huldrych Zwingli.

Think of the great rivalries across history: Ali v Frazier, The Beatles v The Stones, Tom v Jerry. Well, right up there with them is Martin Luther versus Huldrych Zwingli. They should have been on the same side. Well, they *were* on the same side; they just couldn't admit it. On the face of it they had so much in common: born only seven weeks apart, both spoke German, both passionate reformers with a habit of calling their opponents rude names. And yet they ended up bitter rivals.

Zwingli couldn't stand that Luther got all the credit for this reform business. He hated being called a Lutheran. 'I will not have the papists call me Lutheran,' he said, 'for I did not learn Christ's teaching from Luther, but from the very word of God.'

He certainly did things his own way. And his story is one of soldiers, scripture and – strangely – sausages . . .

Huldrych Zwingli was born on 1 January 1484 – just a few months after Luther – in the mountainous central Swiss canton of Glarus.* His home was the rather exciting-sounding Wildhaus in the Alpine valley of Toggenburg. It's all very Wagnerian.

He was educated at Basel, Berne and Vienna – and perhaps in Paris as well. This was a man who got around. He was not intensely religious like Luther, but he did visit Rome (and had a similar violent reaction to all he saw). When his education was over, he returned to Glarus to become a priest in September 1506.

Like Germany, Switzerland was a confederation of semi-autonomous cities and small republics. These territories (called 'cantons') had gained their independence from Austria in 1291, but their small size meant that they often found themselves pawns in various power struggles which went on between France, Spain, the papacy, the Holy Roman Empire and anyone else who wanted to have a go. All of which meant that they had to learn how to fight, and the Swiss developed a reputation as fearsome troops. Switzerland was a poor region – this was a long time before they discovered that flair for international finance which has brought them so much happiness – so these soldiers became something of a major export industry. Armed with their pikes, their William Tell-esque crossbows and, of course, specially designed penknives, Swiss soldiers were feared as mercenaries on the battlefields of Europe.

They were a particular favourite of our old friend, the warrior pope, Julius II, who employed Swiss muscle both in his army and as his personal bodyguard.† Zwingli was one of those who served under Julius. After returning to Switzerland, he served for some time as chaplain to one of these troops of mercenaries, accompanying them to Italy, where they fought under the Pope's command. He saw both sides of the coin. At the Battle of Navarra, in June 1513, he tasted victory when Swiss troops surrounded and destroyed the French forces of Louis XII. Two years later, it

---

* He's also known as Ulrich Zwingli. And in some older books, his surname is given as Zwingle. For some reason that always makes me laugh.
† The Swiss guard have been the official security force for the Vatican ever since.

was a different story: at the Battle of Marignano, some ten thousand Swiss troops were massacred by French and Venetian forces.

Zwingli was a fan of the Pope. He had even written 'The Ox', a poem praising him.* But this massacre shocked him. He returned home with a pension from the Pope of 50 gulden a year, a lifelong suspicion of foreigners in general and Italians in particular, and a copy of Erasmus' *Adages* in which he had underlined the proverb 'War is only sweet to the inexperienced.'

In 1516, he became a parish priest in Einsiedeln, in the neighbouring, and vowel-less, canton of Schwyz. He also bought himself a copy of Erasmus' Greek New Testament, hot off the press. Using this, he sat up at night and taught himself Greek, copying out the letters of Paul by hand in order to fix them in his memory and understand them. (He also began studying Hebrew as well, so that he might read the Old Testament just – as he saw it – as God had dictated it.) He began to reflect on what he was reading (and writing), and to wonder why the life of the early church seemed so different.

He went to visit Erasmus in Basel: 'It was an extraordinary proof of kindness that you did not despise an insignificant man, an unknown ignoramus', he wrote. But Zwingli was not to be unknown for long.

In August 1518 an indulgence salesman called Bernard Samson came to the region. Zwingli didn't read Luther's Ninety-five Theses until 1519, but he had the same allergic reaction as Luther to the practice of indulgences and his powerful preaching forced Bernie to bolt. It was preaching like that which could get a young Swiss ex-mercenary noticed, and later in the year he went to Zürich, one of the wealthiest and most powerful Swiss cantons, taking up a post at the Grossmünster, Zürich's main church. It

---

* In the poem, the noble ox (Switzerland) was lured into a foolish alliance with the leopard (France) or the lion (Holy Roman Empire) in their battles against the fox (Venice).

was not a universally welcomed appointment, not just because he seemed like a bit of a yokel – a village boy with a thick accent – but more because rumours were circulating that he had a somewhat chequered sexual history: it was suggested that, more than once, he'd had what you might call a Swiss roll. There were tales of him seducing the daughter of a prominent official. Zwingli was forced to admit that although he had 'firmly resolved not to touch any woman . . . I succeeded poorly in this'. In Glarus, he said, the resolution lasted six months, 'in Einsiedeln about a year for no one would participate in such a resolution with me'. He was forced to admit that he had slept with the girl. But in his defence she was (a) the daughter of a barber and (b) 'she seduced me with more than flattering words'. Despite this, and the rumours that he had got her pregnant (although he claimed the father could be any one of a number of people!), he was appointed to the post.*

It was a new start in a number of ways. On New Year's Day 1519 Zwingli broke with the standard procedure and declared that he would preach his way more systematically through the New Testament. 'After the Gospel according to Matthew, I continued with the Acts of the Apostles to show to the church in Zürich how and through whom the gospel had been planted and propagated', he wrote. He soon became known for his powerful preaching.

Then, in 1519, the plague came to Zürich. More than one and half thousand people died in the city, and Zwingli was very nearly one of them. He was brought to the very brink, and when he recovered he was a man on a mission. From now on he would serve God whatever happened. 'I am your vessel, to use or to discard,' he promised God. This, in a way, was Zwingli's version of Luther's *Turmerlebnis*, although somewhat less toilet-based.

---

* The other candidate, Laurentius Mär, fell out of the running when it was revealed that he had six children by his mistress and already had a number of other benefices.

But it was Zwingli's 'conversion' experience. Once he recovered, he began to preach with a new zeal.

He also started reading Luther. The Ninety-five Theses came his way, along with a commentary on the Lord's Prayer. Although he seemed quite keen on these at the time, later he came to deny that they had much influence. 'I began to preach the gospel in 1516,' he wrote in 1523, 'long before anyone in our region had ever heard of Luther . . . Luther is, as I gather, an admirable warrior for God, who earnestly searches the scriptures . . . I do not wish to bear Luther's name, for I have read little of his teaching and have often purposely desisted from reading his books in order to conciliate the papists.' He accuses Luther of 'yielding to the weak' and holding back on real reform. 'Not that he says too much; rather he does not say enough . . .'

Zwingli's high view of scripture was the energy behind the Reformation in Zürich. Zwingli was convinced that the scriptures could and should be easily understood by all. Human beings were created with a kind of inbuilt thirst for scripture. (In his 1522 book, *The Clarity and Certainty of the Word of God*, he argued that if humanity is made in the image of God, then we always long for the word of God – even when we don't realise we long for it. And scripture brings clarity – in the sense that it illuminates and enlightens our lives. 'The word of God is certain,' he wrote, 'and cannot fail; it is bright and does not let man err in the darkness; it recalls itself, it makes itself plain and illumines the human world with all salvation.')

Still, for all of his reading of Erasmus and systematic Bible-based preaching, he remained a Catholic. But all that changed after Sausagegate.

Sausage party

One of the chief events of the Church's calendar was Lent. For forty days before Easter, Christians were supposed to fast. They would give up 'choice' foods: meat, milk, butter, cheese and, in Switzerland, presumably, Toblerone.

But in 1522, on Ash Wednesday, the first day of Lent, at the house of a printer called Christopher Froschauer, some Christians dared to eat some smoked sausage and cooked egg. Or maybe they smoked some sausage and cooked some egg. Either way, it was a sausage party. Zwingli was present, although he did not inhale, as it were: he did not actually eat of the forbidden wurst.

It was a scandal. Immediately, the city council began an investigation into Sausagegate, as it has been called.* When the city council asked why Froschauer had defied the Church in this way he answered that he was . . . er . . . hungry. And anyway, he continued, Huldrych Zwingli had said it was OK. Zwingli was interrogated, but he pointed out that there was nothing in the Bible about Lent, never mind sausages. Fasting, he pointed out, was a human tradition. 'If you like to fast, do it,' he said. 'If you don't like meat, don't eat it, but do not touch a Christian's freedom.'

From this point, things moved swiftly. Zwingli and his supporters began to disrupt services where priests were preaching what the reformers believed to be non-biblical ideas. For example, Franz Lambert, a monk from Avignon, was preaching on the veneration of the saints and the Virgin Mary, when Zwingli started shouting at him: 'Brother, this is where you err!' Again, it was not that he was casting all his Catholic past away – Zwingli himself preached 'A Sermon on the Eternally Pure Maid Mary', praising her as the mother of God, a perpetual virgin and a model Christian. What he opposed was the idea of adoration, or the idea that the Virgin Mary could mediate between man and God.

As these new ideas caught on, the city began to change. In July 1522 the ministers of Zürich petitioned the Bishop of

---

* It's only been called this by me, actually. But I'm hoping it's going to catch on.

Konstanz to abolish celibacy for the clergy. In this, they were simply seeking to legitimise a widespread practice. As we've already seen, several popes had not exactly been strictly celibate – with either gender. But further down the clerical ladder it was widely acknowledged that a huge amount of rumpy-pumpiness was widespread. (Not least with Zwingli himself.) Many Catholic clergy had 'housekeepers', who would do a lot more than the odd bit of dusting their knick-knacks.

Nevertheless, the Bishop of Konstanz rejected the idea out of hand. He was against it partly because it was a clear violation of canon law, but also because it would have cost him money. It was common for the clergy to raise families with these house-keepers, and the bishops would turn a blind eye to the practice for the payment of a small fee. In Konstanz, there were reputed to be some one and a half thousand children, which raised a not-insubstantial sum for the diocese through the fees.

By now, though, Zwingli was looking to the Bible as the authority in such matters – not the clergy or the authorities. So, in 1522 he was secretly married to a young widow called Anna Reinhart. However, it was all very hush-hush. They did not cele-brate their marriage publicly until two years later, by which time it was becoming hard to hide, since she was six months pregnant.*

The decisive split came in August 1522 when Zwingli wrote a tract, *The First and Final Defence*, repudiating the right of the bishop to be the final arbiter. His writings inspired the Zürich city council to hold a consultation on 29 January 1523. The debate was a huge spectacle: more than six hundred rulers, coun-cilmen, dignitaries, clerics and general spectators participated, all crammed into the town hall. On one side there was the bishop and his delegation, armed with the might of the Church, and vigorously questioning the presumption of a small Swiss city in daring to challenge orthodox doctrine. On the other side was Zwingli, armed with his Greek New Testament, his Hebrew Old

* They went on to have several children, most of whom sadly died in childhood.

Testament, his Latin Vulgate and, significantly, a document he had drawn up – a programme for reform outlined in sixty-seven theses.

It was five years since Luther hadn't nailed his Ninety-five Theses to anything. But Zwingli's were no copycat production. The Ninety-five Theses were almost all concerned with the indulgence scandal; Zwingli's sixty-seven theses were a comprehensive outline of Reformation thought.

They open with a positional statement: 'All who say that the gospel is invalid without the confirmation of the Church err and slander God.'

And what is that gospel? It is summed up in Jesus: 'The sum and substance of the gospel is that our Lord Jesus Christ, the true Son of God, has made known to us the will of his heavenly Father, and has with his innocence released us from death and reconciled God.'

Zwingli goes on to condemn 'clerical (so-called) ordinances' whose 'splendour, riches, classes, titles, laws' are nothing but 'a cause of all foolishness'. For Zwingli it is all very clear-cut: 'For in the faith rests our salvation, and in unbelief our damnation; for all truth is clear in him.'

The remainder of the theses are a no-holds-barred, all-out attack on abuses, superstitions and anything else which Zwingli doesn't agree with, including, but not limited to, clerical property and wealth, fasting ('the decree about cheese and butter is a Roman swindle,' he complains), pilgrimage, monk's hoods, clerical celibacy and 'orders, sects, brotherhoods, etc.'. Purgatory is rejected, since it is not in scripture. Priests, likewise, since 'About the form of consecration which the priests have received recent times the Scriptures know nothing' and 'they [the Scriptures] recognise no priests except those who proclaim the word of God'.

There was more. Zwingli argued that Christ's death on the cross was a complete sacrifice and so does not need to be repeated constantly in the Mass. This challenged the very purpose of the priesthood, for celebrating Mass was what they did.

It was all about Jesus, and he – not the Pope – was the head of the Church. And scripture – not the Pope, nor the clerical laws, nor the Church Fathers – was the foundation. Only trust in Christ, not our own good works, can save.

These were inflammatory, socially revolutionary statements. 'God does not desire our decrees or doctrines if they do not originate with him,' argued Zwingli. And Christians only owe allegiance and obedience to the secular authorities, 'in so far as they do not command that which is contrary to God'.

The document ends with an ominous warning: 'All the clerical superiors shall at once settle down, and with unanimity set up the cross of Christ, not the money-chests, or they will perish, for I tell you the axe is raised against the tree.'

The axe was poised. And Zwingli was the man with the chopper.

Zwingli of Zürich

The white walls

Zwingli won. Just before lunchtime, the city council decided in Zwingli's favour – presumably so they could all nip off for some egg and sausage. The council immediately ruled that only preaching that was biblical would be legal in Zürich. Now Zwingli had power. Now the *real* reforms could begin.

Of course, when you call clerics 'lying, greedy maggots' as Zwingli did, people tend to get a bit overexcited. His supporters took all the talk of axes and chopping as permission to attack. They started 'cleansing' the churches of idols: statues were destroyed, stained-glass windows smashed, icons burned. It was bordering on anarchy.

The council began to regret their early lunch. So they called a second public disputation, which took place over three days in October 1523. Like all proper sequels, it was bigger: over nine hundred people were present including 350 ministers. And the council, worried that unrest was spreading, decided to press the pause button on all reform. The idea was not that it should be stopped, just that it would be better to have some teaching of the basic principles before people took matters into their own hands. Zwingli agreed and he wrote a book, *A Short Christian Introduction*, which was distributed to local clergy. In it, he warned that Christians did not have the liberty to take matters into their own hands. (Which was a bit rich, since he already had.) Still, the trajectory was in favour of reform and, by June 1524, the council was prepared to get going again. The council commanded that all images, statues and paintings be removed from the churches.

This time it was supposed to be done in a measured way, 'with good behaviour', not 'wantonly'. Indulgences, penance, pilgrimage, prayers to the saints, the monastic life, all were abandoned. In midsummer 1524, bands of clergy, council officials and workmen entered every church, locked the doors, and proceeded to purge them of all their visual splendour. Zwingli had a kind of fear of beauty. He felt people might idolise it. God was invisible, intangible, so he must be worshipped in an invisible kind of way; spiritually, not through the senses. Anything visual, then, was removed; crucifixes, candles, altars, rood screens, images and relics were destroyed. It took thirteen days, after which Zwingli happily declared, 'The walls are beautifully white!'

He was not wrong. Zwinglian style was austere: whitewashed walls, clear windows, the plainest furnishings. He rejected church music, 'which not the hundredth part understands'. Despite fellow reformers trying to persuade him of the merits of congregational singing, it remained banned in Zürich and worship services took place in a Quaker-like silence.*

Great Moments in Reformation History

NUMBER 15: In Zürich Zwingli's iconoclasts get to work.

They've got weapons of Mass destruction.

* Church music only returned in 1529 after Zwingli's death.

The reforms were extensive. Anything 'Roman' was fair game. Monasteries and convents were closed, sold off, and the money used to feed the poor or for education. It was all very Karlstadt: 'pastors' replaced 'priests' and nobody wore vestments, just their ordinary clothes. Zwingli's emphasis on scripture meant that the Bible was seen as the basis for all the law. The marriage laws were revised along Old Testament lines (this had some 'modern' outcomes: since marriage was a civil ceremony and not a sacrament, divorce was permissible).

Perhaps the most important reform, however, took place on Easter Day 1525. And it reflects the real heart of the conflict between Zwingli and Luther.

Zwingli rejected outright the theory of transubstantiation. He believed that the bread and wine were symbols, nothing more. The Eucharist was a purely memorial celebration. Thus, under Zwingli, the Lord's Supper took the form of a simple meal. Gone were the vestments and the gleaming silver; instead there were wooden cups and plates, plain bread rolls, a jug of wine. It was served from a table in the midst of the congregation. The words used were simply taken from the account of the Last Supper in the Bible. Not a word of Latin was spoken; everything was in ordinary German. There was no music or chanting. And in Zürich, the Lord's Supper was only celebrated four times a year: Christmas, Easter, Pentecost and early September.

Furthermore, just as Karlstadt had done four years earlier, the people were given both the bread and the wine.

It was a complete break with the Roman Mass.

And everyone in Zürich was expected to toe the line. Internal obedience was enforced through a Court of Domestic Relations, with Zwingli as the chief consultant. He established a strong education system, starting with a grammar school (for boys, of course). In June 1525, Zwingli founded a theological training school. The *Prophezei* was the first proper reformed Bible

TOP REFORMERS

Huldrych Zwingli

Born: Wildhaus, Switzerland, 1484
Died: Kappel, nr Zurich, Switzerland, 1531

AKA: Ulrich Zwingli, Huldrych Zwingle

Former mercenary chaplain and leader of the Reformation in Switzerland. In Zürich he developed a plain, austere form of Reformation worship. He banned icons and images and argued that Communion was purely symbolic. Always denied being influenced by Luther with whom he argued bitterly. He persecuted the Anabaptists and was killed in battle.

Fun Fact: Zwingli could play six instruments. But he banned the use of music in church.

INFLUENCE	78
THEOLOGICAL IMPORTANCE	72
FACIAL HAIR	0
GENERAL GLOOMINESS	56
ABUSIVENESS	18
HAT QUALITY	66
PROPENSITY TO VIOLENCE	98

college.* Zwingli based the name on 1 Corinthians 14, where

* It not only trained clergy but produced resources, such as numerous Bible

Paul urged Christians to desire 'the gift of prophecy'. Zwingli, curiously, interpreted this as being the ability to teach the Bible – which is probably not at all what Paul had in mind. As well as interpreting 'prophesying' as preaching, he also insisted students were 'given the gift of tongues', by which he meant, not some charismatic experience, but learning Latin, Hebrew and Greek. Clergy, canons, even older school pupils would gather to study the Bible for five days a week (they had Sundays and Fridays off). Teaching was given in Latin and German. And much of the course was taught by Zwingli and his friend Oswald Myconius.

Initially, the Pope was reluctant to take action against Zürich and Zwingli, because he still needed Swiss troops.* Other states, though, looked on with some alarm at what was happening in Zürich. Opposition began to harden among the Swiss confederation. In April 1524, the five 'inner' cantons – Lucerne, Uri, Schwyz, Unterwalden and Zug – formed an alliance, *die fünf Orte* ('the Five States') and pledged themselves to defend the Catholic faith and to 'root out this Lutheran, Zwinglian, Hussite, erroneous and faulty teaching from all our territories and jurisdictions and, as far as we can and our power enables us, to attack, punish and suppress it'.

They called a meeting – the Baden Disputation – which took place at Baden in 1526. Johann Eck arrived to take on the Swiss reformers and to stop this second Reformation in its tracks. Zwingli refused to attend, because he could not be guaranteed his safety. The outcome was exactly as you might expect: Zwingli was condemned as a heretic; he was to be banned and his writings were no longer to be distributed.

However, it was noticeable that three of the Swiss cantons – Basel, Berne, Schaffhausen – refused to condemn him. The sides were forming.

---

commentaries. The year 1529 saw the publication of the Zürich Bible, published five years before Luther finished his translation.
* The Pope was still writing friendly, even flattering letters to Zwingli in 1523, in the hopes that troops would be forthcoming.

14 Politics and popes

Town councils

There had been one reason why Luther had been reluctant to marry Katie: he thought he was going to die. He had no doubt in his own mind that he would be burned or beheaded or generally deaded in one way or another. But it didn't happen. And as time went by, it grew less and less likely.

One of the truly remarkable things about the Reformation is that it succeeded. With the forces ranged against it – the Catholic system which had been entrenched for a millennium, the power of the Emperor, the opposition of many other political and economic forces – it could so easily have been destroyed. And yet it wasn't.

Socially and culturally, as we've seen, the timing was perfect – the rise of print, and the increasing wealth of the merchant classes gave the Reformation teachings huge momentum. But just as importantly, *politically* the time was right.

Power was changing hands. The Reformation was an urban movement, and the cities were gaining in power all the time. For example, despite the Emperor's express condemnation of Lutheranism, out of the sixty-five Imperial cities, more than fifty accepted Reformation ideas at some point in the sixteenth century. It was town and city councils which approved the reforms, which took over the monasteries, appointed pastors and announced local legislation to abolish the Mass.

This was also a time when the idea of nation states began to crystallise. The Emperor was not able to enforce his will on the city-states and regions within his empire by sheer will alone. City-states like Zürich felt able to defy the Emperor's commands.

Another key political factor was the military situation. The Holy Roman Empire itself was embroiled in a series of long-term conflicts. There was the threat from outside, from the Ottoman army, which in 1529 was at the gates of Europe, besieging Vienna. And there was the threat from the inside: for nine years, Charles was fighting the French in Italy. Or possibly fighting the Italians in France. It was all very confusing.

All of which meant that Luther – and others – had the time and opportunity to write, to travel, to preach and generally to get their ideas out there. The result was that reform spread beyond Germany. It went into Switzerland. It seeped into France. The Hussites were resurgent in Bohemia. In Denmark, the ruling classes embraced Lutheranism as a chance to get rid of the clerics; in Sweden they embraced it as a chance to get rid of the Danes. Reform it was, but not uniform. There were many different shapes and emphases. But at its root there were some things which all the movements had in common: an emphasis on scripture, on preaching, on belief in justification by faith and, of course, on a complete rejection of any allegiance to the established, Catholic Church.

'Talking of that,' I hear you interrupt, 'what of Rome? What was the Pope doing about all this?' Great question. Even if it was a bit rude to interrupt.

Well, the fact is, that for most of the Reformation period, the popes were, to use a technical term, utter pants.

More hopeless popes

Pope Leo X died in December 1521, after catching a chill at a riotous all-night banquet. Throughout his papacy he never recognised what was really happening in Germany – he persisted in the belief that it was simply a local spat featuring some German nonentity. And, despite the fact that income from the German arm of his indulgence sales team had dried up, he carried on spending, meaning that when he died he left the papal treasury full of nothing but IOUs. Even the candles used at his funeral were second-hand: leftovers from a cardinal's funeral the day before. As the cardinals gathered that winter to elect a new pope, there was no heating in the Vatican, and some of the windows were boarded up because the glass had been broken and no one could pay for a replacement. They were given virtually starvation rations, and rudimentary sanitation. One elderly cardinal had to be carried out half dead.*

There were the usual political manoeuvrings, agreements, dead-locks, broken agreements, underhand dealings, *really* broken agreements. Then a letter was produced from Charles V, Holy Roman Emperor, King of Spain, War of the Worlds and Bringer of Light, 'recommending' a sixty-two-year-old Dutchman, whom no one had heard of, but who had once been the Emperor's tutor.

He seemed to have a number of things going for him:

1. No one had heard of him. So he hadn't made any enemies.
2. He was sixty-two. So probably wouldn't last long.
3. He was the Emperor's preferred choice. And the Emperor had a big army.
4. Everyone wanted to go home.

And that is how Adrian Florensz Dedal, a man from Utrecht, became Pope Adrian VI.

He quickly proved himself to be one of the most annoying popes ever. He annoyed the Italians because he refused to learn the language and no one could understand his Latin. He refused

---

* Leo had not only used up all the money; he'd spent all the goodwill as well. He was so unpopular that, when the cardinals gathered to choose a new pope, they needed bodyguards to protect them.

to take sides in the conflict between Charles V and the French – thus annoying the very Emperor who had recommended him. He annoyed all the painters and architects because he didn't care at all about art and even threatened to have the Sistine Chapel whitewashed and all that classical statuary – 'heathen idols' as he called them – chucked in the River Tiber. Most of all he annoyed a lot of people because he was so irritatingly holy. He lived like a monk. He spent just a crown a day on catering and his only domestic staff was his old Flemish housekeeper, who did all his cooking, washing and cleaning.

Given all this, he might actually have made a success of things. But he died in September 1523, just over a year after he'd arrived in Rome. That's annoying.

The cardinals had learned their lesson: no more barbarians from the north – for the next four and a half centuries, all the popes were Italian. Of course, Adrian's death meant that they had to return to another conclave. It opened in the autumn this time, but conditions were just as bad. To encourage a decision, the midday and evening meals were reduced to a single course; then the rations went down to just bread, wine and water. Even so they stuck it out for fifty days.

The English were backing Cardinal Wolsey but it was the Emperor's choice – surprise, surprise – who got the gig. It was another member of the Medici family, Cardinal Giulio de' Medici, who became Pope Clement VII in November 1523. He was forty-eight, tall and slim, thin-lipped, with an almost perpetual frown. He was hard working, pious and almost completely unlikeable. He was described as 'somewhat morose and disagreeable, reputed to be avaricious, far from trustworthy, and naturally disinclined to do a kindness'. He was also constitutionally incapable of coming to a decision. All of which meant that Clement VII was another disaster.

But his reign illustrates precisely the kind of internal strife which allowed the Reformation to flourish while everyone's attention was elsewhere. Clement VII owed his election to the Emperor, but he chose to make secret agreements with the French and constantly manoeuvred against the empire. Enraged, Charles V sent two letters to Rome in September 1525. The first accused the Pope of failing in his duties. The second called on the cardinals to call a General Council for the reform of the Church, no matter what the Pope thought. This was a direct challenge to papal authority. If the Pope was not going to reform the Church, then Charles V would do it. (In an uncanny way, Charles was making himself the head of the Church . . . Hmmm . . .)

Then a series of events rocked Rome and the papacy.

In August 1526 the Sultan Süleyman the Magnificent won a decisive victory at Mohács in Hungary, destroying the Hungarian forces led by Louis II. A month later, Rome was attacked in an attempted coup. Soldiers from the rich and powerful Colonna clan – who hated Clement – smashed through the Gate of St John Lateran and poured into Rome. The Pope was forced to flee through an emergency passage while the Colonna troops looted and plundered the Vatican, broke into the Sistine Chapel and tore the tapestries from the walls. The Pope was eventually able to regain power, but it left him a broken man. 'The Pope', wrote the envoy from Milan, 'seems struck dead . . . He looks like a sick man whom the doctors have given up.'

A few months after that, Rome was attacked again, this time by the forces of Charles, Duke of Bourbon, a Frenchman who was fighting for the empire and leading a mixed force of Germans and Spaniards. At four in the morning of 6 May 1527, his troops scaled the walls of Rome. The Duke of Bourbon was killed in the first wave (the painter Benvenuto Cellini claimed responsibility) and it seemed as though the attack would fail, but in the end the Imperial army took the city and embarked on an orgy of destruction and murder. The sack that followed has been described as 'one of the most horrible in recorded history'. For four days and four nights it was a bloodbath. Churches, palaces, houses of any size were ransacked and destroyed. Monasteries were plundered, the more attractive nuns were sold in the streets.

Paintings, sculptures, whole libraries were destroyed. Virtually every street was strewn with corpses. One Spanish soldier reported that his company alone had buried nearly ten thousand and thrown another two thousand into the river.*

Once again the Pope fled, escaping in disguise to Orvieto. An embassy from England found the Pope living in squalid conditions, in 'an old palace of the bishops of the city, ruinous and decayed . . . it were better to be in captivity in Rome than here at liberty'.

Eventually a peace deal was brokered between the French and the empire. The Emperor even made the journey across the Alps for the first time, for his Imperial coronation. He had been nearly ten years on the throne and hadn't bothered before – a sign of the waning power of the Pope. Nevertheless, for a man who valued his role as a religious authority he could hardly call himself Holy Roman Emperor without the official blessing. On 24 February 1530 Charles received from the papal hands the sword, orb, sceptre and, finally, the crown of the Holy Roman Empire. It was the last time in history that a pope was to crown an emperor; the end of a 700-year-old tradition, which had begun when Pope Leo III had laid the Imperial crown on the head of Charlemagne.

---

* Cardinal Giovanni Maria Ciocchi del Monte, the future Pope Julius III, was hung up by his hair. Six months after the destruction, thanks to subsequent starvation and widespread disease caused by the still-unburied bodies, Rome's population was less than half of what it had been before the siege.

15 Danish blues

'But Nick,' I hear you cry, 'what about Scandinavia? What about Sweden, Denmark, Norway, Finland and Iceland, which, as everyone knows, constituted a single federation under Danish rule?'

All right. No need to show off.

Well, interestingly, it was in Scandinavia that Lutheranism really took root. The home of Lutheranism was in northern Germany, so it was natural that Lutheran evangelists should head across the border into Denmark.

The political situation was unstable because the Swedes were revolting. The ruler of this Scandi-kingdom was the cultured, cruel and occasionally unhinged Christian II. But in 1518 the Swedes rose up against Danish rule. Christian fought back and eventually, with the aid of a large army of French, German and Scottish mercenaries, he managed to gain control. His opponents promised allegiance to Christian provided he give an amnesty for their past actions. Christian agreed to allow his opponents to retreat from Stockholm, and to grant pardons to those involved. His position as ruler was confirmed at a church service in Stockholm's Storkyrkan Cathedral and a few days later he invited many Swedish leaders to a private conference at the palace, where they found a batch of Danish soldiers waiting for them. The next day they were summarily tried at a council headed by the Catholic Archbishop Trolle, who accused them of heresy. Over eighty of the king's opponents were hanged or beheaded, including two bishops and many ordinary citizens of Stockholm. It is an event known, in a title just begging for a Scandi-noir thriller, as the Stockholm Bloodbath.

It led to outrage. Not least from the Pope, who was not used to having his bishops beheaded, and to whom Christian apologised. If he thought that would put an end to things, he was completely wrong. One of the victims was a minor nobleman called Erik Johansson. His son was Gustav Vasa (don't ask. I've no idea how that naming works) and little Gustav immediately started rallying support for a new revolt. The result was the Swedish War of Liberation. The Danes were finally expelled.

Gustav needed money, and he saw his opportunity in closing the monasteries. So Sweden turned towards Lutheranism. A meeting of the Swedish Diet at Västerås in 1527 dissolved the monasteries and confiscated their property to the benefit of the nobility. However, Gustav wasn't that keen a reformer: the main motivators were the Petri brothers. Olaus Petri was an alumnus of Wittenberg University, who became royal chancellor. His brother Laurentius, Archbishop of Uppsala, translated the New Testament into Swedish.

Gustav actually fell out with these two and even threatened Olaus with death at one point. In 1571, a church order drafted by Laurentius was made official throughout the kingdom, but it was not until forty years later, under the alliterative King Karl IX, that Sweden properly became Lutheran.

Back in Denmark, after losing Sweden, Christian tried to bring in some reforms of his own. He was actually quite interested in what was happening down Wittenberg way, and he invited some leading reformers to come and advise on changes to the church in Denmark. One of those who went was Karlstadt, who had a mini-break in Denmark in 1521. But he took one look at the king and the fragile political situation and immediately fled back to Germany. And if a situation was too bonkers for Karlstadt . . .

In the end, though, Christian changed his mind. And the political reforms he tried to institute (some of them very progressive) were deeply unpopular. Eventually he was exiled, the crown being taken by his uncle, Duke Frederick of Holstein. Who became Frederick I of Denmark. And he was a Lutheran.

Well, sort of. He certainly helped to spread Lutheran teaching throughout Denmark. But he also protected Catholicism as well. He ordered that Lutherans and Roman Catholics should share the same churches and encouraged the publication of the Bible in Danish. But frankly, he was more an exploiter of Lutheranism than a follower.

Lutheranism had been taken into Denmark by Lutheran missionaries, notably Hans Tausen, a peasant's son and former monk who had studied at Wittenberg and who took the good news of Martin Luther back to his home region of Jutland. He faced armed opposition, but when Frederick I visited the region, he took Tausen under his protection. Tausen was the first Danish priest to take a wife. He used the Danish language in the liturgy, instead of Latin. The Danish for evensong is . . . er . . . *Even song*.

Frederick saw in Luther's ideas a chance to crush the power of the Catholic Church, and, just as importantly, to confiscate a lot of their property and cash. In 1527 Frederick began a programme to close monastic houses and monasteries.

So, at the National Assembly in Copenhagen in 1529, a Lutheran confession of faith, the *Herredag*, was drawn up and adopted. The next year the Danish Assembly adopted the Augsburg Confession. After Frederick's death, though, things descended into civil war, as Catholic forces tried to stop the accession of Frederick's son, Christian III, and to reinstate the deposed King Christian II. It was Christian's Christians versus Christian's Christians. Anyway, Christian won. Christian III, that is. To be frank, I'm wishing you hadn't asked about any of this. Anyway, it was Christian III who really got into the spirit of the Lutheran reformation, abolishing the rank of bishop and reorganising church property. Denmark went all Lutheran.

So much so that when, in 1605, a Brummie bloke in London penned a play called *Hamlet* about a young and very confused

Danish prince, he made his hero a student who was home for the holidays from the University of Wittenberg.

'But what,' I hear you ask, 'about Norway. Or possibly Nørweg.'

Oh, I don't know. I think Christian III tried to spread Lutheran ideas to Norway but they were less keen, being much more focused on things like skiing and knitting and fjishing in their fjords. But I know there was a bloke called Jørgen Erikssøn, who was dubbed 'the Norwegian Luther'. He was Bishop of Stavanger and did a lot of reforming stuff. Beyond that, you'll have to fjind things out fjor yourself.

16 The radical reformation

Baptisms and bluecoats

What was happening in Zürich has clear parallels with the reforms that Karlstadt had initiated in Wittenberg, and which Luther had halted. Zwingli went much further with reform in Zürich than Luther did in Wittenberg. But there were many in the city who thought that these reforms still hadn't gone nearly far enough.

Perhaps it was the altitude, but reform in Switzerland always seemed to go straight to people's heads. In Zürich a new, radical strain of reformed thinking started to emerge, a reform that would out-Zwingli Zwingli. It began around the time of the October 1523 debate – the one where the council told everyone to calm down a bit. That meeting put on hold the abolition of the Mass – a decision which outraged two of Zwingli's followers, Conrad Grebel and Felix Mantz. They accused Zwingli of vacillating and compromising and generally being a bit of a scaredy cat – only turning against Catholic doctrine when it was safe to do so and when he had permission from the council.*

Grebel, Mantz and some others went away and started meeting together to explore the Bible. As they made their way through the book of Acts they worked out what conversion looked like. First you had preaching, then preaching led to repentance, repentance

---

* They weren't entirely wrong. But Zwingli, like Luther, recognised that you needed a certain level of authority in order to pursue your agenda. In fact, Zwingli carried on officiating at Mass until it was abolished in May 1525.

led to faith, and faith led to baptism. Boom. Tick all the boxes and you were in. But then they looked at the Church and saw that it wasn't doing things in this order at all. In their Four-Step Programme to How to Become a Proper Christian, baptism came last, after you had heard and believed the message. But in the Church, infants were baptised, and they hadn't even done step one – which involved staying awake and listening to a sermon – let alone all the repenting stuff. If, as Zwingli himself argued, the sacraments had no mystical powers in and of themselves, but were merely expressions of faith, then baptism had to be the same: it was for believers – those who had some faith to express.

Grebel found no infant baptism in the Bible, but he did find the words 'Believe and be baptised.' And so they ditched the idea of infant baptism in favour of believer's baptism. Zwingli hated them. He called them pseudo-baptists and catabaptists (anti-baptists) but the nickname which stuck – and which is still used today – was anabaptist. Which means re-baptiser.

These radicals adopted other things from the New Testament. They refused to swear oaths, since Jesus had specifically told them not to, and many of them rejected the use of violence. Jesus said 'love your enemies' and 'do not strike back at those who strike you'. So they would follow his example.*

The epicentre of these radical ideas was Zollikon, Witikon and Höngg, which is not a Swiss legal practice, but three lakeside villages where many of the Anabaptists lived and preached. When the church authorities in Zürich heard that the villagers were refusing to have their newborn children baptised (in Zollikon, the font was actually smashed), they did what they always did and called another emergency council meeting, at which the practice of infant baptism was, to coin a phrase, confirmed. On 17 January 1525, the council passed legislation under which anyone who

---

* In October 1524, Karlstadt came to Zürich to meet with the Anabaptists. Although nothing more came of their meeting. Grebel also wrote to Müntzer, urging him not to take up arms; a letter which was returned to him, unread.

refused to bring their child for baptism within eight days of their birth would be deported from Zürich. Grebel and Mantz were ordered to stop preaching and holding illegal meetings.

The Anabaptists responded to this ban on secret meeting by . . . er . . . holding a secret meeting, convened four days later at the house of Mantz's mother. There, Grebel disobeyed the council even more by baptising a former Catholic priest George Cajacob (nicknamed Blaurock or Bluecoat).* Then others asked Blaurock if he would baptise them. 'Each confirmed the other in the service of the gospel,' wrote a chronicler, 'and they began to teach and keep the faith. Therewith began the separation from the world and its evil works.'

Zwingli took action. Separation was, indeed, the problem. Infant baptism was about inclusion, about making sure that everyone entered the Church, part of the fabric which bound society together. Grebel's ideas would essentially turn Christianity into a voluntary organisation which you chose to join. So he excluded the exclusionists: he banished them from the city.

But the Anabaptist ideas were spreading like a virus. As the example of Blaurock's impromptu baptism shows, you no sooner dunked one person than they would go out and dunk ten more. Soon, Anabaptist ideas were reaching beyond Zürich, and 'the Swiss Brethren' – as they became known – gained a significant following in Basel, Schaffhausen and St Gallen. Mantz, Grebel and Blaurock refused to stop spreading their teaching. In October 1525, Grebel and Blaurock were captured in a field at Grüningen. Mantz was arrested a few weeks later.

While these were in prison, the government of Zürich clamped down even further. The council decreed that anyone who continued to perform unauthorised baptisms would be executed. And, in a decision which they must have thought was oh-so-funny,

---

* He got this nickname because he spoke up at a meeting once and no one could remember his name, so they called him 'the bloke in the blue coat'. Fascinating story, I'm sure you agree. Blaurock went on to become an influential leader within the movement.

they decided that the method of execution would be drowning. 'You see? They want to baptise adults; well, we'll *really* baptise them!'

The three ringleaders were sentenced to life imprisonment, but they escaped through a window. Grebel escaped from the region, but Mantz and Blaurock were recaptured in a forest, near Grüningen. (Something tells me Grüningen was not the safest place to be in, so I don't know why they kept going there.) And, crucially, while he was on the run, Mantz had baptised somebody. An example had to be made. So, on Saturday 5 January 1527 his hands and legs were bound together. He declared to the waiting crowd that he was ready to die for the truth. He sang words from Psalm 31 – 'Into your hands, O Lord, I commend my spirit'. And then he was thrown into the water and drowned.

Blaurock (who had not baptised anyone during his escape) was stripped to the waist, beaten and expelled from the city. He shook the dust from his shoes as he staggered away. After some time as an itinerant preacher, he left Switzerland and joined an underground Anabaptist congregation in the Tyrol, Austria. But the Catholic authorities hated the Anabaptists just as much as the Zwinglians did. Blaurock was captured, tortured and burned to death in September 1529.

The Anabaptists were the reds under the bed of the Reformation. And they were treated brutally by both sides. Zwingli, in particular, treated them harshly. Blaurock called Zwingli 'a heretic, a murderer, a thief, the true Antichrist who had misinterpreted the Bible worse than the Pope'. They believed, in fact, that at one time he had been convinced that infant baptism could not be found in scripture, but that 'since he wished to please men rather than God, he contended against the true Christian baptism'. But he wasn't the only one. Catholics, Lutherans, Calvinists and Zwinglians disagreed on many things, but they all hated and persecuted Anabaptists. The believers were harried and chased, exiled and executed. 'True believing Christians are sheep among wolves, sheep for the slaughter,' observed Grebel ominously. 'They must be baptised in anguish and tribulation, persecution, suffering and death.'

'The truth is unkillable'

The major intellectual force behind Anabaptistism was Balthasar Hubmaier. He was the protégé of Luther's arch-enemy Johann Eck and soon became a prominent Catholic scholar and preacher. But then he moved to Waldshut, near the Swiss border, where, in his forties, he had a kind of theological midlife crisis and completely changed his opinions. He read the Bible with new eyes and went on a fact-finding tour through the major centres of reform. He met Erasmus at Basel. Or possibly Basil at Erasmus. And he became a zealous convert. He accused the Catholic hierarchy – of which he had once been a part – of promoting 'courtesans, fools, whores, adulterers, procurers, gamblers, drunkards and buffoons, whom we would not entrust with our pigs or geese, let alone accept as the shepherds of our souls'. Sounds like he'd been to Rome, then. Not to be left out, in 1524 Hubmaier issued his own set of theses – only eighteen this time – and challenged his former Jedi master Eck – whom he called 'The Elephant of Ingolstadt' – to a debate. It was the Elephant in the Debating Room. He was summoned to stand trial by the Bishop of Konstanz, but refused and, in the end, fled to Schaffhausen, where he wrote an influential book: *On Heretics and Those Who Burn Them*.

The book is a passionate defence of the freedom of ideas. Hubmaier argued that maybe, just maybe, torturing and burning those we disagree with might not be the best way to teach people about God's love. Instead, persuasion and example and gentle Bible teaching were the way to lead people to the gospel. He declared the burning of heretics 'an invention of the devil' and ended the book with his personal motto: *Die warheit ist untödlich* – 'The truth is unkillable'.

By Easter 1525, he was living in the town of Waldshut, which had embraced Anabaptism. Zwingli launched a war of words with Hubmaier, but in Hubmaier he more than met his match – after all, Hubmaier had spent years honing his skills in disputation, argument and logic. Unlike other Anabaptists, Hubmaier believed in the right of self-defence and was known to carry weapons. And they would need them: he had encouraged the people of Waldshut to reject Austrian rule and to oppose tithes. He knew that they could not rely on Zwingli for any assistance. They would have to defend themselves.

Sadly, they were no match for the Austrian forces. In December 1525, Austrian soldiers attacked Waldshut. Because the town was now Anabaptist, the other Swiss reformed cantons refused to come to its aid. Hubmaier escaped across the border into Switzerland and went into hiding in Zürich, where he was captured and interrogated by Zwingli.

Under enormous pressure, Hubmaier agreed to recant. He was taken to the Fraumünster and stood in the pulpit, in which it was intended that he should give a public admission of his errors and heresies. But to Zwingli's horror, he changed his mind. 'Oh, what anguish and travail I have suffered this night over the statements which I myself have made,' Hubmaier suddenly announced. 'So I say here and now, I can and I will not recant.' He launched into a statement of defence, but Zwingli silenced him and accused him of being possessed.

Hubmaier was taken to Wallenberg Prison, a tower on an island in the Limmat River. There, he wrote a statement of faith: *Twelve Articles of Christian Belief*. Zwingli increased the pressure. Literally. Hubmaier was tortured on the rack and, unsurprisingly, broke under the strain. In the end he issued a public recantation and, broken in body and spirit, he was thrown out of the city.

Zwingli. Reformer. Bible believer. Torturer. Executioner. Figure that one out.

TOP REFORMERS

Balthasar Hubmaier

Born: Friedberg, Germany, c.1485
Died: Vienna, Austria, 1558

AKA: Hubmair, Hubmayr, Hubmeier, Huebmör, Hubmör and Friedberger

Originally a student of Johann Eck, he became a convert to Zwingli's ideas and then an Anabaptist leader (although not a pacifist). A passionate defender of freedom of ideas. He suffered several periods of imprisonment and torture. Finally he was executed in Vienna.

Fun Fact: All of his publications contain his favourite motto: 'the truth is unkillable'

INFLUENCE	20
THEOLOGICAL IMPORTANCE	80
FACIAL HAIR	40
GENERAL GLOOMINESS	10
ABUSIVENESS	0
HAT QUALITY	80
PROPENSITY TO VIOLENCE	5

Hubmaier went, like so many other Anabaptists and radicals, to Moravia, which, ever since the time of Hus, had been a kind of nature reserve for religious radicals. The Lichtenstein family owned large tracts of land in the country and they offered sanctuary to Anabaptists. Baron Leonhard von Lichtenstein was even baptised by Hubmaier. There, Hubmaier started to recover. He once again took to writing and preaching and, freed from fear and persecution, he found new energy and purpose. In one year alone he baptised some six thousand converts and published seventeen tracts.

It couldn't last. In August 1526, Louis II of Hungary and Bohemia was killed by Ottoman forces at the disastrous Battle of Mohács. He died without an heir, so Moravia was taken over by Archduke Ferdinand. He was a member of the Habsburg Imperial family. And so persecution started in Bohemia and Moravia. Lichtenstein could not resist the pressure and in the summer of 1527 he reluctantly handed Hubmaier over to the authorities. He and his wife were sent to Kreuzenstein Castle, a ruined fortress which was used as a jail.

Faced again with the terror of torture, he appealed to Ferdinand, asking for mercy. He agreed that 'faith alone is not sufficient for salvation', but still clung to the doctrine of believer's baptism, and still wanted everything proven from scripture. Ferdinand was in no mood to compromise.

Hubmaier was taken to Vienna, tortured on the rack and finally executed on 10 March 1528.

'I may err – I am a man,' he wrote before his death, 'but a heretic I cannot be, because I ask constantly for instruction in the word of God.' He made no more compromises; he resisted the pain and refused to recant. A witness claimed that he remained 'fixed like an immovable rock in his heresy'. He recited verses from scripture as he was marched through the city. At the stake he prayed, 'I give you thanks that you will today take me out of this vale of tears.'

When soldiers rubbed gunpowder and sulphur into his beard to increase the torment, Hubmaier joked, 'Oh, salt me well.'

As the flames took hold he asked the crowd to pray 'that God will forgive me my guilt in this my death. I will die in the Christian faith.' His wife was drowned three days later – cast into the river with a huge stone around her neck.

Swords v staffs

The Anabaptists were never a Church, or even a coherent movement in the sense of Lutheranism or Calvinism. But they did
make attempts at some kind of uniformity.

In 1526, with Grebel gone, and Mantz and Blaurock in prison,
the Swiss Brethren regrouped under a new leader, Michael
Sattler. He was another former monk, having previously been
prior of a Benedictine abbey in the Black Forest. There, presumably when he wasn't making gateaux, he began to study the
New Testament and soon became convinced of the need for
reform. He joined the Anabaptists during those early days in
Zürich and was expelled in November 1525, during one of the
many crackdowns.

In February 1527, Sattler chaired a secret conference of
Anabaptist leaders at the village of Schleitheim, near Schaffhausen
on the German-Swiss border. There, they produced a joint statement: the Schleitheim Confession, which outlined the foundational
principles for their movement. The true Christian community,
the Anabaptists maintained, had to be separate from the world.
It had to model what Christianity actually looked like, and you
couldn't do that while making accommodation with the powers
that be. So the Schleitheim Confession stated that true believers
could not serve in the army. It called those who wanted to work
with the secular authorities – people like Luther and Zwingli for
example – 'magisterial' reformers – i.e. people who colluded with
the magistrates. Believers, they stated, should have nothing to do
with 'the devilish weapons of force'. Because of their commitment
to non-violence they even advocated non-resistance to the Muslim
forces who were invading Eastern Europe.

While he was at the conference, the Catholic authorities in
Bavaria uncovered Sattler's network, and as soon as he returned
home he was arrested. In May 1527 he and thirteen other
Anabaptists were put on trial. The charges included sedition;
rejection of transubstantiation, infant baptism, extreme unction;

211

and refusal to swear oaths. Sattler had also married and left his monastic order, which only added to the charges.

Sattler argued that the court had no right to try him. He pointed out that the Edict of Worms only specifically condemned Lutheranism. Nothing had been said about Anabaptism. He admitted to preaching non-violence, but pointed out that he was only obeying what Jesus said in the Bible. (Although he didn't help his case by saying that if he had to fight, he would rather fight against the empire than against the Turks, because at least the Turks had an excuse: they didn't claim to be Christians.)

The Anabaptists were found guilty, of course. Sattler was mutilated, his body dragged to the place of execution and dismembered along the way while he was still alive. He was tied to the stake and burned, and when the flames burned through the ropes, he raised his two forefingers to heaven – a secret Anabaptist sign of victory. Faced with the horror of Sattler's execution, some of the Swiss Brethren recanted. Sattler's wife, however, refused to recant: she was drowned a week later.

The horror of Sattler's treatment actually inspired many followers.* Wilhelm Reublin, an Anabaptist leader and the man who had baptised Sattler, wrote an influential account of Sattler's martyrdom – which inspired and energised the movement.† Not for the first time, the authorities discovered the danger of making martyrs.

The constant attacks, the injustice and the persecution caused intense debate among the Anabaptist movements. Shouldn't they

---

* And even mainstream reformers raised questions. Martin Bucer – not an Anabaptist by any means – called Sattler a 'dear friend of God'.

† His story also appeared in a later collection, called *Martyrs Mirror* or *The Bloody Theatre*, first published in Holland in 1660. The full title of the book is *The Bloody Theatre or Martyrs Mirror of the Defenceless Christians who baptised only upon confession of faith, and who suffered and died for the testimony of Jesus, their Saviour, from the time of Christ to the year A.D. 1660*. The American edition published in 1749 ran to 1,512 pages and was the largest book printed in pre-Revolutionary America. It differs from Foxe's *Book of Martyrs* by only including non-violent martyrs.

try to fight back, to resist this evil? Anabaptists like Hubmaier were moderate pacifists. In his work *On the Sword*, he argued that it was the government's duty to defend the innocent and the helpless, and that, if called to fight in a just cause, he should do so. Others argued that all violence was wrong, whatever the cause. They split into two camps: the Stäbler and the Schwertler. The Stäbler – people of the staff – were non-violent pacifists. The Schwertler – people of the sword – believed in the right to self-defence.

There were other differences as well. Some Anabaptists went too far even for the rest of the Anabaptists. They rejected the doctrine of the Trinity on the grounds that it was nowhere stated in the Bible. An Anabaptist preacher and bookseller called Hans Hut (who had been among Müntzer's followers in the peasants' defeat at Bad Frankenhausen) asserted that Christ was only a 'great prophet'.

After 1529, the Anabaptists were exiled from Moravia. Most of them kept their heads down, trying to live quiet, inoffensive lives, building small communities and practising a Christian communism. Some of the Stäbler found refuge in Austerlitz, where they banded together for safety, sharing possessions, making sure that no one was in need. They formed a Brotherhood. But even these powerless people were subject to power struggles. An influential Anabaptist called Wilhelm Reublin arrived in 1530 and tried to wrest control.* Eventually he departed with some three hundred followers, went to Auspitz, declared himself the chief minister and was expelled when a load of money was discovered stashed under his mattress. Leadership fell to a man called Jakob Hutter. Not a great deal is known about Hutter (although we do know, entertainingly, that he was born in a town called Moos) but his brief leadership had a profound effect on these believers. He was captured and burned alive in Innsbruck in February 1536, and his followers became known as Hutterites.

---

* Reublin was the man who baptised both Balthasar Hubmaier and Michael Sattler.

- Part Five -
Crash Diets

❖

17 Protesting cities

A protestation

From the perspective of Charles V, Holy Roman Emperor, King of Spain, Lord of the Rings and Soup of the Day, one thing was clear: 'If you want a movement crushing, you have to crush it yourself.' So in 1529, he called an Imperial Diet of all the German rulers, at Speyer.

The idea was simple: they'd all get together and agree the whole thing was a mistake. Germany would revert to its medieval self and they'd say no more about it. But the landscape had changed. Germany was split by a north–south divide: the north was mainly Lutheran; the south mainly Catholic. And the Lutherans had powerful supporters who weren't budging. Frederick the Wise had died in 1525, and the new leader of Electoral Saxony was his brother John, who became known as John the Constant because, well, he just kept on with the same approach. And there were other allies, the most prominent of whom was Philip, Landgrave of Hesse. Philip was an enthusiastic convert to Lutheranism, especially when it came to confiscating ecclesiastical revenues. Sixty per cent of the confiscated cash went to fund four hospitals and the new University of Marburg. But the rest helped to pay for his own court.

Charles also made a mistake in not attending himself. Instead, he delegated authority to his brother Ferdinand. He sent Ferdinand a letter suggesting that he pursue a conciliatory line, but Ferdinand either never got the letter, or ignored it, and instead announced that the Edict of Worms would be enforced and that everyone was now to be Catholic again, so there. And there was to be absolutely no more reforming or else there would be Words. Zwinglians were declared heretics, and Anabaptists were to be put to death.

A lot of the assembled leaders went along with all this, but a significant number – six princes and fourteen cities – refused. They delivered their refusal in an official letter of protest to the Emperor, a document which became known as the Protestation.

And that, children, is where the name 'Protestants' comes from.

It is these political leaders who were the first 'protestants' and it's really a political grouping, not a religious one. Indeed, during the Reformation period itself the term was hardly used outside German politics.*

Charles and Ferdinand were unable to force the issue because they had another nasty flare-up of the Turks. The Ottomans were at the gates of Vienna. So the Imperial forces rushed off to deal with what was happening in Austria. But in the words of another famous Austrian, they would be back.

Christian unions

Two of the Imperial cities which signed the Protestation – Strasbourg and St Gallen – were not Lutheran but Zwinglian. St Gallen, noted for its enormous and wealthy abbey, had adopted reforming ideas in 1527. The leader there was Joachim von Watt, who (here we go again) had Latinised his name to Joachim Vadian or Vadianus. He was a humanist, a doctor, friend of Zwingli and

---

* At the coronation parade of Edward VI a special place was reserved for the 'Protestants', by whom was meant the visiting dignitaries and VIPs from the states that had signed the Protestation.

also brother-in-law to the Anabaptist Conrad Grebel, although he had married Martha, Conrad's sister, a long time before Conrad went all radical.

Strasbourg, one of the most important of the Imperial cities, was under the control of Martin Butzer or Bucer. Bucer is usually ranked as the fourth most important reformer – just out of the medals, behind Luther, Zwingli and Calvin. Born in 1491 in Sélestat, France, he came from a family of barrel makers, but, tired of all that scraping, he became a Dominican monk, and studied humanist scholars such as Erasmus. Bucer was struck by Luther's arguments in his Ninety-five Theses and he adopted the reformed cause. He was excommunicated and fled to Strasbourg, where he eventually rose to prominence. Though he was notoriously long-winded, he brought to the Reformation a strong sense of civic and communal duty. And he was to be a major influence on a certain John Calvin. (Of whom, more later.)

Bucer spent his life trying to bring unity. You've got to admire his optimism. In Strasbourg he created a new order of service, which he later proposed to reformers in Wittenberg and Zürich as a common order of service for the entire Reformation movement. Beginning in 1524, he made a fruitless attempt to mediate between Luther and Zwingli over the issue of the Eucharist, spending many hours and covering many miles in his efforts to gain some form of consensus on the question. He was prepared to accept other evangelicals as his brethren as long as they agreed on the fundamentals of faith. In March 1526, Bucer published his *Apologia*, which outlined his views and proposed that different understandings of scripture were acceptable, and church unity was assured so long as both sides had a 'child-like faith in God'.

Naturally neither side agreed with this, they being more childish than childlike.

Later Bucer was to write, rather plaintively:

If you immediately condemn anyone who doesn't quite believe the same as you do as forsaken by Christ's Spirit, and consider anyone to be the enemy of truth who holds something false to be true, who, pray tell, can you still consider a brother? I for one have never met two people

TOP REFORMERS

Martin Bucer

Born: Sélestat, Alsace, France, 1491
Died: Cambridge, England, 1551

AKA: Martin Butzer

A former monk, he became the leading reformer in Strasbourg. As well as helping Calvin, he tried to mediate between Luther and Zwingli, and even unite Protestants and Catholics. In 1549 he was exiled to England where he advised Cranmer. Six years after his death his body was exhumed and burned for heresy.

Fun Fact: Bucer probably died of tuberculosis, which was exacerbated by the damp climate of Cambridge.

INFLUENCE	45
THEOLOGICAL IMPORTANCE	65
FACIAL HAIR	0
GENERAL GLOOMINESS	20
ABUSIVENESS	5
HAT QUALITY	0
PROPENSITY TO VIOLENCE	17

who believed exactly the same thing. This holds true in
theology as well.*

Typically, Luther continued to attack him to the end of his life.
Bucer replied with a kind of shrug. 'We must seek unity and love
in our relationships with everyone,' he wrote, 'regardless of how
they behave toward us.'

But, like Lutheranism, Zwinglianism was also spreading.
Berne was the largest state in the Swiss confederation. When
Zwingli's ideas started filtering in, the Small Council of Berne
stayed aloof, but the Greater Council, which was more varied
in social background, and which included merchants and artisans, gave approval to reformed ideas. By 1528, then, Berne had
become a Protestant canton. Church properties were confiscated
(although, unlike in Zürich, the Berne authorities do not seem
to have spent the resulting revenues on either education or
alleviating poverty. It's probably still in a Swiss bank somewhere).

The city set up its own *Prophezei* school and Zwingli visited
the city to share his ideas. Another man who arrived was a Hebrew
scholar and preacher who had assisted Erasmus with his Greek
translation. His name was John Huszgen, but he chose to go by
the Greek name Oecolampadius. Given that Huszgen means
'house lamp', you can't blame him. (Oecolampadius means
exactly the same in Latin, but it sounds a lot posher.) Anyway,
the people of Berne saw the (house) light. Inspired by
Oecolampadius, they exiled their bishop, and, after a brief flir-
tation with freedom of worship, decided that everyone had to
adopt Zwinglianism.

Basel followed in 1529. This was a more fiery transition: there
were riots in the streets and image burning and destruction reminiscent of the early days of Wittenberg. The works of art taken

* His tolerance only extended so far. He later tried to persuade Philip of Hesse
to ban Jews from all trades except very menial work.

from the cathedral burned for two days and nights. The now-elderly Erasmus, who was living there at the time, fled in disgust. Schaffhausen joined the other cities in September 1529, under the leadership of a former Dominican friar, Sebastian Wagner, or Hofmeister.

These reformed Swiss states realised that they had to work together to survive. So they formed a 'Christian Union'. Not that kind of Christian Union: they didn't meet in the lunch hour at school; no, this was a proper CU with weapons and everything. Zürich, Konstanz, Berne and St Gallen allied together in April 1529 and were soon joined by Basel, Schaffhausen, Biel, Strasbourg, Mühlhausen, Uncle Tom Cobley and all. Against them was the Christian Alliance, formed of the five 'inner' cantons that had condemned Zwingli in 1524. They were, as you will no doubt recall, Lucerne, Uri, Schwyz, Unterwalden and Zug. They chose to ally themselves with Charles's younger brother, Archduke Ferdinand of Austria.

Sides were being taken. Tension was rising. All it needed was a spark to light the fire. And that spark came in the shape of, well, a spark actually, when one of Zwingli's followers was arrested and burned at the stake in Schwyz. Zwingli interpreted this as an aggressive act against the Christian Union and started agitating for war. He drafted *Ratschlag über den Krieg* (*Advice About the War*) which sought to justify a pre-emptive attack on the Catholic states. Clearly he had got over his traumatic experience with the mercenaries. However, the Berne authorities were less keen and sent delegates to try to argue for diplomacy. 'You cannot really bring faith by means of spears and halberds', wrote one of their delegates, Niklaus Manuel. But Zwingli was determined to provoke a fight and threatened to resign if the Zürich authorities refused to march.

So, on 8 June 1529, war was declared. The forces met at Kappel and battle was joined. Or, rather it wasn't. Because, at the last minute the leaders of Berne and Zürich decided to deny Zwingli

TOP REFORMERS

Johannes Oecolampadius

Born: Weinsberg, Germany, 1482
Died: Basel, Switzerland, 1531

AKA: Johann Hussgen, Heussgen, Hausschein

A preacher in Basel, he took up Luther's ideas for a while, then gave them up and became a monk. Then left that to become a reformer again. Led the Reformation in Basel and supported Zwingli against Luther. More a leader than a theologian. His wife, Wibrandis Rosenblatt, later married Bucer. Among others.

Fun Fact: His real name means 'house lamp'.

INFLUENCE	25
THEOLOGICAL IMPORTANCE	20
FACIAL HAIR	81
GENERAL GLOOMINESS	10
ABUSIVENESS	0
HAT QUALITY	65
PROPENSITY TO VIOLENCE	0

his punch-up and they brokered a peace deal. The Catholics agreed to dissolve their alliance with Austria, and to allow a limited freedom of worship in their areas. Zwingli was livid. It left him alienated from the authorities in Zürich and his influence started to decline.

But he couldn't rest or retire from the fray. Only a few months later, he had another battle. But this time it was with Martin Luther.

18 Disunited we stand

Hoc est corpus meum

What with the Imperial Diet at Speyer, and the opposition from
Catholic cantons in Switzerland, it was clear to the Protestant
leader Philip of Hesse that it was vital that the evangelicals stood
united together. The problem was that they weren't united. There
was Zwingli in Switzerland with his iconoclasm, and his abolition
of the Mass. And there was Luther in Wittenberg who could
disagree with anyone. Even with himself. While Zwingli undoubtedly believed in justification by faith alone, he never quite gave
it the weight that Luther did. Zwingli was far more influenced
by Erasmus. Like Erasmus, Zwingli thought of Christ as an
example for us, more than as our Saviour. Luther kept robes and
some rituals; Zwingli dismissed them.

Zwingli always denied that Luther had any influence on him.
'I will have no name except that of my captain, Christ, whose
soldier I am,' he rather presciently declared. Despite that, he
added, 'Yet I value Luther as highly as anyone alive.' Sadly, the
feeling was not mutual. Luther always viewed anyone who disagreed with him as either a traitor, a heretic or possibly possessed.
Or all three. He wrote, 'I regard Zwingli as un-Christian, with
all his teaching, for he holds and teaches no part of the Christian
faith rightly. He is seven times worse than when he was a papist.'

Their biggest argument was over the matter of the Eucharist.
As we have seen, Luther hated the term transubstantiation, largely
because he hated scholastic theology with its logic-chopping and

convoluted arguments. But he continued to believe in the real presence – that Christ was truly present in the Eucharist – because, well, Christ had said it. So he still believed that the bread and wine were, in some way, the real body and blood of Christ. Christ, he claimed, was 'ubiquitous' – he was everywhere – so that made it possible for him to somehow be physically present. He used the analogy of an iron rod placed into a fire. The fire somehow merges with the metal, it unites as a red-hot iron, yet both are also distinct. All right, it's not a great analogy. And it doesn't really explain much. Don't blame me, blame Luther. Anyway, he believed Christ's body and blood are present 'in, with and under', as he put it, the forms of bread and wine. It's a kind of transubstantiation-lite.*

Zwingli rejected all that. To him the event was purely a memorial, a symbolic commemoration of Christ's sacrifice. Mind and spirit were assisted by eating and drinking, and partaking of Communion signified our membership of his body. But there was no presence, no magical transformation. Bread was bread, wine was wine, sausage was sausage and that was that. This is known as memorialism, and groups which commonly follow this tend to refer to the event as 'Communion' or 'the Lord's Supper'.

Calvin, on the other hand, believed that Christ is not present literally in the bread and the wine, but that he is spiritually present. In other words, it's all about receiving the bread and wine in the faith that through the power of the Holy Spirit you get the actual body and blood of Christ. This is why it's sometimes known as 'wishful-thinkingism', sorry, 'receptionism'. 'The rule which the pious ought always to observe', wrote Calvin, 'is, whenever they see the symbols instituted by the Lord, to think and feel surely persuaded that the truth of the thing signified is also present.'

* It's sometimes known, by those who care about these things, as consubstantiation, although Luther himself never used this term. Luther still called the commemoration 'the Mass'.

This idea is strongly reflected in Anglican practice. Track 27 on the bestselling album *The 39 Articles* says that, 'the means whereby the body of Christ is received and eaten in the Supper is Faith'. Or, as John Donne put it (a lot better):

> He was the Word that spake it;
> He took the bread and brake it;
> And what that Word did make it;
> I do believe and take it.

Luther could not accept all this 'imagination'-type stuff. It challenged his most cherished notion: that we are justified by faith not works. If we have to use our imagination about the Lord's Supper, that means we have to *do* something – and then, for Luther, the Lord's Supper becomes about works, not grace. He could not accept that the presence of Christ depended on us, on whether we had nice thoughts about him.

Philip of Hesse, though, was clearly one of nature's optimists. And he viewed it as crucial that Luther and Zwingli should agree. So, in early autumn 1529, he arranged a summit meeting at his castle in Marburg in southern Germany, and persuaded a number of reformers to attend. It was an all-star line-up: there was Luther and Melanchthon from Wittenberg, Zwingli from Zürich, Bucer from Strasbourg, Oecolampadius from Basel, Stephan Agricola from Augsburg, Uncle Tom Cobbleianus from Yorkshire, etc. Zwingli came willingly. Or possibly zwillingly. He knew that the Swiss reformation was poised on a knife-edge. If the Austrians got involved everything might be lost. Luther was less bovvered. Not only was Wittenberg more secure, but he'd already made his mind up on all the main issues. And, at this point, at least, he was unconvinced about using military means to defend the gospel.

In the end they did manage some measure of agreement and issued fifteen articles which outlined their common positions on the Trinity, original sin, redemption, Church tradition and other issues. But they could not agree on the key issue of the Eucharist.

Anyway, the argument was not very constructive. Luther stated his argument in typically bullish, drama-queen terms. He strode to the table and wrote '*Hoc est corpus meum*' – 'This is my body' – on it in chalk.* That was his position. Those were Jesus' words and he meant them literally.

Zwingli – who was a better scholar than Luther – countered that in ancient Aramaic, Jesus could only have meant the word

---

* Thinking about it, he could have meant that the table was the body of Christ.

'represents'. And he stressed the next words of Jesus: 'When you eat this bread, do it in memory of me.' Jesus was therefore speaking metaphorically. Jesus meant 'this *signifies* my body'. Oecolampadius pointed out, logically enough, that Jesus often used metaphors. When, for example, he said, 'I am the door', he was not, at that moment, a large piece of wood with hinges. When he said, during the same event, 'I am the vine', he hadn't suddenly sprouted branches and leaves.

Luther said, 'Don't tell me things I already know.'

Oecolampadius said that to think Christ was in the bread was an opinion and not a fact.

Luther said it was all about faith. And that Bucer didn't teach the Trinity properly.

Bucer said, 'We so do, you are such a fibber . . .'

Luther replied. 'Yer mum.'*

The debate went nowhere. Admittedly there were inconsistencies on both sides. In the book of Acts, Jesus is described as 'standing at the right hand of God'.† Zwingli took this literally – Jesus was literally in heaven, literally standing to God's starboard. Luther viewed this as figurative. After all, Christ's resurrection body could not be a mere body, else how would Christ be present with all believers?

Anyway, it all showed just how complicated *sola scriptura* was. Both Zwingli and Luther avowed the primacy of scripture, but both read it differently. And in the end, both sides claimed victory.

Zwingli, in his account, called Melanchthon 'uncommonly slippery' and accused Luther of peddling 'countless inconsistencies, absurdities and follies . . . If ever a man was beaten in this world it was Luther – for all his impudence and obstinacy – and everyone witnessed it too.'

---

* Actually he is recorded as saying, 'It makes no difference to me how you teach in Strasbourg. Since you do not want my teaching I cannot have you as my disciples.' But it amounts to the same thing.

† Acts 7:56.

Luther, with his usual good grace, refused to shake hands at the end.

He said to Zwingli, 'Call upon God, that you may receive understanding.'

Oecolampadius retorted, 'Call upon him yourself, for you need it just as much as we!'

And then they all went home.

Signatures of the reformers on the Marburg Articles – at least the ones they agreed to – including Luther, Melanchthon, Oecolampadius, Zwingli and Bucer. It was more what they couldn't agree on which was the problem

Diet at Augsburg

The Ottomans arrived at the gates of Vienna in late September 1529. It had been a difficult journey. A lot of the troops were ill, having marched across Eastern Europe in the rainy season. The Turks had had to abandon a lot of their heavy artillery, not to mention a lot of camels. Meanwhile, in the city the Viennese commemorated this difficult time by inventing the croissant, said to be modelled on the crescents on the Turkish flags. And the Viennese Whirl, modelled on their own sense of panic. And the Viennetta, modelled on their . . . er . . . lack of central heating.

Anyway, to cut a long siege short, the city held out. The Turks gave up and went home. With the siege lifted, that meant Charles could once again return to the thorny problem of all those Protestants, and in 1530 he called another Diet, this time at Augsburg.

This time the attempt was not about crushing disagreement, but rather about trying to find some kind of consensus – a tricky task, not least because, as we've seen, even the various Reformation groups didn't agree among themselves. And the Catholic states, while obviously not supporting the Lutherans and the Zwinglians, were reluctant to do anything that might increase the power of the Emperor and the Habsburg family.

Luther was obviously unable to attend – he was still a banned heretic. So he chose to monitor proceedings from the safety of nearby Coburg and sent the far-more-patient and far-less-potty-mouthed Philip Melanchthon to represent him. Melanchthon made a heroic effort to bring everyone together in One Big Happy Holy Roman Imperial Family by presenting a statement of faith to the Diet, a document which became known as the Confession of Augsburg. But even though it skirted over contentious issues such as purgatory, and went as far as it could go towards Catholicism, it didn't *exactly* work. Although some leaders signed it, notably nine princes of the empire who were sympathetic to Luther's ideas, the Emperor refused to have anything to do with

231

it. And, typically, Luther didn't agree with it: he thought it far too mealy-mouthed. It focused mainly on things like justification by faith and the importance of preaching. So it's a bit ironic that the Confession of Augsburg has since become the standard Lutheran confession of faith, the definitive statement of Lutheranism.

Augsburg didn't heal the rift, but it did help to unite the Protestant side. Having failed to reach agreement with the empire, they decided they had to prepare to defend themselves, and in 1531 they formed a military federation with the unwieldy name of the Schmalkaldic League. They offered membership of the league to other European states, but only if they signed the Augsburg Confession. This effectively ruled out the Zwinglian Swiss federations. They were on their own.

Not that Zwingli was worried. Once back in Zürich he continued to agitate for war. The Five States were organising themselves again. Re-arming. And they had refused to honour the terms of the peace treaty – in particular, the agreement to allow freedom of worship.

Zwingli pushed through an economic blockade, hoping to starve them into submission. But it was not enough. In the summer of that year, a comet was seen in the sky.* A portent of war.

The Catholics declared war on Zürich on 4 October 1531, and a week later the two sides met in battle. Zwingli led his troops, but this time his side was woefully unprepared. A hastily gathered force of only 5,300 Zürichers faced a Five States army five times bigger. It was all over very quickly. Outnumbered, terrified, the Zürichers fled. Five hundred men were killed, some drowning in the Mühlbach River, hampered by their armour as they tried to flee.

And among the casualties was Huldrych Zwingli. Mortally wounded, he was discovered by enemy soldiers and offered the

---

* It was what would become known as Halley's Comet. Although Halley wasn't yet born.

last rites by a priest. He refused. He was stabbed to death by the unfortunately named Captain Fuckinger of Unterwalden.

They cut off his head. His body was hacked into pieces and burned. The ashes were mixed with pigs' offal to stop them ever becoming some kind of relic. He was forty-seven years old.* Zürich was forced to sue for peace and the defeat put an end to Zwingli's hopes of a unified, Protestant Switzerland.

When Luther heard of Zwingli's death he declared it to be divine judgement on an evil ruler: 'They that take the sword shall perish by the sword.'† He had a point: Zwingli was a man who believed that killing people could solve some of his problems, whether the people he killed were enemy soldiers or Anabaptists drowned in the river. But the lack of empathy, sympathy or any other kind of 'pathy' in Luther's statement is typical.

There was a backlash in Zürich against Zwingli and his ideas.

The city council declared that all reformers would be kept out of political decisions from then on. They appointed Heinrich Bullinger as Zwingli's successor. He was a milder, less forthright personality. Under his rule, Zürich became a strong centre of Protestantism and Bullinger himself was an influential figure who engaged in extensive correspondence with English reformers.

Talking of which . . .

---

* A legend grew up that three days later (no coincidence there) some friends found Zwingli's remains on the battlefield, from which his heart suddenly rose into the air. They divided it up to keep as relics. This seems an odd legend, not least because Zwingli was deeply opposed to the idea of relics.
† He also believed an erroneous report that Karlstadt had been killed in the battle, which made him even happier. For a moment. And Oecolampadius snuffed it in November 1531. Erasmus celebrated the fact that 'We are freed from great fear by the death of the two preachers, Zwingli and Oecolampadius, whose fate has wrought an incredible change in the mind of many. This is the wonderful hand of God on high.'

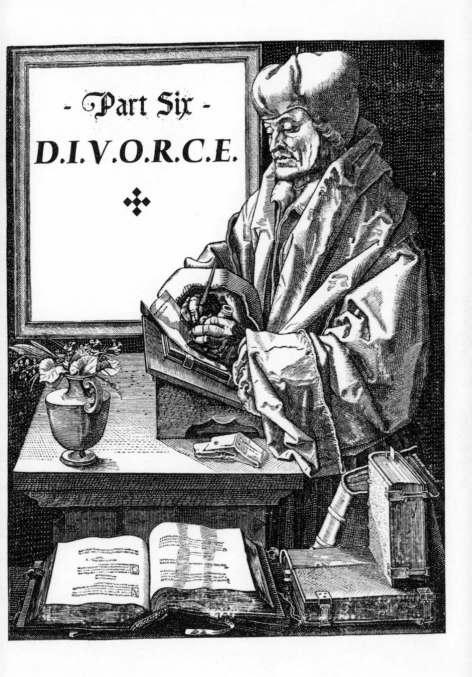

- Part Six -

D.I.V.O.R.C.E.

19 William Tyndale

'If God spare my life'

'But Nick,' I hear you ask patriotically. 'What about England? What about old Blighty?'

Good question.

Because parts of Germany were Protestant. As were parts of Switzerland. But the first actual, entire country to declare itself free of the Pope was England. Gosh, it makes you feel proud.

Or it would if it wasn't, basically, all because King Henry VIII couldn't keep his codpiece to himself.

OK. Slight over-simplification, but it's true to say that the Reformation in England was not motivated by quite the same theological imperatives that fuelled it in the rest of Europe. It really happened because Henry VIII (a) needed a male heir and (b) fancied Anne Boleyn. For a start, Henry was a vehement opponent of Luther, and his anti-Lutheran writings, as we have seen, earned him the title 'Defender of the Faith', not to mention winner of 'Best Polemic' in the Anti-Luther Book Awards 1521. 'Defender of the Faith' is still one of the tediously long list of titles owned by the monarch of England, although, ironically, it is a somewhat different faith that they defend these days.

Nevertheless, despite Henry's mixed motives and general ambivalence, within the space of thirty years, England moved from being one of the most Catholic countries in Europe to being one of the most anti-Catholic. How did that happen? Part of the answer lies in England's history of seditious, heretical thought.

Since the time of Wycliffe and the Lollards there was a sizeable underground church that was, at the very least, sympathetic to Lutheran ideas. So, although the English Reformation was a programme initiated by, and largely supporting the interests of, the ruling class, it was also welcomed by a great many people on the lower rungs of the social ladder. Like many English things – irony, tea drinking, cricket – the English Reformation operated to rules which those in continental Europe found hard to comprehend. To them it happened in a very English way: i.e. slowly, sporadically, and often on the wrong side of the road.

The Church in England in medieval times had been in reasonably good shape. It varied widely, of course, but on the whole the clergy were respected. I mean, they weren't always listened to, or obeyed, but *pretending* to listen is one of the chief ways in which the English show respect. Anyway, they weren't hated. Most people just muddled along, living their lives around the three main obsessions of the English: the weather, beer and innuendo.

But gradually things changed, as new Lutheran ideas began to seep in from *le continent*. People began to take notice. London, in particular, was a hotbed of reformed thinking, not least because of a long-standing dislike of the clergy. (In 1529, the Imperial ambassador Chapuys wrote, 'Here nearly all the people hate the priests.') Gradually people began to realise that maybe those continental Johnnies had something important to say. It wasn't just in London, either. Miles away from the metropolitan medieval elite, in rural Gloucestershire, a young tutor got into an argument with a local cleric over the Pope. When the priest stated that, 'We were better to be without God's laws than the Pope's', the young man was outraged.

'If God spare my life,' he replied, 'before many years I would cause the boy that drives the plough to know more of scripture than you do.'

God did spare his life. Not for long, but long enough; long enough for him to make good on his word.

His name was William Tyndale. And he is one of the greatest figures in English history.

Signs of the times

You won't, though, find Tyndale mentioned in many history books and his face is never found on stamps or bank notes. (Although, looking at the only portrait of him, that may be a blessing in disguise.) And yet this man has had more impact on the English language – and on English culture – than any other writer, including Shakespeare, Kipling, Dickens and J. K. Rowling.

William Tyndale was born in Gloucestershire – we don't know where – and after studying at Oxford, went to work as a tutor and chaplain in the house of Sir John Walsh at the splendidly named Little Sodbury. 'He was very frugal and spare of body', according to a contemporary account, and throughout his life he was known for his piety and courage.

It was around this time that he heard of what was happening in Wittenberg; in particular, he heard about Luther's New Testament, and he began to think about doing the same thing, but in English.

This was a radical notion. In England, unlike other countries, translating the Bible into the native tongue was banned. It had been banned ever since the time of the Lollards, because the authorities believed that if you allow common people to read the Bible they get all kinds of ideas in their heads and become even more uncontrollable than they are already.

The authorities were right, of course. But Tyndale refused to be put off. He started work on a translation. He was a bit naive, though. Thinking that he could do with some official backing, he took his project to London, where he approached John Colet, the Bishop of London, for help. Colet was a humanist, a fan of Erasmus, but he was horrified, and refused to have anything to do with the idea.

Undaunted, Tyndale continued to work in secret, but then his work was discovered and he had to flee the country. He went to Germany. First to Cologne, where, assisted by a former friar called William Roye, he began to prepare his translation for the press. Sadly, one of his printers had a bit too much to drink and was overheard saying that they were printing a book which would make England Lutheran. This account reached Johannes Cochlaeus – Luther's spirally opponent – who informed the authorities. There was a raid, and Tyndale had to flee again, hastily grabbing a few of the sheets that had been printed.* He and Roye took a boat down the Rhine to Worms, which was safer territory, and within a year, in 1526, Tyndale had succeeded in producing his landmark work: *The newe Testament As it was written and caused to be written by them which herde it.*†

Tyndale, like Luther, based his text on Erasmus' Greek New Testament. It followed Erasmus in translating *presbuteros* as elder instead of priest; *ekklesia* as congregation; *agape* as love instead of charity; *metanoeo* as repent instead of 'do penance'. Tyndale was a gifted linguist – he had mastered Latin, Greek and Hebrew – but his real genius was in English. He was, simply, one of the greatest of English writers. Ever. And I'm including Enid Blyton in that. His writing pulses with vigour and energy, and many of our most cherished and most used English phrases come from his words; not just the religious phrases – 'lead us not into temptation but deliver us from evil'; 'knock and it shall be opened unto you'; 'let there be light' – but everyday phrases as well. From Tyndale we get 'the powers that be'; 'the salt of the earth';

---

* Only thirty-one pages of that original edition survive. They are in the British Library. And no, you can't borrow them.

† The first edition was published anonymously. The 1534 edition has as its title, *The newe Testament dylygently corrected and compared with the Greke by Willyam Tindale.* They had a more flexible approach to spelling in those days. Either that or his quill didn't have autocorrect.

TOP REFORMERS

William Tyndale

Born: Gloucestershire, England, c.1494
Died: Vilvoorde, Belgium, 1536

AKA: Tynsdale, Tindall, Tindill, Tyndall, Tindale

The translator of the first modern English New Testament (and parts of the Old Testament). A writer of genius, he worked in exile and on the run. He was burned at the stake. His various writings were smuggled into England and his work became the basis for all subsequent English Bibles of the sixteenth and seventeenth centuries.

Fun Fact: In his translations, Tyndale introduced new words into English, including 'Passover' and 'scapegoat'.

INFLUENCE	88
THEOLOGICAL IMPORTANCE	56
FACIAL HAIR	21
GENERAL GLOOMINESS	12
ABUSIVENESS	25
HAT QUALITY	28
PROPENSITY TO VIOLENCE	0

'under the sun'; 'signs of the times'; 'pour out one's heart'; 'the apple of his eye'; 'the parting of the ways' and many more. More than any other man, Tyndale laid the foundation for modern English – and since modern English is now a world language, that makes him one of the most influential writers who ever lived.

So the book was readable and memorable. It was also smuggler-friendly, pocket-sized. You could *hide* this thing. And hide it people did. Lots of merchants and tradesmen supported the Protestant cause, and they smuggled many copies of Tyndale's New Testament into England, hidden in bales of cloth, under beams of timber, behind barrels of wine. Soon copies were available on the black market at nine pence a shot.

In the best time-honoured traditions of English politicians, Somebody was Instructed to Do Something. And the Somebody in question was Bishop Tunstall, who conceived the magnificently stupid idea of suppressing the book by buying up every copy of it. He instructed a merchant in Antwerp called Augustine Packington to purchase the entire print run and burn it. In October 1526, Tunstall personally oversaw a burning of some 2,000 copies. Which meant, of course, that the first edition sold out.

Tyndale was thrilled with the sales figures. The profits from Tunstall's bulk purchase paid off all his debts and gave him enough money to print a second, corrected edition. And there was another knock-on as well. People found the Bible biblioclasms in London rather disturbing. Some onlookers were very uneasy about the burning of 'God's word'; others began to wonder what was so dangerous about this book, and where they could get hold of a copy for themselves.

Those caught smuggling Tyndale's work faced stiff penalties. Several people died in custody. In Northamptonshire one smuggler, Robert Barnes, escaped by writing a fake suicide note, and leaving a bundle of his clothes by the river. By the time the authorities realised that he wasn't actually dead, he had legged it across the channel to Antwerp. He eventually settled in Wittenberg and became a friend of Luther's.

A man for all hunting seasons

Oddly, even while Tyndale's translation was being hunted out by theological sniffer-dogs, there were signs that things might be changing in England. By 1529, Henry was a king desperately in search of a new queen. The problem was that he already had a wife – Catherine of Aragon, the Spanish princess and the widow of Henry's late brother, Arthur. Diplomatically, it was a cracking bit of foreign policy which allied the up-and-coming power of England with the already-established world power of Spain. But in other ways it proved less productive: Catherine gave birth to a daughter – Mary – but no son. Henry had a receding heir line.

This was no problem. Henry was a staunch Catholic and, as we've seen, he'd already scored a lot of papal brownie points by writing a book attacking Luther's ideas in 1521. So, he was confident that the Pope could be persuaded to grant an annulment and let him marry another woman who could act as an heir restorer. He'd already sorted out a replacement: Anne Boleyn.

All they needed was a loophole. And Henry found one by reading the Bible. Using a rather clever reading of Leviticus he argued that, technically, he had married his brother's wife, so the whole thing was a bit sinful. Which was why God had clearly cursed the marriage and denied him an heir. Case proven.

It wasn't that easy though. Catherine denied her marriage to Arthur had ever been consummated, so argued that she and Henry had done nothing wrong. More to the point, Catherine's nephew was Charles V, Holy Roman Emperor, King of Spain, Best of Both Worlds, Top of the Class, Sign of the Times, etc. And when Henry made his request it was a little after that moment when the Emperor's troops had sacked Rome and forced Pope Clement VII to flee to Orvieto – so there was no way he was going to annoy the Emperor any further. Instead the Pope simply prevaricated, and, in the end, nothing happened.

Henry blamed Wolsey for all this nothing happening, and replaced him with Sir Thomas More.*

Sir Thomas More is, officially, a saint. He has the certificate, the official regulation halo and the saint's day to prove it. He's not only a saint in the Catholic Church (he was canonised by Pope Pius XI in 1935), which, given his opposition to Henry's later policy, is understandable; he's also commemorated in the Anglican calendar of Saints and Heroes of the Christian Church. And that is baffling, because More's main contribution to the English church was to try to suppress every copy of the English Bible, and to torture and burn any evangelical heretics he could lay his hands on.

More pursued heretics with an efficient, unyielding, murderous zeal. And chief of the heretics, their ringleader, was Tyndale, who, by now, had learned Hebrew so that he could start on the Old Testament. He published a copy of the Pentateuch – the first five books of the Bible – in English in Antwerp in 1530, probably with the help of his assistant Miles Coverdale. More hated the idea of the Bible being translated into English. He argued that there was no point in translating it because not enough people could read, an argument which rather falls apart when you consider the numerous heresy trials which he oversaw, which showed only too clearly that ordinary people could read. It was precisely all that reading which got them into trouble.

Another argument More used – a real lawyer's argument if ever there was one – was that the problem was not so much the Bible as the marginal notes that Tyndale had added, which made doctrinal comments on the text. Since Tyndale was a heretic, clearly the notes were heretical – and that made the whole book heretical. So it wasn't so much that they were burning the New

* Wolsey was stripped of all his property, including the magnificent residence of Hampton Court, which Henry decided to keep for himself. Disgraced and accused of treason, Wolsey died a year later. His last words, reputedly, were, 'If I had served God as diligently as I have done the King, he would not have given me over in my grey hairs.'

Testament; rather that they were burning the notes. The English translation of the New Testament was just collateral damage. More also objected to Tyndale's use of congregation, elder, etc., but this was trickier for him to argue against, since More's great friend Erasmus had done exactly the same. (In the end, More argued that Erasmus did not have a seditious intent, but Tyndale clearly did. More didn't object to heresy if it was done by his friends.) More stated that anyone trying to expound the Bible for themselves should have 'an hot iron thrust through their blasphemous tongues'.

It was not just Tyndale's Bible that More hated. Tyndale also wrote tracts such as *The Parable of the Wicked Mammon* (1528), which explored Luther's ideas of justification by faith (and which More denounced as 'a very treasury and well-spring of wickedness') and *The Obedience of a Christian Man*, which is his most influential work. In the book, Tyndale took aim at the clergy, who worried about making the slightest mistake in the Mass but thought nothing of sleeping with prostitutes or sending men to war. He mocked the Church and its obfuscations: 'to keep us from the knowledge of the truth they do all things in Latin. They pray in Latin, they christen in Latin, they bless in Latin: only curse they in the English tongue.' A cracking bit of classic Tyndale prose.

And Tyndale tried to argue against the 'seditious rebel' tag. He argued that the Bible taught that the monarch was not to be resisted but was 'in this world without law and may at his lust do right or wrong and shall give accounts but to God only'. Henry – whose lust was being frustratingly thwarted by the Pope – was pleasantly surprised: 'This is a book for me and all kings to read,' he is rumoured to have said.

He was less pleased, though, with Tyndale's 1530 work *The Practyse of Prelates*, because that opposed Henry VIII's divorce on the grounds that it was unscriptural. Tyndale didn't help his case by arguing some seriously unpopular (with the aristocracy at least) ideas. He disagreed with the death penalty for theft. Or for heresy. He argued, even more radically, that God commanded us to love the Turks and try to convert them.

More, aided by clergymen like John Stokesley, Bishop of London, responded to all this by launching a ferocious programme of heretic hunting. Their first victim was Thomas Hitton, who was captured in Kent after smuggling in copies of Tyndale's New Testament. Hitton was burned at the stake in Maidstone in February 1530; More called him 'the devil's stinking martyr'.

Richard Bayfield, who brought in at least three big consignments of illegal Lutheran books, was burned at Smithfield, in central London, which was to become one of the most notorious of the execution sites. Indeed, such was More's zeal that he took his work home with him. In April 1529 John Tewkesbury, a London leather merchant, who had been found in possession of copies of Tyndale's New Testament and *The Practyse of Prelates*, was taken by More to his house in Chelsea and so badly tortured and beaten that he was almost unable to walk. Tewkesbury was subsequently burned at the stake.* There were other victims: John Bent, burned for denying transubstantiation; three men, hanged for breaking into Dovercourt church and destroying the rood screen; Thomas Harding, spotted secretly reading a book of prayers in English, hunted down by a mob and burned at the stake; James Bainham, a London lawyer, executed for possessing Tyndale's New Testament and who said, as the flames rose, 'The Lord forgive Sir Thomas More.' Thomas Bilney – a Cambridge scholar who had been converted by reading Erasmus' *New Testament*, was arrested after giving an ex-nun a copy of

* More always denied that he used torture and claimed that any heretics detained in his household suffered 'never . . . so much as a fyllyppe on the forehead'. 'Fyllyppe on the forehead' is not a reference to the enormously foreheaded Philip Melanchthon, but refers to the word fillip, which means, 'A movement made by bending the last joint of a finger against the thumb and suddenly releasing it (so as to propel some small object, or merely as a gesture); a smart stroke or tap given by this means.' Which is, I guess, why we talk of flipping a coin. There. You learn something new every day.

Tyndale's *Obedience of a Christian Man.* He was burned in the ominously named Lollards Pit in Norwich. John Frith, Tyndale's associate, was captured during an ill-advised visit to England. He was tortured, then burned at Smithfield in July 1533, chained back-to-back with a tailor from Kent.

More rejoiced: 'after the fire of Smithfield, hell doth receive them, where the wretches burn forever'.

20 Horrid Henry

A vote for Hexit

More was keen on heretic hunting, but less keen on Henry's obsession with divorce. As a vehement Catholic, he had a lot of reservations about that. But Henry was determined and handed over responsibility for obtaining the annulment to Thomas Cromwell, who was aided by a churchman, Thomas Cranmer, a former Cambridge don.

They thought it might help their case to get some expert opinion from theologians at various universities throughout Europe. So Cranmer went on a research trip. And that meant he started coming into contact with some radical ideas. Some radical, *reforming* ideas. He talked to people like Simon Grynaeus, a Basel-based humanist who was a disciple of Zwingli and Oecolampadius. He went to the Lutheran city of Nuremberg, where he saw the Reformation in action. In Nuremberg he took an even more extreme step by marrying Margarete, niece of the reformer Andreas Osiander. It meant that he broke with his vow of celibacy. Clearly, by 1532, Cranmer was going native . . .

After the failure of the embassy to Orvieto, Henry tried an economic embargo: in 1529, he stopped the ancient papal tax known as Peter's Pence. But it soon became apparent that the Pope was not going to cooperate. So Henry decided that if the Pope would not annul the marriage, then he would annul the Pope instead.

Aided by the astute organisational skills of Thomas Cromwell, Henry secured legislation in Parliament which divorced, not only

Henry and Catherine, but England and the Pope. First, the Ecclesiastical Appeals Act of 1532 forbade appeals to the Pope on religious or other matters, and instead made the king the final legal authority in all such matters. The wording of the statute is significant. For a start, it proclaimed that 'this realm of England is an Empire . . . governed by one Supreme Head and King having the dignity and royal estate of the imperial Crown of the same'. Not only was this a bid for freedom from the Holy Roman Empire; it was a geographical statement. Unlike the landlocked city-states of Europe, England was a distinct, geographical entity. It was easier for this island to be perceived as a fully sovereign state.*

It was followed by the First Act of Supremacy (1534) which made Henry 'the only supreme Head in earth of the Church of England called *Anglicana Ecclesia* . . .' From now on, he – not the Pope – could tell people what to think, and how to interpret the scriptures. He, it was, who had the authority to 'repress and extirpate all errors, heresies, and other enormities'. And if you didn't want your enormities repressed by Henry, tough luck. The wording of the act made it clear that Parliament was not inventing something, or changing something; it was recognising an already obvious, existing fact.

Henry was leaving Europe. It was a vote for Hexit.

Henry's moves had left More isolated. In 1532 he asked to be relieved of his office, citing ill health. Henry agreed. His place as chief enforcer was taken by Cromwell. And now the pendulum swung: Cromwell instituted a series of high-profile treason trials which brutalised and executed those who refused to support Henry's defiance of the Pope. One of the most notorious cases was that of Elizabeth Barton, a young nun from Canterbury whose ecstatic visions and spiritual wisdom had won her the nickname 'the Holy Maid of Kent'. She prophesied that if Henry divorced Catherine

---

* It proved that England was an empire by appeals to 'divers sundry old authentic histories and chronicles'. These showed that England was founded by Brutus, who came to England after the fall of Troy. No, really. It's true. He lived at Stone Henge, I'm sure of it.

and married Anne he would cease to be king within a month. When the king visited Canterbury, Elizabeth announced that he was 'so abominable in the sight of God that he was not worthy to tread on hallowed ground'. Cromwell had her arrested and tortured. She was forced to admit that her prophecies were false. She and five associates were executed at Tyburn in April 1534.

It turned into a reign of terror. Anyone who refused to give up their allegiance to the Pope was killed – either gruesomely executed or simply left to rot in prison. Two deaths, in particular, shocked powers in Europe: that of Bishop John Fisher of Rochester, and of the former deputy Defender of the Faith, Sir Thomas More. They were both beheaded because they refused to swear the oath required by the Act of Supremacy. More was the only layman who refused to swear the oath: it was a step too far. He had been prepared to acquiesce to Henry's divorce. He was even prepared to lie to Parliament about it. But he refused to swear an oath. And once he'd taken that step he was outspoken about the rest of Henry's plans: he declared the Act of Supremacy to be 'repugnant to the laws of God and his holy church'. This principled stand has allowed More to be portrayed as a martyr, a man who died for his principles. Hmmm. More lied to Parliament, lied to the public, tortured his opponents and reintroduced the burning of heretics. For which he was canonised and made the patron saint of politicians and statesmen. You couldn't make it up.

Cromwell was driving reform forward, but Henry was no reformer. He was no Lutheran. He was more what would become Anglo-Catholic. By now Catherine had been put into storage, and Henry had unwrapped his fresh, new wife, Anne. His fresh, new *evangelical* wife: Anne was a keen sympathiser with the Reformation and was known to have read all the latest Reformation authors. Her Catholic enemies called her a 'harlot' and a 'goggle-eyed whore'. Charming. But she was key in encouraging the reformed parties at court, not only Cromwell, but the new Archbishop of Canterbury, the newly married Thomas Cranmer. From 1534, Cranmer and Cromwell started to dismantle the old church systematically. A set of royal injunctions were introduced in 1536 and 1538 that aimed to ensure that all dissent was 'repressed and utterly extinguished'.

Despite this momentous change, Henry had not forgotten his enemies. Two years after the Supremacy, with the help of English agents, Tyndale was betrayed, arrested and imprisoned in the castle of Vilvoorde near Brussels. From his cell he wrote, plaintively, 'I ask to have a lamp in the evening; it is indeed wearisome sitting alone in the dark. Most of all I beg and beseech Your Clemency to urge the Commissary that he will kindly permit me to have the Hebrew Bible, Hebrew grammar and Hebrew dictionary, that I may pass the time in that study.' The Old Testament had not been completed.

It was too late. Tyndale was condemned for heresy and in October 1536, in a square in Antwerp, he was burned at the stake. As an act of mercy and in light of his fame, he was allowed to be strangled at the stake before the flames were lit. His last words, according to Foxe's *Book of Martyrs*, were a prayer for Henry VIII, that the king's eyes would be opened. But it was not Henry who killed him. He was executed on the authority of Charles V. The Low Countries, where Tyndale was killed, were at that time owned by Spain. But Henry did nothing to stop it, and Cromwell made only a token effort.

By the time of Tyndale's death it is estimated that some sixteen thousand copies of his translation had been distributed in England. And his work found new forms. In 1535, while Tyndale was in prison, Miles Coverdale, who had been Tyndale's assistant in Antwerp, published the first complete Bible in English.* He compiled this from Tyndale's translations, with the rest translated from various Latin versions and Luther's Old Testament. In 1537 a new Bible appeared which was called the Matthew's Bible,

---

* Coverdale was a kind of one-man Bible publishing industry. As well as the Bible named after him, he also worked on the Great Bible, and in the 1560s he helped prepare the Geneva Bible, while on the run in Europe.

named after its translator, one 'Thomas Matthew'. But Thomas Matthew didn't exist – he was probably a man called John Rogers. The fact that he chose to use a pseudonym indicates that there was still anxiety about the English vernacular versions.

In the end, Henry bowed to the inevitable and issued instructions for the publication of an official, authorised English translation of the Bible. The so-called 'Great Bible' was issued in 1539. And Cromwell secured a royal order instructing every parish in England to buy a complete Bible.

One look at the title page tells you all you need to know about this Bible: the Great Bible has a large image of Henry with a tiny Jesus hovering over him like a bird. Henry is presenting Bibles to laymen on one side and clerics on the other. Thomas Cranmer, Archbishop of Canterbury, passes the Bible to the bishops; Thomas Cromwell gives it to the nobility. Below the bishops, a preacher expounds the scriptures to the common people, who celebrate by shouting 'Vivat Rex' – long live the king.*

Henry didn't want people reading the Bible. He wanted to stop them, in fact. Publication of the Great Bible in 1539 was followed by an act of 1543 in which Henry attempted to restrict Bible reading to certain groups, on the grounds that uneducated people wouldn't be able to understand it properly. Noblemen could read it to their families; noble- and gentle-women, and merchants, could read it to themselves; but lower-class merchants, women, apprentices, yeomen, labourers were all banned from reading the scriptures.

Henry banned any version of the New Testament except the official one. He also banned works by certain authors, especially Wycliffe, and the Bible translators Tyndale and Coverdale. What he didn't realise – because nobody told him – was that the 'Great Bible', his own authorised version, with his picture on

---

* The royal proclamation, which declared that every church had to buy a copy, was good news. Especially for Cromwell, who had been granted a five-year deal for exclusive printing rights to this Bible.

253

the title page, was not only edited by Coverdale, but it contained most of Tyndale's version, with some extra bits from the Vulgate to make the Bible more acceptable to conservative English clerics.

TOP REFORMERS

Miles Coverdale

Born: Yorkshire, England, c.1488
Died: London, England, 1569

AKA: Myles Coverdale

A one man Bible-translation industry. Because of his beliefs he had to flee to Antwerp – the first of several periods of exile in his life – where he produced the 'Coverdale' Bible – the first full-length English Bible. He had a hand in several subsequent English Bibles. He was bishop of Exeter for a while, then a leader of the Puritans.

Fun Fact: Although the Great Bible was commissioned by Henry VIII, it was mainly printed in Paris because English printers weren't up to the job.

INFLUENCE	25
THEOLOGICAL IMPORTANCE	15
FACIAL HAIR	7
GENERAL GLOOMINESS	6
ABUSIVENESS	0
HAT QUALITY	15
PROPENSITY TO VIOLENCE	20

Tyndale's text was hidden in the very pages of the official Bible itself. Now that really is Bible smuggling.

Defender of the eighth

Henry's attitude to the Bible shows his essential conservatism. Henry didn't want to abolish the papacy so much as replace the Pope. But not everything worked out as planned. The main aim of all his reforms – marrying a new wife and securing a male heir – hadn't succeeded. First Anne miscarried a son, then she compounded this crime by giving birth to a daughter, Elizabeth. Henry was already infatuated with another mistress – Jane Seymour – so charges were fabricated against Anne. In May 1536, Henry, the old monster, had her executed on charges of treason, incest and, significantly, Lutheranism. He had the decency to import a French swordsman, so that the cut would be precise. Henry married Jane Seymour, who did give him a son – the future Edward VI – but who died in childbirth. Meanwhile, Cromwell and Cranmer were still working to change things more significantly. Cranmer was still there, clinging on in the bewildering landscape of Henry's court. And through it all he continued to push the reformed cause.

Cranmer was a masterly writer, a thoughtful and sincere man, although he was more than capable of some pretty low-down behaviour, and was complicit in the deaths of several heretics and Catholics. But if any man is the architect of the English Reformation it is Cranmer. It was a slow, and not-at-all straightforward task. Reforming a country is not as easy as reforming a city. What Cranmer oversaw was not a matter of changing some bylaws, or even altering the decoration of a few churches, but a gradual dismantling of a way of life. The saints' days were banned, old ceremonies abandoned. Other Catholic practices that were outlawed included pilgrimages to local shrines, votive candles, kissing images and even the use of rosary beads. But it was not enough to ban the practices: you had to get rid of the things and the places that attracted such practices.

TOP REFORMERS

Thomas Cranmer

Born: Aslockton, England, 1489
Died: Oxford, England, 1556

The architect of the English Reformation, as Archbishop of Canterbury he annulled Henry VIII's first marriage. (And his second one. And his fourth one.) A master of English prose, he wrote two versions of the Book of Common Prayer. He was burned at the stake by Mary Tudor.

Fun Fact: He was thrown out of university for marrying a woman called 'Black Joan'. But she died in childbirth so he was allowed back in again.

INFLUENCE	75
THEOLOGICAL IMPORTANCE	63
FACIAL HAIR	65
GENERAL GLOOMINESS	42
ABUSIVENESS	5
HAT QUALITY	35
PROPENSITY TO VIOLENCE	12

In 1536 Henry issued the Ten Articles, which limited the sacraments to just baptism, the Eucharist and penance, and upheld the doctrine of justification by faith. But, as we've seen, Henry was less in favour of reform than he was in favour of (a) power,

(b) changing wives and (c) money. And having obtained (a) and done (b) at least twice, he now decided it was time to go for (c). England had cut itself adrift from Catholic Europe, and it was time to cash in. So he authorised Cromwell and Cranmer to dissolve the monasteries (not literally, just closing them down and selling the contents off). Cromwell, who now had the title Vicar-General, commissioned a report on the abuses and corruption of the monastic system. Like all government reports before and after, it was carefully designed to come to the right conclusions, i.e. the monasteries were hopelessly corrupt and should be closed down.

In 1536, Parliament passed an act dissolving the smaller monasteries. The larger ones followed in 1539. Some seven hundred and fifty religious houses were suppressed between 1536 and 1540. Henry sold off most of the monastic lands to nobility or anyone with enough dosh. The abbeys were torn down, their relics dispersed, their treasures sold off. Many precious manuscripts were simply given up to the fire. The desecration more than doubled the wealth of the Crown. At least until Henry spent it all.

There was no doubt that the monasteries and the abbeys had many faults. But they were institutions which had survived for centuries, and in a few years these places of prayer, learning and support for the surrounding communities were destroyed. Those who protested were arrested or worse. The abbots of Glastonbury, Reading and Colchester were brutally executed. Anything saleable was taken, and then workmen were sent in to tear the buildings down. Many people bought up the monastic lands and used the stone to build fancy new houses. Among the many catastrophic losses were the contents of some of the great monastic libraries, including huge numbers of Anglo-Saxon manuscripts, which were torn apart just for their precious bindings.

Many people were only too happy to profit from this.* Others,

* In my own village of Eynsham, the people were so distraught at the destruction of the famous abbey that they could only console themselves by stealing all the stone and using it as building materials for their own houses.

however, were upset. *Very* upset. They looked on, bewildered, as thousands of nuns and monks were made homeless. In the north of England the dissolution provoked a rebellion. The so-called Pilgrimage of Grace was a brief armed uprising in 1536, which was brutally suppressed. But it showed that not everyone was mad for reform.*

In 1538 a wave of iconoclasm swept through the country. Shrines were dismantled, relics destroyed. Even the bones of Thomas Becket – England's No. 1 saint – were dug up and destroyed. He had disobeyed a king: that in Henry's eyes made him not a saint but a traitor. Some relics – in a carefully orchestrated piece of PR – were revealed to be fakes. Among the objects which fell victim to this purge was the celebrated Rood of Grace from Boxley Abbey in Kent. This was a wooden cross, with a figure of Jesus that could turn its head, roll its eyes and move its lips. As one mocking ballad put it, 'he was made to joggle, his eyes would goggle'. This was displayed as a fraud and a cheap trick before being sent to London, hacked to pieces and burned. (But we shouldn't assume that people were taken in: they just might have been fans of puppetry.)

Sometimes the burning of these images fuelled an even darker destruction. A Franciscan friar called John Forest was burned to death for the crimes of having been confessor to Queen Catherine of Aragon, of defending the papal primacy in the Church and refusing to swear the oath of loyalty. He was burned to death at Smithfield, London, on 22 May 1538, and part of the fuel for his fire was an enormous wooden statue of St Derfel from the pilgrimage site of Llandderfel in north Wales. This, in a rather grim joke, was seen as the fulfilment of a prophecy about the statue, which claimed it would 'one day set a forest on fire'. The

---

* The conservative areas – the north and the south-west – were still attached to the old faith. East Anglia, the south-east, and especially London, were more Protestant. Henry Brinkelow gushed that 'The gospel was never more successfully preached in the time of the apostles than it hath been of late in London.'

horse on which St Derfel originally sat remained in the church and was venerated for centuries, despite having lost its rider.

Among those who tried him were Thomas Cranmer and Hugh Latimer.* All I will say at this stage is, what goes around, comes around.

We should note that some more 'extreme' evangelicals were also killed: John Lambert was arrested because of his Zwinglian views on the Eucharist: he denied the 'real' presence of Christ in the bread and wine. He was tried before the king in November 1538, pronounced guilty by Cromwell, and burned at Smithfield six days later.†

The journey to reform was never a straight line. By 1539, Cromwell himself was falling out of favour and a more conservative faction was taking over. In June 1539 the Ten Articles were replaced by the Six Articles, which upheld traditional concepts like transubstantiation, Communion 'in one kind' (i.e. people getting the bread only) and enforced clerical celibacy. This proved to be a popular move: the French Ambassador, Maurillac, reported that 'the people show great joy at the King's declaration touching the Sacrament, being much more inclined to the old religion than the new opinions'. He may have been telling his masters what they wanted to hear, but there was no doubt that there was still a great affection for the old faith, not least inside Henry's head.

Cromwell rolled the dice. With England now opposed to the great European powers of Spain and France, the country needed to find new friends. So Cromwell sought the support of Protestants in Germany, and the method he chose was the standard procedure: i.e. find Henry another wife. The lucky woman he chose was Anne of Cleves. Henry was persuaded to marry Anne on the basis of the Tudor equivalent of a photoshopped picture. She

---

* Latimer had been at one time 'as obstinate a papist as any was in England'. The oration for his Bachelor of Divinity degree had taken as its subject a denunciation of the teaching of Melanchthon.

† Cranmer condemned his views, but he was later to adopt them himself.

looked good in the painting he'd seen, but when she arrived she looked . . . different. It was the first recorded dating website scandal. Henry packed her off to the country and Cromwell was sent to the Tower for false advertising.

The charges against Cromwell were laid on thick. He was accused of supporting Anabaptists and other Protestant heretics, of consorting with 'sacramentarians' (i.e. those who denied transubstantiation) and even plotting to marry Lady Mary Tudor, the daughter of Henry and Catherine of Aragon. He was condemned to death without trial and was executed in June 1540.

With his death, a renewed wave of persecution broke out which engulfed all sides of the religious spectrum. At one execution three evangelical preachers who professed Zwinglian views – Robert Barnes, William Jerome and Thomas Garrard – were executed alongside three Catholic priests – Thomas Abel, Richard Featherstone and Edward Powell. All six were drawn through the streets on hurdles, with a Catholic and a Zwinglian on each hurdle. He was an ecumenical monster, was Henry VIII.

Thomas Howard, Duke of Norfolk and leader of the pro-Catholic party, was now in favour. He had used the Anne of Cleves debacle to bring down his enemy Cromwell, and even better, the king married his niece, Catherine. This sudden switchback made life very difficult for Cranmer. But he was helped by the fact that Catherine was a somewhat flighty character. And, indeed, in the past she had managed to land in some dodgy nests. She took a lover behind the king's back. (Not literally, although by now he was so big that it would have made a reasonable hiding place.) Archbishop Cranmer told the king what was going on: Catherine was executed.

Suddenly Cranmer was back in favour. And, naturally, he organised for Henry to marry a sixth time. This time it was another Catherine, but Catherine Parr, a good Protestant. Henry married her on the very day of Catherine Howard's execution. A good day to smuggle out the bad news. From then on, Cranmer remained in favour. Indeed, he was so vital to Henry that, when

Great Moments in Reformation History

NUMBER 18: After six wives, Henry VIII tries
another approach.

the old ogre died in 1546, he passed away holding the Archbishop's
hand, which is not a euphemism.

Henry was a tyrant. Although he initiated the English
Reformation, there was, in the end, only one cause which Henry
VIII really believed in – and that was Henry VIII. He was a
Henrician above everything else. Not so much a Defender of the
Faith; more a Defender of the Eighth.

He and his cast of thugs tore down the Catholic institutions,
executed priests, abbots and monks. But they also killed those
on the evangelical side who disagreed with them. In January
1546, the radical Protestant John Hooper felt it necessary to live
abroad for his own safety. He wrote that 'Our king has destroyed
the Pope, not Popery.'

When he died, the king who created the Church of England
left instructions that Masses should be said for his soul.

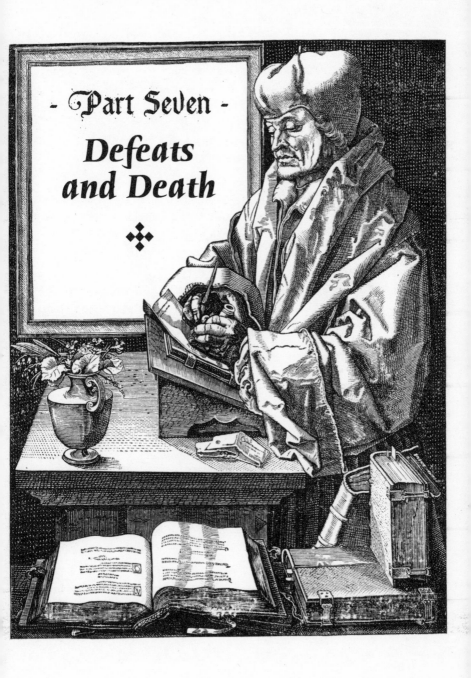

- Part Seven -

Defeats
and Death

✤

21 Jean Cauvin

True articles

'Mais Nick,' j'écoute vous ask. 'Où est la plume de ma tante?
Et aussi, what about la belle Français?'

Bonne question.

On 18 October 1534, King Francis I of France woke up to find
a poster on his bedroom door.

This came as something of a shock to him, (a) because he
hadn't blu-tacked it there; and (b) because it was not a picture
of his favourite band. Instead, the poster was titled 'True Articles
on the Horrible, Great and Important Abuses of the Papal Mass,
Devised Directly Against the Lord's Supper of Jesus Christ', and
was a fairly dense piece of text directly attacking the theology
of the Catholic Mass. It was like Luther's Theses all over again.
Only this time with an actual door.

What is more, Francis had no sooner downed his coffee and
lit his first Gauloise before news came in that these placards were
plastered all over Paris. 'Sacré bleu!' he exclaimed. 'Et sacré vert,
sacré rouge, sacré orange aussi! C'est un outrage! Je suis très
annoyed!' He launched un crackdown immediatement. Some
ringleaders were conveniently found and executed, mainly artisans – a shoemaker, draper, printer, weaver, stonemason and
bookseller. The king went on to lead a penitential procession to
atone for the sacrilege, and along the way the processional route
was lit by pyres on which more suspected Protestants were burned.

In fact the tension had been rising for some time. Initially, the young French king, Francis I, was broadly in favour of reform. Paris was, after all, home to one of the leading universities, and a centre of humanist thought. But then an anonymous iconoclast had knocked the heads off the Virgin and Child in Paris – a statue known for its miracle-working powers – and he changed his mind. He blamed the Lutherans, which rather ignored the fact that Luther himself was against iconoclasm. So when, on All Saints' Day 1533, the new rector of the University of Paris, Nicolas Cop, gave a sermon which was widely interpreted as showing Lutheran sympathies, he was immediately kicked out and forced to flee south.* And not only him, but also all his associates and supporters and anyone who might have had a hand in this seditious sermon.

Among those who fled was a twenty-five-year-old law student by the name of Jean Cauvin.

Or as we know him, John Calvin.

Converted by stages

Jean Cauvin (Calvin derives from the Latin version of his name) was born on 10 July 1509 in the agricultural market town of Noyon, in Picardy, north-eastern France. His grandfather was a bargee on the River Oise; his father, Gérard, had obtained a somewhat drier post, becoming a lawyer serving the cathedral. And Jean, in many ways, was to become the driest of them all.†

Calvin's father wanted young Jean to become a priest. He secured for his son two small benefices, the money from which went to pay for his education. (It is one of the ironies of Calvin's life that he was educated using money from parishes for which

---

* Hence the expression 'cop out'. He apparently contrasted slavery under the law with salvation gained through Christ's sacrifice. He was accused of minimising the effects of good works.
† His mother, Jeanne le Franc, was an innkeeper's daughter from Cambrai. Just thought you ought to know.

he was nominally the priest, but which he never went near: Calvin's education was supported by the very clerical abuses the reformers fought against.) He was a precocious child. At the age of twelve he was working for the bishop as a clerk, a post which brought him some influential support. Aged about fourteen, he went to the University of Paris to study theology. First he went to the Collège de la Marche, then he joined the Collège de Montaigu, a theological boot camp famous – or notorious, perhaps – for both its intellectual and moral rigour, not to mention frequent penitential floggings. The college has a fascinating list of alumni from this time, including Erasmus, Calvin, Ignatius Loyola (founder of the Jesuits), the Scottish reformer John Knox and the French writer Rabelais, who called it 'a lousy college'. Rabelais' opinion of the college was not shared by Calvin, whom the regime suited down to the ground.*

He was always a man who loved discipline, and as a student he began practising the kind of abstinence and self-denial that was effectively to ruin his health. Erasmus – who also hated the college – recalled how students lived under a harsh regime of 'fasts, vigils and work'. 'I know many who even today cannot cure the infirmities contracted in Montaigu,' he said. Certainly, for Calvin, it was the beginning of a lifelong unfitness regime. His physical health was also affected by the rigour of his studies: he drove himself to study the Greek and Latin Church Fathers.

Calvin had been destined for the Church, but then his father changed his mind. It had become apparent that his son was not going to land some plum sinecure, so he decided Jean should study the law. How this went down with Calvin, we don't know, but he left Paris and went first to Orléans and then to Bourges, where he soon became bored by his lecturers' 'pomposity'.

What we do know is that as soon as his father died, two years

---

* Mind you, I shouldn't have thought it likely that Rabelais' opinions on anything were shared by Calvin. Rabelais claimed that Moors and criminals were treated better than students.

later, in 1531,* Calvin gave up the law and devoted himself again to theology. He returned to Paris, started studying Hebrew as well, and became an enthusiastic, fully signed-up humanist like his hero, Erasmus.

By now, he had begun to read the works of reformers like Luther. And he was also influenced by his cousin, Pierre Robert. Pierre, like Jean, worked long hours. He was given the nickname 'Olivétan' because of his olive-oil-fuelled lamp that was always burning as he wrote late into the night. Olivétan produced a translation of the Bible into French by the time he was twenty-nine.

It was at this time in Paris that Calvin seems to have experienced some kind of conversion. It is hard to ascertain what happened, because Calvin rarely talked about himself and, anyway, he was not the type of man who was given to over-emotion. Or much emotion at all, come to that. But in his commentary on Psalms he recalled how he had been 'firmly addicted to the papal superstitions' until 'God by a sudden conversion subdued and brought my mind to a teachable frame'. Not for Calvin the dramatic toilet-based moment of Luther, or the near-death experience of Zwingli. In Calvin's words, 'we are converted little by little to God, and by stages'.

The result was that by 1533 the authorities had him in their files as a 'Lutheran'. Which is why, in the fall-out from Cop's speech, they arrived at his lodgings with a warrant for his arrest. But when they burst into his room, Jean was gone. Calvin had escaped just in time, lowering himself out of his window on a rope made out of bed sheets. He made his way to Nérac in southern France and he was there in 1534 when the incident of the posters occurred. Calvin – who was never one for direct action of that kind – wrote a pamphlet blaming the Anabaptists. But France was now too dangerous for him, so he slipped across the border and into Switzerland.

* Of testicular cancer, apparently. Men: check yourself regularly.

Instituting the Institutes

He went to Strasbourg and then to Basel. And there he started producing the item for which he has become famous: men's underpants. No, sorry, wrong Calvin. I mean, his *Institutes of the Christian Religion*. Easy to get the two items muddled up, because, like many men's underpants, *The Institutes* were designed to systematically arrange some very important fundamentals. And like many men's underpants, as the years went by, *The Institutes* got bigger and bigger. Also, like many men and their underpants, Calvin just couldn't stop tinkering with the contents.

Calvin's *Institutes* are a kind of primer or handbook to the basics of reformed theology. The first edition was published in 1536, but over the next twenty years he continually added to it. By the time he'd finished, the *Institutes* were fourteen times the length of the Bible.

It was, in its first iteration at least, a small pocket-sized book, just six modest chapters which take the form of a kind of cate-chism.* Calvin hoped that it would be carried throughout France, disseminating the gospel and spreading reform. He even dedicated the book to King Francis I, which was optimistic on two counts: (a) that the king might still be interested in the cause of reform, and (b) that he might actually read the darn thing.†

The *Institutes* take their name from the Latin *Institutio*, which means 'basic instruction', and that's what this book was supposed to be: a simple textbook introduction to reformed Christianity. Calvin's purpose 'was solely to transmit certain rudiments by which those who are touched with any zeal for religion might be shaped

---

* In the enormously expanded, completely rearranged later editions, virtually all these original six chapters are still there, hidden away like a tiny village swallowed up by a massive city. The 1539 edition expanded to seventeen chapters. The final versions (Latin 1559, French 1560) have swollen to eighty chapters in four books.

† He called on the king to end the persecutions in France and not to listen to 'the whisperings of the malevolent'.

to true godliness'. His big theme was the glory and holiness and authority of God. When we turn from the glory of God we can only look on our sinful selves with shame: it is only the free, undeserved grace of God which can rescue us from our own depravity.

In the later, fully developed, structure of the *Institutes*, Book One is all about 'What it is to know God'; Book Two deals with how we know God through Christ, and Book Three with salvation. Book Four is concerned with how all this is applied in the real world – it deals with the Church, sacraments and civil government. (And in Book Five, the heroes go to Mordor and drop the ring into Mount Doom. Or something like that.)

The Institutes are not a kind of manifesto of 'Calvinism'. Nor do they contain very much about the idea which has come to be associated with Calvin more than any other: the idea of predestination.

Predestination casts a bit of a disproportionate spell over the perception of Calvinism. But you only find predestination in Book Three, chapter 21 – a somewhat exhausting fifty-six chapters in. Out of the entire 1,521 pages, only a mere 67 treat the topic. Some would say that this is still around 66.5 pages too much, but I suppose it does imply that predestination is not really central to Calvin's systematic theology. Nevertheless, it has come to overshadow our thinking about Calvin and his theology. And that's because it's really a rather shocking, some would say horrible, idea.

It's not that he was preaching anything radically new. Calvin believed that God 'elected' those whom he intended to save – but so did Augustine. So did Thomas Aquinas. What differed with Calvin – and those who followed him and interpreted his works – was that he looked, unblinkingly, at the logical consequences of election. God is in charge of everything, isn't he? So if he's decided that some are elected to salvation, then he must have decided on the fate of the rest. Or as the chapter heading has it: 'Of the Eternal Election, By Which God Has Predestinated Some To Salvation, And Others To Destruction'.

It begins, like the *Institutes* themselves, with an affirmation of God's majesty and authority. Whatever happened in human history, God was in complete control. There was no such thing as 'chance' – didn't scripture say that every hair on our head was numbered? If God was *fully* in charge, then every single event in human history has to be not only known about, but ordained by God. Salvation, especially, was in God's hands. As Luther had argued repeatedly, human works were of no avail. So, logically, if someone becomes a Christian, they are the elect. God has chosen them to be saved.

But if God has chosen some people to be saved then . . .

Yep. It's called 'double' predestination. Calvin believed that, from all eternity, God predestines some men to salvation because of His Goodness, and predestines most to hell because of His Justice. God has chosen who will be saved and who will be damned. And there's not much you can do about it. And what is more, he has created swathes of human beings knowing that they would be damned.

Calvin didn't blink. He looked into the logic of predestination, dispassionately confronted its darker side, and endorsed it. Luther, typically, agreed with 'double predestination' (salvation and damnation from the beginning of time) but he chose not to talk about it. Melanchthon didn't like the idea at all and pretty much deleted it from the Augsburg Confession. Most Lutherans followed Melanchthon in downplaying this idea.

How did you decide on who was in and who was out, though? Well, you couldn't, not really. You could only look at people's response. If they responded to the Word and acted on it, then they must have been elected. If they didn't, well, not so elected, then.

For Calvin this showed the majesty of God, but then it was OK for him, because he's in the elect. It also, handily, explained the failure of the Reformation in areas like France. It was not so much a disappointing failure as predestined. The doctrine of election thus became a great comfort to people who felt ostracised, outcast and abused: it wasn't because they were wrong, it was because the other side were not the elect. And like all groups who consider themselves chosen, it began a process which continues to this day: an endless splintering of just who is chosen and who isn't.

TOP REFORMERS

John Calvin

Born: Noyon, France, 1509
Died: Geneva, Switzerland, 1564

AKA: Jean Cauvin, 'the Frenchman'

Fun-loving, wild, wacky, happy-go-lucky – all words which have nothing to do with Calvin. A man of iron self-discipline and deeply penetrating intellect; Calvinism became the dominant Protestant ideology after his death. He transformed Geneva into his ideal city. He would have hated being made into a playing card.

Fun Fact: Calvin preached over two thousand sermons. Although, admittedly, they don't exactly fit into the 'fun' category.

INFLUENCE	90
THEOLOGICAL IMPORTANCE	90
FACIAL HAIR	72
GENERAL GLOOMINESS	85
ABUSIVENESS	10
HAT QUALITY	5
PROPENSITY TO VIOLENCE	22

A Frenchman in Geneva

In 1536 Jean Cauvin left France for good. He didn't intend to; it was a bit of a mistake – insofar as you can have any mistakes in Calvin's world. In 1535 the pressure in France eased a little and Calvin took the opportunity to nip back home to settle some family business. After that he planned to go to Strasbourg, but the road from Paris to Strasbourg was heavily militarised because of the ongoing conflict between Charles V and Francis I. So he took a route to the south and ended up in the Swiss city of Geneva.

He was to spend most of the rest of his life in the city. You know how it is: you only intend to stay one night, but somehow you find yourself organising a city-wide Reformation. Happens to the best of us.

Geneva was a big city, larger than Zürich or Berne, with some ten thousand inhabitants. Calvin arrived to find the city in some turmoil. This was not that unusual; Geneva was a city of splits and factions. Not only was there a divide between the posh town at the top of the hill and the slummy area down the bottom, but it couldn't really decide whether it was French or Swiss. However, the turmoil this time was to do with the Reformation.

In 1532 a young French émigré called Guillame Farel had arrived in the city. A red-headed firebrand, he was appointed preacher at the church of St Gervais and began to promote a strong reformed agenda. His ideas caught hold. A few years later the city council voted to abolish the Mass and evict the bishop. They took an oath to live 'by the holy law of the gospel'. Monastic houses were dissolved and a tough moral code was enforced. Blasphemy was outlawed, along with card-games and dice. Citizens had to attend sermons or pay a fine.

The city had a new motto: *Post tenebras lux* ('After darkness, light'). But if it was a light, it was flaming torches and roving searchlights. There was disorder everywhere: a confused, roiling, ferment of mob activity which included image smashing, and casting the consecrated bread to dogs. Some thirty years later, on his deathbed, Calvin recalled the city when he arrived: 'When I first arrived in this church there was almost nothing. They were preaching and that's all. They were good at seeking out idols and burning them, but there was no Reformation. Everything was in turmoil.'

The problem was that Farel was better at tearing things down than setting them up. But when the author of the already-famous *Institutes* arrived in his city, Farel sensed a solution. He persuaded Calvin that his duty lay, not in going to Strasbourg to waste time in all that studying stuff, but in staying in Geneva and making sure the Reformation stuck. Calvin had deep reservations, but he was constitutionally incapable of ignoring the call of duty, especially if it meant unpleasant self-sacrifice: 'I felt as if God from heaven had laid his mighty hand upon me to arrest me,' he recalled.

The result was that Calvin was installed as Reader in Holy Scripture at the church of St Pierre.

In January 1537, Calvin and Farel presented their programme for ending the turmoil. First, they put forward a new, evangelical confession of faith which they had drafted. Obviously, people were free to disagree with this, but if they did, they would have to leave the city. I mean that's only fair, right? Second, they proposed major reforms to the celebration of Communion, which would now be held monthly and which anyone could attend as long as their behaviour was up to scratch.

Communion was a stick. Or a carrot.* A network of overseers was to be established to monitor the population and report any whose lives hinted that 'they do not belong to Jesus'. Once identified, these outcasts would be denied Communion and ostracised until they mended their ways. And if they didn't mend their ways

---

* Not literally. It was still bread and wine. Although given some of the bread and wine I've tasted over the years, I think I'd prefer being hit by a stick while eating a carrot, actually.

they would be hauled before the council on grounds of showing contempt for God.

In a small city like Geneva, this would be humiliating for anyone identified in this way. And while the council accepted his ideas, the people hated them. Calvin was never a charismatic figure. Thin-lipped, with a ragged beard, suffering from colds and migraines and illness, he was assailed by frequent attacks of catarrh and neuralgia and seems to have had a permanent cold. He lived an austere, disciplined, self-contained life.

Worst of all, he was foreign. He was *'ille Gallus'* – 'the Frenchman'. He was even accused of being a French spy. The citizens of Geneva found it incredibly insulting that two Frenchmen should be the arbiters of who got to live in their city. 'I mean, they come over here, excommunicating our priests . . .'

There were riots in the streets and shots outside his window. They started to fall out with the judiciary – when one of Calvin's preaching colleagues decided to out some magistrates as 'drunkards', they locked him up. Farel and Calvin were eventually banned from preaching.

Calvin, typically, refused to comply. To him, opposition was just a sign that he was in the right. And the greater the opposition the more right he must be.

The council disagreed. And in 1538 Calvin and Farel were evicted from Geneva.

22 Münster

Mainlining the Apocalypse

The Reformation is a celebration of the law of unintended consequences. Evangelicals like Luther encouraged the reading of the
scriptures, provided that the scriptures were read in the right way.
But people would insist on learning to read, reading the Bible
and then coming to all kinds of conclusions. It was very annoying.

One book in particular caused problems: the Revelation, or
Apocalypse, of St John. Of course, this had been a perennial
favourite – think back to Dürer and his popular prints – but as the
turmoil around people increased, as the old certainties fell one by
one, Revelation became more and more of a magnet. The febrile,
theologically hyper-oxygenated atmosphere of the Reformation
made more and more people certain that they were living in the
end times.

In 1524 a magistrate in Toulouse ordered an ark to be built
on the top of a nearby hill, to provide escape in the forthcoming
flood. A little later, an Anabaptist preacher and bookseller called
Hans Hut – who had been among Müntzer's followers in the
defeat at Bad Frankenhausen – stated confidently that Christ
would return in 1528. 'Subjects should murder all the authorities,'
he concluded, 'for the opportune time has arrived.' He was
arrested and died in prison on 6 December 1527, just a few weeks
short of seeing how wrong he was.*

___
* Although he was tortured in prison, he actually died as a result of asphyx-

Another itinerant preacher, a travelling fur-trader called Melchior Hoffman, also believed the end of the world was coming. Hoffman identified himself as one of the two witnesses mentioned in Revelation chapter 11, from which he logically deduced that Strasbourg, where he lived, would be the New Jerusalem, from where he would send out an army of evangelists (this being Revelation, there would be 144,000, of them) to share the good news. And all this would be achieved before 1533 when, fifteen hundred years after the death of Christ, the millennium would begin. Then a fellow prophet proclaimed that the Second Coming would occur after Hoffman had been in jail for six months. This was a problem, because, at that time, Hoffman wasn't actually in jail. So, in order to speed things along, he had himself arrested. He was locked in a cage and eventually died. Ten years later.

Meanwhile, in the German city of Münster, Westphalia, a former Lutheran pastor with the name of Berni Rothmann started to preach – guess what – the imminent Second Coming of Christ. (He also preached all the normal Anabaptisty stuff such as holding all things in common, adult baptism, etc. etc.) Rothmann's words fell on fertile ground. The area had been devastated by bubonic plague and was ruled by a prince bishop, who imposed heavy taxes on the citizens in order to pay for a war against the Turks. This sense of deprivation and grievance added to Rothmann's followers day by day. Alarmed, the city authorities tried to expel Rothmann, only to find a large, heavily armed group had gathered outside St Lambert's church in the city centre. The council realised that they weren't facing the pacifist kind of Anabaptist, or even the self-defence kind of Anabaptist. They were facing a new kind: the all-out, berserker-attack kind of

---

iation when a fire broke out. It was the day before his trial, but the authorities didn't let a little thing like the fact that he was dead stop them from due process. He was duly sentenced to . . . er . . . more death. And his corpse was burned at the stake in one of the more pointless executions of all time.

Anabaptist. The authorities backed down and backed away, and Rothmann and his followers took over the city.

Soon the news was spreading among the radical Anabaptist community: Münster was the place to be. One of those who heard the news was a convert of Hoffman, a Dutch baker called Jan Matthijs.*

With Hoffman in the clink, Matthijs had become a prominent leader in Haarlem. Hoffman had preached a non-violent creed, typical of Anabaptist teaching. But Matthijs had different ideas. He left his wife and married a woman called Divara or Dieuwertje. He started to send out 'disciples' two-by-two, to proclaim the imminent millennium. He sent two 'missionaries' to Münster – Gerrit Boeckbinder and Jan Bokelson† – where, naturally, they were greeted as the two witnesses from Revelation. I've now lost count of how many versions of the two witnesses there are. Anyway, Rothmann and many others were re-baptised by Matthijs's missionaries and the city became a magnet for apocalyptic revolutionaries who arrived from all parts. It was Anabaptist Central. The New Jerusalem.

One of the arrivals was Jan Matthijs himself, who came in February 1534 to oversee things. The city was now under the control of the extremists. Catholics were exiled from the city, as were any Protestants who disagreed with the new leaders. They started to institute the kind of religious law that made Geneva look like Las Vegas. Anyone refusing to accept adult baptism was ejected from the city, without their belongings. Matthijs exercised dictatorial, summary justice. A city official who suggested Jan was possessed was executed. There was complete social equality, all goods were held in common, and the city declared itself no longer bound to any earthly ruler or authority.

* Aka Jan Matthys, Jan Matthijsz, Jan Matthyssen, Jan Mathis (actually, I've just realised that's Johnny Mathis).

† Aka Jan of Leiden, Jan Beukelsz, Jan Beukelszoon, John Bockold, John Bokelson. Gerrit is also known as Gerrit boeckebinder van Nyewenhuys and Gerrit thorn Closter. Fun this, isn't it?

This made said earthly authorities very annoyed. An army of some three thousand arrived to take back the city. Surprisingly, it was an ecumenical force, made up of both Catholics (who obviously didn't like being kicked out) and Protestant troops from Philip of Hesse (who didn't like anything that these radical loonies stood for). This army gathered outside the city and put it to siege.

In the city, Matthijs was mainlining the Apocalypse. He believed he'd had a vision showing him that he would defeat the enemy army. God had revealed to him that he would win the siege through his mystical visionary power. Convinced that he was the rider of the white horse mentioned in Revelation, he rode out alone to face the enemy forces.

And was hacked to pieces.

In the ensuing power vacuum, leadership passed to one of Matthijs's messengers, Jan Bokelson. A former tailor, he was handsome, charismatic and borderline insane. (As his first public act, he ran naked through the town in a frenzy, before falling into a silent, visionary ecstasy which lasted three days. Something to look forward to when your next mayor is elected then.)

When he recovered, and put his clothes on, he gathered all the people together and announced that God had revealed to him an entirely new set of rules for the town. The people were to surrender all their gold and silver to him. All books were banned except the Bible. There would be a strict code of morality, which would purify them in preparation for the coming Day of the Lord.

Everyone would have to make do on less. Well, not *everyone*, obviously. Some of them would actually get a bit more. Like Bokelson himself, for example, who, in September 1534, proclaimed himself king. He married the former wife of Jan Matthijs, who became Queen Divara.* But Divara was not the

---

* She was given luxurious clothes, a necklace and a crown of gold, and her own residence and court. She also took a prominent role in the distribution

279

only queen. Bokelson announced that, like the monarchs in the Old Testament, he would practise polygamy. He chose a number of new wives (some accounts say sixteen, some say twenty-two), none of whom was older than twenty. While the self-styled King of the New Jerusalem sat on a golden throne and dined in splendour, there was starvation on the streets.

'Now I am given power over all nations of the earth,' Jan declared, modestly, 'and the right to use the sword to the confusion of the wicked and in defence of the righteous. So let none in this town stain himself with crime or resist the will of God, or else he shall without delay be put to death with the sword.' And use the sword he did. Bokelson presided over a reign of terror as the city became a cult-like compound. When people objected, Jan had them executed. Forty-seven rebels were executed by firing squad and buried in two mass graves. He also executed one of his wives, Elisabeth Wandscherer, who was beheaded after publicly questioning him. Rothmann, who had become Bokelson's PR man, announced that 'God has raised the promised David and armed him for vengeance and punishment over Babylon and its people.' He would stamp out the 'Babylonian power' of their opponents. It was language straight out of Luther.

Of course, it could not end well. With the New Jerusalem stubbornly slow in arriving, Bokelson confidently assured the starving people that the Lord would send a miracle by Easter 1535. No miracle came, just bloodshed. In June 1535, some four hundred of the besieging troops managed to break into the city. They opened the gates for the rest of the army and wholesale slaughter broke out.

The bodies of the dead were dumped in mass graves. Rothmann was cut down by the troops. Jan and two of his deputies were captured, publicly tortured and brutally executed. Their bodies were hung in cages from the tower of the city church. The strange,

---

of Communion to between two thousand and six thousand people in the town square. She had a child by Jan of Leiden, a daughter called Averall.

rectangular, crate-like cages still hang there today, dangling from the central windows of the tower.

After Münster

The virus of Münster was not confined to the city walls. In January 1535, Anabaptist plots were foiled in Wesel, Maastricht, Utrecht and Leiden. There were Anabaptist uprisings in Groningen and a small battle in Friesland. John of Geelen marched with his followers through Amsterdam shouting 'Woe! Woe! The wrath of God falls on this city!' Since he and his followers were stark naked at the time, no one took the threat that seriously. But in May 1535, he entered the city hall during a banquet, killing the burgomaster and several others.

A man called Jan van Batenburg led gangs of followers known as Batenburgers. They believed that they were God's chosen children and that therefore they had a perfect right to make their living by stealing from those who . . . er . . . weren't God's children. Like the Münsterites, they were polygamists, but by now the authorities had got really serious about this kind of thing, and the Batenburgers posed as Lutherans or Catholics. Batenburgers could only be identified to other members of their sect by secret symbols displayed on their houses or their clothing, by certain ways of styling their hair, and by a curious addiction to a marzipan-covered cake.*

---

* Van Batenburg was captured. (Coincidentally, he was captured in Vilvoorde – the place where Tyndale was executed.) He tried to save his own skin by giving the authorities the names and addresses of as many Anabaptists as he could, but he was executed in 1538 and the Batenburgers ended their brief existence as a band of common thieves. They were later led by a man called Cornelis Appelman, who murdered his own wife because she denied him permission to marry her daughter. The Batenburger sect further fragmented into any number of splinter groups, all dedicated to robbery and murder. One of them, the Children of Emlichheim, seems to have been solely dedicated to killing non-believers. However, their most notorious massacre was

Münster – and the activities of violent Anabaptists like the Batenburgers – made it possible for their opponents to depict all Anabaptists as rabid, violent, debauched extremists. The Anabaptists as a whole were highly moral, peace-seeking communities, but these violent sub-sects were used by the propagandists to define them in the popular imagination as dangers to society. The truth was, of course, that every group in the Reformation – be it Catholics, Lutherans, Zwinglians, Calvinists or Young Conservatives, had their violent fringe. But all those groups had places of safety, lands and territories where they could find shelter. The Anabaptists had no such luxury.

Even those radical Anabaptists who eschewed violence learned how to conceal themselves. A group of former Münsterites coalesced around David Joris, a stained-glass craftsman and poet who persuaded them that he was actually the new King David. In his youth he had been an enthusiastic protester: in Delft, he had led an attack on a procession in honour of the Virgin Mary for which he received a flogging and had a hole bored in his tongue. Not surprisingly, this rather put him off public protests, and he and his followers stayed firmly under the radar from then on. He ended his days as a respectable citizen, living under an assumed name in Basel.

Perhaps the most unusual of these hidden Anabaptist sects – and certainly the group with the most hippyish name – was the Family of Love, whom we have met before in Antwerp, where they were covertly supported by the printer Christopher Plantin.* They appear to have been founded by a wealthy merchant called Hendrik Niclaes. He avoided the Münster debacle, concentrating rather on inner enlightenment and encouraging his followers to believe that they were so full of the Holy Spirit that they were really divine themselves: they were part of the Godhead. While they were evangelistic – Niclaes himself appears to have made

---

the assassination of 125 cows that belonged to a local monastery.
* Page 46. Do pay attention.

missionary trips to England during the reign of Edward VI and, more daringly, Mary I – they kept things very quiet, and only talked to sympathisers. They attracted artists and scholars – people who *knew* themselves to be part of the elite so didn't need to make a show about it. As well as Plantin, their members included the cartographer Ortelius and the painter Peter Brueghel the Younger. One of their most notable outposts was in the Cambridgeshire village of Balsham, whose vicar, Dr Andrew Perne, was notorious for the flexibility of his opinions. A keen Protestant under Edward VI, he recanted when Mary came along and was made Master of Peterhouse College, Cambridge. Under Elizabeth he made another U-turn, denounced the Pope and happily signed up to the Thirty-nine Articles. He donated a weathervane with his initials to Peterhouse College, and it was said that 'A.P.' stood for A Papist, A Protestant, A Puritan' depending on which way the wind was blowing. Anyhow, he allowed known Familists to become churchwardens and even get buried in the church.*

Münster changed things. It made everyone more fearful. Luther had initially argued that the Anabaptists should be won back through persuasion. He felt compassion for them. In his treatise *On Anabaptism* (1528) he wrote: 'It is not just, and I am pained because these miserable people are so wretchedly killed, burned and horribly slaughtered. One ought to let everyone believe what he will . . . With fire, one accomplishes little.' After Münster, however, he argued that Anabaptists should be hunted down and slaughtered. Melanchthon believed they should be killed because 'they repudiate the public ministry of the word and teach that one can be saved without preaching or worship'. Heaven forbid anyone should be saved without hearing a few hundred sermons first. The Anabaptist Melchior Rinck accused Lutherans of

---

* Perne was no stranger to self-concealment. It was rumoured that he was the homosexual lover of John Whitgift, later the Archbishop of Canterbury. Certainly in old age he moved in to Lambeth Palace to live with his friend.

'shameful deeds, persecutions, tyrannies, betrayals and the shedding of so much innocent blood'.

Some of the more reasonable Anabaptists tried to pick up the pieces from this reputational disaster. Melchior Hoffman was still alive in jail when Münster happened. His movement was given a completely new direction by a Dutch Anabaptist called Menno Simons. A former Catholic priest, Simons had begun to read the Bible seriously when friends mocked his lack of Bible knowledge. He started to preach and gain followers, and when he heard of the beheading of an Anabaptist in Leeuwarden, he investigated. In January 1536 he renounced his calling as a Catholic priest and joined the Melchiorites.

Simons was a pacifist – a 'staff' man. He became their leader and dedicated his time to rescuing the Anabaptist movement from its association with anarchy and violence. The Melchiorites rebranded themselves as the Mennonites. 'We leave iron, metal, pike and swords to those who unfortunately consider human blood to be worth no more than the blood of pigs,' Menno Simons said.

His reward was always to be hounded, always to be on the run with a reward placed on his head. Yet under his patient leadership the movement was shaped into a communal-living, non-violent, often heavily bearded group of people. And, as the Mennonites, the movement he reshaped still exists today.

To be Anabaptist was to be associated with sedition, revolt, sectarianism. Almost sixty years after the event, the English writer Thomas Nashe recounted the example of Münster in his book *The Unfortunate Traveller* as a moral lesson: 'Hear what it is to be Anabaptists, to be Puritans, to be villaines . . .'

Anabaptists. And worse. *Puritans*.

(Of whom, more later.)

TOP REFORMERS

Menno Simons

Born: Witmarsum, Netherlands, 1496
Died: Wüstenfelde, Germany, 1561

AKA: Minne Simens

Former Catholic priest who became an Anabaptist. He took over leadership of the Dutch Anabaptists after Münster. For 25 years he shepherded the movement. A pacifist, his followers became known as Mennonites and have since spread throughout the world.

Fun Fact: His brother, Pieter, was killed taking part in an armed Anabaptist revolt.

INFLUENCE	60
THEOLOGICAL IMPORTANCE	45
FACIAL HAIR	80
GENERAL GLOOMINESS	20
ABUSIVENESS	0
HAT QUALITY	25
PROPENSITY TO VIOLENCE	0

23 Losing Luther

On the Jews and their lies

1534 was a big year for all things Reformation. In England, Henry VIII introduced the Act of Supremacy. In France, there was the affair of the posters. The Anabaptists took over Münster. Pope Clement VII died, worn out by all the disasters of his papacy, to be succeeded by Paul III (of whom, more later). And in Wittenberg, Luther completed his translation of the Old Testament. He had been working at it for years and published it in sections: the Law in 1523, Samuel, Kings and Chronicles in 1524, the Prophets ten years later. Compared with his sprint through the New Testament, this was a marathon. 'Dear God,' he complained, 'it is such hard work and so difficult to make the Hebrew writers speak German!'

He was tired, he was ill, he was feeling old. In the same year as he finished the Old Testament, he had the first in a series of heart attacks. He had an 'open, flowing ulcer on his leg', dizzy spells, severe headaches, loud ringing and roaring in his ears, haemorrhoids, heart congestion, and kidney stones which caused him 'great agony'. He joked that he was being 'stoned to death like Stephen and to give the pope an occasion for pleasure, but I hope he won't laugh very long'. In the winter of 1542-3, he seems to have suffered one of his many bouts of depression. He put it rather graphically to his table guests: 'I am ripe shit, so is the world a great wide asshole; eventually we will part.' Charming.

And there were still so many battles to be fought.

His reputation had been established and he had seen

Reformation ideas adopted not only in Germany, but also in Switzerland, England, Scotland, Denmark and other places. I mean, people didn't always adopt them in the exact way that he wanted – which was a source of frustration – but at least the power of the papacy had been broken in those places. Yet Luther's later years were a struggle. There is a sense of disappointment and anger, of frustration and even disillusion.

Political leaders failed him. In 1539, Philip of Hesse decided to get married. Which wouldn't be a problem, except for the fact that he already *was* married. So he asked Martin Bucer in Strasbourg to prepare a theological defence of bigamy, confident that that would make it all right. Strangely, Bucer did not reject the proposal. He agreed, albeit reluctantly, and on condition that the marriage be kept secret. And together with Luther and Melanchthon, he prepared a document which claimed that bigamy could be sanctioned only under rare conditions. Philip, delighted, went ahead and married.

Philip of Hesse. Wearing a heck of a hat

It is hard to keep a marriage a secret, especially when the man marrying is the ruler of his own state. News inevitably began to spread and the reformers had to decide what to do. They decided on lying. Luther advised Philip to deny it, Bucer advised him to hide his second wife and conceal the truth. When the scandal was revealed it left Philip severely damaged politically and Luther damaged reputationally.

Luther lived long enough to see the seeds he had planted grow. But if sometimes he saw flowers, just as often he saw weeds. He saw how the writing which he had poured out in that incredible burst of energy from 1520 onwards inspired thousands, and often in ways he didn't like.

Few men can survive their ideas being taken seriously by so many.

Nevertheless, there is, in Luther's later writing, a horrible anger and bitterness. And it reached its absolute nadir in his writings on the Jews.

In his earlier years he had been optimistic about the possibility of Jews converting to Christianity. He was friends with many Jews and he reasoned that what had been putting them off was not Christianity, but Catholicism. Once that was out of the way then they would surely see the light. In 1523 he wrote a pamphlet titled *That Jesus Christ Was Born a Jew*, which critiqued the common treatment of Jews by Christians and which argued that the Jews are 'blood relatives' of Christ and should therefore be treated with respect. He dedicated the book to a Jewish friend (admittedly one who had converted). He would later support this friend and his son at great personal cost.

But then all the reforms came in and still the Jews didn't rush into the open arms of Lutheranism. Turns out that it wasn't Catholics who had been putting them off Christ, but Christians. By the time he wrote *Against the Sabbatarians* in 1538 his attitude was beginning to change. He talks of 'obdurate' Jews who 'are given to babbling and lying'.*

* Luther wrote at least five treatises on the subject of 'the Jews': *That Jesus*

And so Luther became angry. The Jews had rejected what he had to offer them. They were deliberately perverse and disobedient. They were just the same as those 'Jews' mentioned in the pages of his beloved New Testament. No, they were worse: nowadays they were in league with the Devil, the Turks and the 'papists'. He started condemning them in much more extreme ways.

He was not alone, of course. The history of Christianity is riddled with anti-Semitism. In the late medieval period, Jews were habitually accused of everything from blasphemy to poisoning wells. The most serious accusation was the blood libel: the idea that Jews kidnapped and murdered the children of Christians in order to use their blood as part of their religious rituals. Jews were marginalised in society. Some people did challenge the prevailing hatred. Andreas Osiander wrote a tract which systematically refuted the blood libel charges and pointed out that Jewish dietary laws forbade them even to eat the meat of animals containing blood. (Although written in 1529, it was not published until 1540 and then anonymously.) In response, Luther's old opponent Johannes Eck wrote a truly horrendous document called *Refutation of a Jew-Book*, which basically repeated every anti-Semitic myth and story he could think of and 'supported' it with his own witness testimony. Eck claimed that he had actually 'placed his own fingers in the wound of a child who had died four weeks before at the hand of the Jews of Waldkirch'.

Luther's anti-Semitism reaches its peak in 1542 with *On the Jews and their Lies*. Jews are condemned in the harshest terms. They are 'a defiled bride, yes, an incorrigible whore and an evil slut', a 'whoring and murderous people' who 'curse, spit on, and malign' Gentiles. They practise witchcraft and blasphemy. He argues that the reason they are in exile from their own land is

---

Christ was Born a Jew; Against the Sabbatarians; On the Jews and Their Lies; On the Ineffable Name and on the Lineage of Christ; and On the Last Words of David.

'due to a more heinous sin than idolatry, the murder of the prophets, etc. – namely, the crucifixion of the Messiah'. And, tragically in the light of later history, he advocates banning all rabbinic teaching, burning Jewish homes and synagogues, and expelling from Germany all Jews who would not convert.

Defenders of Luther try as hard as they can to defuse all this. They argue – rightly – that you cannot dismiss all of Luther's ideals because of this aspect of his character. Another defence is that 'some of his best friends were Jews'. Or that 'they did it first' – meaning that Luther was stung into action by some virulent Jewish pamphlets attacking Christianity. Or they recast it as 'theological anti-Judaism', rather than anti-Semitism; he was thinking in terms of religious observance, not racial categories.

They are right to a point. But all these distinctions and excuses still leave you in the same place: that section at the end of the book, where Luther recommends that Jews' synagogues and schools should be burned to the ground, their houses should be 'razed and destroyed', their holy books confiscated, their rabbis forbidden to teach on pain of death. Where he says also that their money should be taken from them, that they should be denied safe conduct on the highways, that they should be subjected to harsh labour.

We cannot blame Luther for the appalling programme of pogroms and genocide which occurred four centuries later. But we cannot entirely absolve him, either. Luther is not to blame for Hitler. But it says something that *On the Jews and their Lies* was proudly displayed behind a glass case at the Nazi's Nuremberg rallies.

'Such was Luther'

Luther died in 1546. Aged sixty-three, he had braved the winter weather to make a journey to his birthplace, Eisleben, where he had been asked to settle a dispute. (A bit like asking an arsonist to put out a fire, but there you go.)

He ate a meal and then experienced pains in his chest, so he went to bed. He died that night, at four o'clock in the morning, on 18 February, surrounded by his friends and supporters, but many miles from his Katie.

Luther died without a priest present, receiving no last rites, having made no final confession. He had broken with the old patterns of religion. Contemporary Catholic writers claimed that a posse of devils had been seen taking him directly to hell, both for his 'theological heresy and for marrying a former nun'.

In fact his body was taken back to Wittenberg and buried under the pulpit.

During the funeral sermon, Melanchthon acknowledged Luther's good side and bad:

> Some well-meaning men have complained that Luther was rougher than he should have been. This I will not deny, recalling that Erasmus often said, 'On account of the great evil in this most depraved time, God gave a rough physician' . . . I will also not deny that Luther was occasionally quite vehement. But no one is altogether without mistakes in light of our natural weakness . . . Such was Luther as we knew him.

For all his 'vehemence' there is something wonderfully human about Luther. He was paranoid because they really were out to get him. And it was because he was a man so keenly aware of his own failings and sin that he discovered the forgiveness of God in such a powerful way. For all the vulgarity, the anger, even the hatred, there is also glory and salvation and love. He mined the traumas of his life for a rich seam of grace. But he was not a saint. And every time you try to present Luther as some stained-glass, pious, saintly figure he swears loudly and makes a rude gesture in your direction.

A few days earlier, when Melanchthon first heard the news, he was teaching some students, appropriately enough, from Romans. He turned to them and said:

Alas, now has died the charioteer and chariot of Israel who guided the church in this last age of the world. It was not through human wisdom that the teaching of the remission of sins and the faith of the Son of God was perceived, but it was disclosed by this man whom we saw to have been aroused by God.

In the Interim

'But Nick,' I hear you cry. 'What of the Schmalkaldic League? How goes it in Schmalkaldia?'

Well, *that* question came out of nowhere. And I think you'll find it's the town of Schmalkalden.

But since you've asked.

When he announced Luther's death to his students, Melanchthon concluded with a foreboding line: 'May we be modest and consider the immense calamities and great changes which will follow this death.'

His pessimism was not unfounded. Four months after Luther died, Charles V, Holy Roman Emperor, King of Spain, Tip of the Iceberg and Nanook of the North, etc. made a final attempt to deal with all those pesky Protestants. No more Diets and councils and colloquies and all that. Now it would be war. The time was right: he had secured a temporary truce with the Turks, the war with France was concluded, and he had persuaded Pope Paul III to stump up the cash for a shedload of mercenaries.

So, over the winter of 1546–7, the Imperial forces fought against the unpronounceable Schmalkaldic League in the unpronounceable Schmalkaldic war. It ended, predictably enough, with a military victory for the Imperial forces: in the final battle of the war, the forces of Electoral Saxony were routed at Mühlberg on 24 April 1547. John Frederick, Elector of Saxony, and Philip of Hesse were stripped of their titles and lost their lands.* Philip was to spend five years in prison.

Militarily then, a victory. Charles imposed what was called the Interim – an official declaration of mainstream Catholicism, with a few concessions to the cause of reform (clerical marriage, and allowing the laity to drink the Communion wine). Protestant cities were forced to accept the Interim and many of their leaders

---

* John Frederick was the son of John the Constant. People distinguished him from his father by calling him John the Magnanimous.

left. Bucer, for example, fled Strasbourg and ended up in Cambridge, where the damp climate of the fens soon killed him. Others made their peace with the Interim. Melanchthon agreed to abide by it, and even wrote a letter with a kind of recantation: 'At times earlier in life,' he wrote, 'I followed Luther too slavishly.' (Many Germans heard a strange whirring sound that spring: it was Luther spinning in his grave.)

Melanchthon and the like were roundly condemned by the hardliners, who called themselves Gnesio-Lutherans – from the Greek *gnesios*, meaning 'legitimate'. In Lutheran Magdeburg, hardliners established a stronghold against the Interim and the illegitimate Lutherans. Nine pastors wrote a document that was to have lasting significance in European political history. The 'Magdeburg Confession' justified resistance against political tyranny and argued that it was OK for 'lesser magistrates' to engage in armed resistance against their so-called superior powers if those powers were working to destroy true religion. This idea took seed in places like Geneva, where religious refugees were seeking haven from persecution in their homelands.

As many military leaders have to keep discovering for themselves, it is one thing to win a few battles, another thing to win hearts and minds. A new association of princes led by the famous prince and hairdressing salon Moritz of Saxony allied themselves with France, and refused to implement the Interim. The Emperor realised that he could not win this. And so, on 25 September 1555, the sides returned to Augsburg and drew up a peace treaty.

The Peace of Augsburg gave Lutherans and Catholics equal rights to practise their religions in the Holy Roman Empire. It did so through a hugely significant principle: in Latin, *cuius regio, eius religio* – literally, 'Whose realm, his religion'. What it means is that the person who is in charge gets to choose the faith. The ruler gets to choose the religion of the subjects. If the subjects disagree with this, well, they can always move to another state. It was only intended as a stopgap, but it remained in force right up until Napoleon put a final end to the Holy Roman Empire.

TOP REFORMERS

Philip Melanchthon

Born: Stolberg, Germany, c.1490
Died: Mühlhausen, Germany, 1525

AKA: Philipp Schwartzerdt

Luther's number 2 in Wittenberg. Melanchthon was an academic, educator and translator. He tried to systematise Luther's teaching and, in doing so, really developed Lutheranism. He dedicated himself to trying to bring unity between reformers and even made significant compromises with the Catholics.

Fun Fact: 'Schwartzerdt' literally means 'black earth'. Melanchthon is a Greek version of the same phrase.

INFLUENCE	65
THEOLOGICAL IMPORTANCE	39
FACIAL HAIR	12
GENERAL GLOOMINESS	35
ABUSIVENESS	5
HAT QUALITY	0
PROPENSITY TO VIOLENCE	5

What the principle really did was to recognise the new reality. It legitimised what was already the case: that many cities, regions and even countries had changed their religious affiliation.

After this, Charles V, Holy Roman Emperor, King of Spain,

Lady of the Lake and Vicar of Dibley, retired from politics. He went to live out his remaining years in the monastery of Yuste in Spain.

For all that *cuius regio* stuff, Augsburg really identified that the only two religions allowed in the empire were Catholics and Lutherans. And there was a lot in Lutheranism that would have been acceptable to the Catholics: crucifixes and icons and priests and robes. The 'Lutheran' Eucharist was known as the Lutheran Mass: some bits of it were even still in Latin. While the treaty recognised Lutherans and Catholics, it completely excluded Zwinglians, the hated Anabaptists and Calvinists.

And there were a *lot* of Calvinists out there.

- Part Eight -
The Counter-Attack

❖

24 The really long meeting

The petticoat cardinal

'Nick,' I hear you say in a rather breathless manner (are you sure you're OK?) 'What's happening back in Rome? Surely they've been planning some kind of response? Some kind of counter-Reformation?'

Well, funny you should mention that.

By the 1530s the Catholic Church had spent some twenty years losing ground. Literally, in some cases; large chunks of territory had gone all Protestant and there didn't seem to be much that anybody could do about it.

Part of the issue was that they tried fighting this new way of thinking with an old set of tools. The authorities refused to acknowledge that things had changed, so they reacted by doing what they always did, i.e. issuing really important documents in Latin, sending papal bulls, burning people at the stake, and generally acting all shouty and tough. None of which had worked.

The truth was that actually, in their quiet moments, quite a lot of Catholic scholars and clerics were sympathetic to the idea of Reformation. In Spain, for example, Cardinal Jiménez – who was created a cardinal in 1507 – had introduced many reforms. He founded the University of Alcalá, which was intended to train clergy properly (and which achieved this largely by cutting down a lot of the tedious hair-splitting debates which scholasticism tended to collapse into). He cracked down on clerical celibacy and on financial corruption. The result was that when the

Reformation came along, Spain was the country least receptive to its ideas.

Meanwhile, many Catholics absolutely agreed with the Protestants on the need for reform.* And one of them was the Pope.

The Pope who followed the ill-fated, and, let's face it, pretty spectacularly useless Clement VII, was an Italian, Alessandro Farnese, who took the name Paul III. He was elected Pope in 1534 at the age of sixty-six. Although, to be fair, he didn't look sixty-six. He looked about eighty-six. He was bent almost double, with a long white beard, and was only able to shuffle along with the aid of a stick. You might have thought that electing someone who looked like Gandalf's dad was a stopgap measure, and perhaps that's how it was intended (he was elected quickly and unanimously: it only took two days). But he went on to reign for the next fifteen years.

Made a cardinal at just twenty-five, he was known as the 'petticoat cardinal', since it was alleged that he'd only obtained the post through the influence of his sister Giulia, who was rumoured to be a favourite mistress of Pope Alexander VI. He certainly acted like a traditional Renaissance cardinal – he had a mistress who bore him four children, so when he came to be Pope, people were expecting more of the same. To a certain extent he didn't disappoint, financing lavish shows for the Roman populace, including bullfights, horse races and firework displays. He even made two of his grandsons cardinals – despite the fact that they were only aged sixteen and fourteen.

So far, so Renaissance. But Paul III turned out to be a dark horse. (Not literally, although even a carthorse would have made a better pope than Clement VII.) He was a bit of a secret reformer. In 1536, he summoned a special commission to make recommen-

---

* Some of the German states, for example, remained Catholic but still broke their allegiance to the Pope. The Duchy of Bavaria, for example, stayed Catholic, but refused to sign up to papal control and stopped sending any money.

dations 'concerning the reform of the church'. Their report – the *Consilium de Emendanda Ecclesia* – was submitted in March 1537 and it was no whitewash. For a start, it recommended the dissolution of all but the strictest religious orders. It not only listed all the abuses, such as the sale of indulgences, the simony and all that, but it laid the blame squarely on the papacy. The report concluded that had the Church actually been, you know, a *tad* more Christian, then all this might not have happened. Naturally, all the cardinals and clerics who had been carefully excluded from the commission did all they could to sweep the report under the carpet. But the report was leaked, and gleefully reprinted in a German translation complete with a cartoon showing foxes sweeping a room with their own tails.

Along with this report, there were still attempts being made to bring Catholics and evangelicals back together. A secret meeting was held in December 1540 between two high-ranking Catholic clerics – Johann Gropper, canon of Cologne, and Gerhard Veltwick, the Imperial secretary – and Martin Bucer and a man called Wolfgang Capito from Strasbourg.* They managed to agree some terms, including positions on original sin and justification, and Bucer sent a document with their draft conclusions to Luther.

He rejected it.

But with the Turks and the French still a threat, the Emperor wanted to stabilise things in Germany. So he made another attempt to bring the sides together, calling a conference in

---

* Capito, aka Köpfel, was an Alsatian. I mean that he was born in Alsace, not that he was a dog. A former doctor, he had been a cleric at Basel, where he came under Zwingli's influence. He was an old hand at these kind of conferences, having been present at Marburg. Typically his efforts to bring together the two sides – especially the Lutherans and the Zwinglians – led to both regarding him with suspicion. He later married Oecolampadius' widow, who was called Wibrandis Rosenblatt. No, really. Capito was her third husband: she was the widow of a Ludwig Keller before she married Oecolampadius. And when Capito died, she went on to marry Martin Bucer. This woman clearly had a bit of a thing for reformers.

Regensburg in 1541. It was another all-star line-up. Eck made another appearance for the Catholics and the Pope sent Contarini as his papal legate. The evangelicals were represented by Bucer and Melanchthon.

Again, they made some progress. Four articles – on the status of man before the Fall, on free will, on the cause of sin, and on original sin – were all agreed. Justification proved trickier, but eventually they managed a statement on that as well. They agreed that we are justified by faith – thus satisfying the reformed parties – but that faith must be active in love – thus ticking the 'action' box for the Catholics. Difficult subjects like church hierarchy, authority and discipline were kicked into the long grass.

A final document was agreed upon and copies sent by deputation to Luther and the Pope.

They rejected it.

'The Holy Scriptures and God's commandment are by nature not ambiguous,' snorted Luther, which kind of makes you wonder if he'd ever read the Bible.*

So the Regensburg conference failed. Contarini returned to Rome, to find himself accused of heresy. He died under house arrest. His role of Cardinal In Charge of Sorting Everything Out was taken by a hardline traditionalist called Cardinal Carafa. Carafa was a nasty piece of work. He was the head of the Roman Inquisition, and so utterly dedicated was he to rooting out Italian Protestants that he had a new house built with its very own dungeons, so that he could work from home.

It was clear that the idea of unity had been put on the back burner. And then the back burner was turned up high enough to incinerate it.

But clearly *something* had to be done. The Catholic leadership had to respond in some way to the threat of Protestantism.

---

* The Elector, John Frederick, also disagreed with it, but Luther asked him not to be too harsh on Melanchthon for approving the justification statement, 'so that he does not once again die of grief'.

Adopting the ancient principle of *Quisquam potestis, possum melior*, or 'anything you can do, I can do better', the Pope knew that they needed a counter-Reformation. And in order to do that, he called a meeting. A really, *really* long meeting.

Council of Trent

As his life was drawing to a close, Luther jokingly asked those assembled around his deathbed to pray 'that all might be well with him, because the Council of Trent and the accursed pope are very angry with him'.

It's a reference to the council which Paul III began on 13 December 1545, in Trent – not the river in Nottinghamshire, but the little city of Trento in the Italian Alps. This was supposed to be a great assembly of the Roman Catholic Church intended to establish her position once and for all. But out of about six hundred Catholic bishops in Europe, only thirty-one actually turned up for the start.*

It may not have been well attended, but it was the start of something big. Or long, at least. In all, the council meetings lasted for a whopping eighteen years, split into three chunks.†
The first phase ran from 1545 to March 1547, but it halted when Pope Paul III tried to transfer it to Bologna. It reassembled at Trent in May 1551, but the French were forbidden by their king to attend and the election of a new pope meant it was halted again. Finally, it reconvened in 1561 and of the three sessions, this was the best attended and most fruitful. When it eventually

---

* It was actually attended by a single cardinal, four archbishops, and thirty-one bishops.
† This proved good news for the hospitality industry in Trent, the members of which put up all their prices and made a killing. The Protestant historian Sleidan, who attended as part of an early kind of press corps, was deeply aggrieved to find that it cost him twelve florins a week for two rooms and two meals a day. Clearly he wasn't on expenses.

concluded in November 1563 it had produced a lot of words: more legislation than had been generated by all previous eighteen General Councils of the Church together. But hidden in all that verbiage there were some significant statements.

First, the Council of Trent rejected the Reformation principle of *sola scriptura*. Trent concluded that the Bible could not be the only source of truth: the Church is also the vehicle of divinely ordained doctrine and traditions. And while clearly the Church could not veto bits of scripture (and, by the way, the council declared that scripture definitely included the Apocrypha), it could veto the way it was read. So the council forbade anyone 'to interpret it in any way that disagrees with the understanding of holy mother Church, the only judge of its true meaning'. So there.

It went on to define justification as 'not only the remission of sins but also the sanctification and renewal of the inner man'. So, where the reformers saw justification as a declaration from God that the sinner has been given the righteous status of Christ – while still a sinner – Trent characterised justification as a process of becoming more holy and so more personally worthy of salvation.

Trent declared anathema (i.e. eternal condemnation) on a lot of alternative views. So, Canon 9 of the council declares that 'If anyone says that the sinner is justified by faith alone . . . let him be anathema.' Two canons later, it underlines this:

> If anyone says that men are justified either solely by the imputation of Christ's righteousness or solely by the remission of sins, to the exclusion of the grace and charity which is poured into their hearts by the Holy Spirit and stays with them, or also that the grace by which we are justified is only the good will of God, let him be anathema.

While Canon 12, just for variety, states, 'If anyone says that justifying faith is nothing else than trust in divine mercy, which remits sins for Christ's sake . . . let him be anathema.'

I think we've got the point. Trent was not against God's grace – *of course* Christians need God's grace – but grace works with will to enable Christians to keep God's law. We are saved by faith *and* by works.

Trent was a wholesale rejection of everything the Reformation stood for. As well as kicking Reformation ideas of justification into pulp, it reaffirmed all the major traditions of the Church, including the seven sacraments, purgatory, indulgences, the priesthood and original sin (a pop at many Anabaptists who denied it). It declared, some 1,150 years after he'd written it, that Jerome's Latin Vulgate translation of the Bible was the official, approved, authorised Latin edition.

The Council of Trent was the first time that Catholicism was called 'Roman'.

Contarini and his party had lost. Rome, in its statements about salvation, was as far from reformed teaching as it ever had been.

However, it was not averse to the idea of 'reformation' as such. And Trent did stipulate a number of actual reforms. It decided that the teaching of the Church should be beefed up, and that there should be a seminary in every diocese. It did, in fact, recognise that changes had to be made, and that the Catholic Church had been beset by corruption and laxity.

But it was, at best, only a partial success. By enshrining a thousand-year-old Bible as the 'official version' and withholding authorisation of any updates, they tried to preserve the historic teaching of the Church, yet only really succeeded in making it look more old-fashioned than it was already. Choosing the Vulgate was the equivalent of stamping their feet, putting their fingers in their ears and singing 'la-la-la, can't hear you'. It was a belated – and futile – attempt to stop all those disquieting discoveries being made by textual scholars as they explored the Hebrew and Greek manuscripts. Even some Catholic scholars knew the Vulgate was an inadequate translation.

And it was hardly pan-European. Because of the ongoing conflict between the French and the Holy Roman Empire, the

French church was often completely unrepresented.* But it did halt the Protestant tide – at least in the south of Europe. And it meant that in the second half of the sixteenth century, the Catholic Church was reinvigorated and renewed. It was a time which saw new, enthusiastic and devoted orders of monks and nuns.

That was the real Counter-Reformation.

---

* It was overwhelmingly Italian; even at its biggest, when over two hundred and seventy bishops were there, the German delegation only numbered thirteen.

25 Getting all Jesuitical

My name is Iñigo López de Loyola.
Prepare to die (to yourself)

I suppose it was natural that a bloke who always looked as though he was on his last legs, should value signs of life. But one of the ways that Pope Paul III responded to the challenges of the Reformation was to encourage those who were actually making a difference. And this period saw the emergence of some new orders intended to breathe new life into the Catholic Church; orders, such as the Theatines and the Ursulines, that were dedicated to living in parishes and promoting spiritual renewal among ordinary people.*

For example, there was a young priest called Filippo Neri, who worked among the poor and the outcast in Rome. He worked with prostitutes – not in the way that a lot of Catholic clergy, and indeed, popes, did – but in a more charitable and helpful way. He founded an order dedicated to helping the many thousands of poor pilgrims who wound up in Rome. He was devoted to evangelism and mission, and also founded the Congregation of the Oratory, a group which would meet in a hall, or 'Oratory', for prayers, hymns, Bible readings, and then a lecture or discussion. Sometimes they listened to choral work by one of his followers, like the composer Palestrina. (Which is why these works

---

*Unlike the Brilliantines, who were dedicated to hair products. Or the Clementines, who were more focused on providing Vitamin C.

307

became known as Oratorios.) Occasionally he took people on trips to see other churches and threw in a picnic on the way.

Perhaps the most significant and influential figure who was encouraged by Paul III, though, was a soldier-turned-monk, a Basque man called Iñigo López de Loyola. Although, due to a spelling mistake at his university – a mistake which he rather liked – he has become known as Ignatius of Loyola.

A former courtier and soldier, Ignatius had a crisis of faith that in many ways was similar to Luther's. He came from an aristocratic Basque family, and as a young man gained notoriety as an arrogant young gallant who enjoyed gambling, duelling and bedding women, although not necessarily in that order. His life changed when, on 23 or 24 May 1521, he was badly wounded in battle. A cannon ball fractured his right leg and badly lacerated his left. It took nine days to get him from the field of battle to the doctor's. And such was the severity of their treatment that he almost died. For the rest of his life he walked with a limp, and his legs were deformed. For a man who had prided himself on his appearance and his valour, the cannon ball injury was a shattering blow in more ways than one. Forced into a prolonged period of convalescence, he appears to have plunged into depression. In the place where he was convalescing he could find nothing to read apart from the Bible, the *Life of Christ* by a monk called Ludolph of Saxony, and *Lives of the Saints* by an Italian Dominican, Jacopo da Voragine. So he immersed himself in those, and this course of intensive reading changed his life. He abandoned his earlier ambitions, and, as soon as he could walk again, set out on a series of pilgrimages. He completely threw off his previous life, giving away his sword and his fine clothes, and even ostracising his family (he was not to speak to his family for ten years). During this time his mood oscillated between delirious happiness and deep depression – there is little doubt that he was a manic-depressive – but his mood can't have been helped by the severe fasting and penances he set himself. He allowed both his hair and his nails to grow long. And, like Luther, he had some intense visionary experiences; one of his recurring visions was a rainbow-coloured snake covered with objects that shone like eyes. He later decided this was sent by the Devil.

He emerged from these depths of intense prayer, however, as a changed man.

Gradually, over the course of several years, he developed a system of spiritual formation which he began to teach to others. Much later it was formalised as his *Spiritual Exercises* – a thirty-day spiritual formation boot camp of prayer, self-examination and surrender to divine will. The *Spiritual Exercises* is one of the most important and influential books in Western Christianity. It was originally designed as an instruction manual to be used and adapted by spiritual directors responsible for guiding others – just as Ignatius guided others through it. Today it remains as influential as ever, and it crosses boundaries, since many Protestants have discovered the benefits of Ignatius' programme.

Naturally, teaching others personal devotion and prayer and holiness and that sort of thing brought Ignatius to the attention of the Inquisition, which was never into personal holiness in a big way, especially in Spain. It's another of the ironies of church history that Loyola – the founder of the Jesuits – had to flee Spain because he was being hunted by the Inquisition. He made his escape in 1528, eventually ending up in Paris, where he joined the same university college attended by Erasmus and John Knox.

In 1534 Ignatius and six other students gathered together in the crypt of the Basilica of Saint-Denis in Paris and committed themselves to a society or fraternity, which took the name the *Compagnia* or Society of Jesus. They also called themselves the *Amigos en El Señor* or 'Friends in the Lord'. They planned to go on pilgrimage to the Holy Land, but the international situation thwarted their plans. So they decided to stay and be holy in Europe instead, and went to offer their services to the Pope. The result was that, in 1540, the Pope granted them a Bull of Foundation. They were now officially an order. This was an eyebrow-raisingly quick promotion, and it engendered a certain amount of resentment among the more established orders. People dubbed these new upstarts the 'Jesuits'.

Ignatius was not a great preacher, but the austerity of his life, his abstinence, his self-control and certainty made him a formidable figure. His followers certainly treated his every word as law. They were different to the other monastic orders. They had no distinctive uniform, no fixed headquarters. They weren't even ordained – even though they did things like preach and hear confession. Their ascent was no doubt helped by the fact that, along with the usual monastic vows, they added a vow of complete obedience to the Pope. And when they said complete obedience, they meant it. There was no one who took loyalty quite as seriously as Loyola. Loyola's *Rules for Thinking within the Church* start with number 1 – 'We should put away completely our own opinion and keep our minds ready and eager to give our entire obedience to our holy Mother the hierarchical Church, Christ our Lord's undoubted spouse' – and then get even more ridiculously stern. Rule No. 17 is frankly the kind of thing you expect in fascist or communist states: 'To arrive at complete certainty, this is the attitude of mind we should maintain: I will believe the white object I see is black if that should be the decision of the hierarchical Church . . .'

This was the kind of uncritical thinking that had got the Church into trouble in the first place. It is hard to see how anyone other than the most blinkered, ignorant follower could have this kind of faith given the popes at the time. And it's hard to see any kind of 'holiness' in wilfully lying to yourself. But at a time when so many people seemed to be ignoring what he said, the idea of an order which would believe him, no matter how stupid or wrong he was, must have come as a welcome surprise for the pontiff. They would believe him and obey him, and since the purpose of the Jesuit order was a bit vague – 'to strive especially for the progress of souls in Christian life and doctrine and to the propagation of the faith' – it more or less meant that the Pope could use the Jesuits for anything.

In 1550, they added a significant couple of words to their mission statement: now they would strive for 'the defence and propagation of the faith'. This meant, in practice, doing battle with the Reformation. When Loyola's assistant Jerónimo Nadal visited Germany in 1555 he was shocked to see so much Lutheranism and he became convinced that the Jesuits must combat it. And so they became one of the key organisations in combating the ideas of the Reformation. They have been called the shock troops – even the storm troopers – of the papacy. They were utterly dedicated, indefatigable preachers and missionaries.

Their history since has been chequered to say the least, but in their early years, they were revolutionary.

The Jesuits were willing to try to reach the parts of Christendom that other orders simply wouldn't reach. From 1580 onwards, many made their way covertly into England. Their mission was strictly forbidden to 'deal in any respects with matters of state or policy of [the] realm' but to serve the Catholics in the country. However, they assumed secret identities (the famous Jesuit missionary Edmund Campion took on the guise of a jewel merchant) and their presence was assumed to be treacherous. Despite the best efforts of the authorities, no direct connection was ever made between the Jesuits and the members of the gunpowder plot, but that didn't matter to the general public. In the popular imagination – and not just in England – they replaced the Inquisition as chief Catholic villains.

But this reputation is unfair – at least in the early years. They never took any part, for example, in any of the Inquisitions, no doubt recalling the problems their founder had had with that notorious institution. Instead they focused on education and set up 'colleges' in some university towns. The colleges were originally lodging houses for Jesuit students, but they expanded to become schools themselves. They also made a strategic alliance with the Ursulines – another fairly recent order – who provided education for girls. Some of their reputation for devious behaviour was fostered by the other Catholic orders, who were envious of the preferential behaviour which the order seemed to be receiving. And the Jesuits didn't help their cause by implying that they were a bit cleverer than the others (which, due to their education, they often were).*

The thing is, the Jesuits were, in a way, a classic Reformation movement: they had no clerical dress, they were not an enclosed order, they wanted nothing to do with the worldly excesses of the other monastic orders, they were committed to evangelism, they valued education and scholarship, and they were devoted to

---

* Chief among their early opponents was Cardinal Carafa, who wanted to remodel the society into a more traditional monastic order. He himself had been one of the founders of a monastic order – the Theatines – and there were suggestions that the two should merge. But he died before the merger could happen.

personal spiritual transformation. Ignatius, like Luther, passionately believed that it was possible to live a holy life in the world. Because the *Exercises* themselves are a distinctly personal, individual experience, there is a sense in which the Jesuits were always following a higher calling – higher, even, than their dedication to the Church.

And they were very efficient at what they did: a lot of the language of the surviving early letters of the order is about business and how the Jesuits might exploit opportunities for expansion. Another thing: although the Jesuit Constitutions bang on a lot about strict discipline, and complete obedience to the leaders of the society and, ultimately, to the Pope, in practice Jesuits often found themselves in positions where they had to exercise their own initiative. While the Superior-General of the order maintained a tight control, there was no regular decision-making body like the 'chapter' of a monastery. When you're hiding in a priest's hole in a country house in England, you have to become good at improvising.

And sometimes, their travels took them a lot further than England.

The X-Men

One of the original group of six students who met in the crypt of Saint-Denis was a young man from Navarre, in Spain. His name was Francis Xavier. And he went on to found the X-Men and establish a school for mutants . . . oh, no hang on. That was the other one.

Xavier decided to take the mission of the society east. A long way east. And in 1542 he arrived in India, where he lived for seven years. Xavier embodied the kind of servant values that the Church needed. When told that he should take a servant with him to do the tasks below the dignity of a papal representative, he replied that, 'It is such dignity that has debased the church of Rome. The way to real dignity is washing one's own underwear.'*

His mission saw big results. At one point he baptised 10,000 people in one month. He also claimed to have seen miraculous healings as a result of his Gospel readings. In 1549 he moved even further east, to Japan. He went there on the advice of a Japanese outlaw whom he had met in India, and who told him, in an early version of TripAdvisor, that people in Japan were very keen to learn about 'both God and the world'. Like much of the advice on TripAdvisor, it proved to be only partially accurate. The Japanese were very polite, but not that keen to hear what Xavier had to say.

He worked hard to convert them, but came up against enormous cultural differences. His monastic poverty – so impressive in other places – only offended the Japanese, who couldn't understand why anyone would be interested in someone who dressed like a beggar. The result was that in Xavier's time in Japan only around two hundred commoners and low-status people accepted Christianity.

He moved on towards China, but it proved a journey too far and in 1552 he died of fever while still waiting to land.

He was a remarkable man and he never did see the full fruits of his endeavours. After his death, back in Japan, some of the local warlords embraced Christianity, and by 1587 there were some three hundred thousand Christians in areas around Nagasaki.

He had his faults, of course. He, like too many missionaries since, confused Christianity with 'European' and forced converts to take Portuguese names and dress in Western clothes, and he encouraged the tearing down of ancient Hindu temples and shrines.†

---

* It was Xavier who famously said, 'Give me the children until they are seven, and anyone who likes can have them afterwards.' Nowadays it's assumed rather a predatory air, but it is rooted in the Jesuit belief in education.
†He also encouraged King João III of Portugal to dispatch the Inquisition to

The Jesuits worked hard throughout East Asia. In Vietnam, they made thousands of converts. In China, a Jesuit named Matthew Ricci arrived in Macau in 1582. There he spent twenty years becoming a Mandarin scholar, before he ever breathed a word about Jesus. This was a man who took a long view. He also understood the culture. But in some ways, that meant a rather un-Jesuit-like compromise. The version of Catholicism developed in China was rather 'liberal': converts were allowed to maintain their traditional veneration of their ancestors and of Confucius. Jesus became more like a Confucian wise man than the Son of God. Even so, by the time he died, some three thousand people had become Christians.

In India, a Jesuit called Robert Nobili took a similarly incarnational approach. He rejected the paternalism of the earlier missionaries and lived with the people, wearing the same clothes and embracing the culture. Those he converted kept a lot of their Hindu practices except those which were completely and utterly opposed to Catholicism, like some forms of idol worship. When the authorities in Rome heard about his approach they were appalled. They accused him of watering down the gospel. He argued that he was not about turning Indians into Europeans; he wanted them to adopt the essential elements of Christianity in their own culture. However, his approach raised some serious questions. He adopted, for example, the Indian caste system, and this meant that he fed Communion to the untouchables – the Dalits – on the end of a stick. Hardly, one thinks, what Jesus would have done.

The Counter-Reformation – and, in particular, the Jesuits – really established missionary work as a core part of church

---

Goa. It has been claimed that he was present at the burning of two heretics in Portugal in 1540, so he must have known what this meant. The Inquisition eventually arrived in Goa in 1560, after Xavier's death, and it acted as an arm of the colonial powers, brutally killing, imprisoning and torturing Jews, Muslims, Hindus and anyone it wanted to, frankly.

activity, for the first time since the days of the early church.* In 1622, the Pope established what was the first mission agency – the Sacred Congregation for the Propagation of the Faith. The Latin version of its name is the origin of the English term 'propaganda'.

---

* The Baptist William Carey has often been called the Father of Modern Mission. Complete bunkum. He didn't arrive in India till 1793, some two hundred years after the Jesuits.

26 Ending Trent

Even more hopeless popes

Perhaps the biggest failing of the Council of Trent was that it left the papacy itself completely unreformed, which, given what the report issued some decades earlier said, seemed to be rather ignoring the root of the problem. Pope Paul III never lived to see the culmination of the council: he died in September 1547 and Trent still had another sixteen years to go.

In fact, the list of popes in the decades after Luther came to prominence contains some *more* of the worst examples of papal misbehaviour in church history. Once again I wouldn't dream of sullying this noble work with their behaviour.

Oh all right then, if I absolutely must . . .

Julius III (Pope from 1547 to 1555)
Paul III was succeeded, after the usual politicking by the cardinals, by a cleric and lawyer who took the name Julius III. There was nothing remarkable about him, unless you count his parties, which were known to descend into homosexual orgies after the main guests had left, and his infatuation with a seventeen-year-old boy with the somewhat ironic name of Innocenzo, whom he had picked up in Parma and whom he immediately made a cardinal. His ending was a little ironic as well: he was renowned as a glutton, yet his digestive system stopped working and he effectively starved to death on 23 March 1555. But despite his personal

habits, Julius, too, was a bit of a reformer, and he did all he could to keep the Council of Trent going before he died of too much irony.

Marcellus II (Pope from 1555 to . . . er . . . a bit later in 1555)
Next in the queue for the papacy was another reformer: Marcellus II, a humanist, translator and scholar. He was the austerity pope, cutting coronation expenses and running costs to the bare minimum. And he was so anti-nepotism that he actually banned all members of his family from even visiting Rome in case they accidentally got appointed to anything. Sadly, after just twenty-two days in office he had a massive stroke and died. Shame. He had potential.

Pope Paul IV (Pope from 1555 to 1559)
The new Pope was elected on 23 May 1555 as Pope Paul IV. But we've already met him in the form of Cardinal Carafa, the DIY home torturer. He was seventy-eight years old – the oldest pope of the sixteenth century. And also the most horrific, which is saying something. An intolerant, authoritarian, anti-Semitic bigot, Paul IV was a medieval pope in a Reformation world. He was a man who turned objection into an art form. He objected to the Reformation, naturally, but he also suspended the Council of Trent. He banned travelling entertainers and dancing, and had fig leaves painted on the nude figures of the Sistine Chapel. Convinced that the Jews were secretly in league with the Protestants, he forced the Jews in Rome into ghettos, forbade them to trade in anything except food and second-hand clothing, and demolished all of Rome's synagogues bar one. Such was the severity of his campaign against the Jews that the Jewish population of Rome was halved.*

---

* Shockingly, the bull which contained these statutes – *Cum nimis absurdum* of 17 July 1555 – remained in force for the next three centuries.

He was a big fan of the Inquisition, and never missed its weekly meeting. Indeed, in 1557 he started one of the Catholic Church's most notorious institutions – the Index of Forbidden Books. It listed some 550 authors whose works were not to be read, including theologians like Luther and Calvin (and Erasmus), works of botany and geography, and the complete run of Venetian Playboy.* Typically it backfired. Because what the Index really did was to draw people's attention to all the naughty books, and thus act as a helpful guide to what to read next. In fact, early copies of the Index made their way very quickly to the enterprising printers in Leiden, Amsterdam and Utrecht, who used them as guides as to what to print. Then, as now, nothing did more for sales and publicity than a ban.†

Paul was the last pope to lead troops into battle. He had never forgiven Emperor Charles for concluding the Peace of Augsburg, which conceded Lutheran territory. So, stupidly ignoring the fact that Charles V was actually a champion of Catholicism, he allied himself with the French and declared war on Spain. He even quarrelled with Mary I of England, who was trying to return the country to Catholicism. He died in 1559, a broken, foolish and widely detested man. When news of his death hit the streets of Rome, the people immediately destroyed the offices of the Inquisition, released all the prisoners and burned all the files. Then they tore down the statue of the Pope, ripped off the head and threw it into the Tiber.

---

* The Index's last major update was in 1948, but it was officially abolished in 1966 by Pope Paul VI, who, like everyone in the 1960s, was probably keen to read some far-out books.

† This is called the Streisand effect. It's named after the American singer Barbra Streisand, who in 2003 attempted to ban photographs of her Malibu residence which had appeared on the Internet. But in making a fuss about it, she actually drew more people's attention to the existence of the photos and everyone went to have a good look at Chateau Babs.

Pius IV (Pope from 1559 to 1565)

Paul IV's successor was Cardinal Giovanni Angelo Medici. He was actually no relation to the great family of the fourteenth century, but was a humble lawyer's son who took the name Pius IV. He restarted the Council of Trent, made up with the Emperor, cut back the powers of the Inquisition and whittled down the Papal Index. He also encouraged artists and scholars, founded universities and printing presses.

In this he was aided by his nephew, Charles Borromeo, who was to prove one of the greatest reformers of his time. Borromeo took over leading the final sessions of the Council of Trent. But he was more than an administrator. He worked tirelessly among the poor and the sick, most notably during the plague year of 1576. Among the many reforms he initiated in his own diocese was the establishment of seminaries, colleges and communities to provide better education for would-be priests. In the 1576 outbreak of plague and famine in Milan he remained when all the other nobility had legged it, and used up all the funds of the religious communities to feed up to seventy thousand people each day.*

But there's always some dark stuff. Borromeo was also very concerned about sorcery, witchcraft and heretics: in a visitation to Catholic cantons in Switzerland, some 150 people were arrested for practising witchcraft. He persuaded 139 of them to repent, but after he left, eleven women and the local priest were condemned to be burned alive. This despite the fact that they acknowledged their 'sins' and, apparently, received absolution and Holy Communion. They even called out to Jesus as the flames took them. The priest he left in charge of the burnings – Father Stoppani – wrote that he had every hope that these unfortunate creatures had won salvation. So that's all right then.

---

* Not that everyone liked him. Some of his reforms made him enemies, among them the Humiliati (Brothers of Humility), who were an order of monks which, although reduced to a mere 170 members, somehow owned 90 monasteries. They tried to have him assassinated, but the bullet missed.

Borromeo comes across as a bit of an Italian Catholic Calvin. Il Calvino? He was austere, humourless, utterly dedicated and uncompromising. Perhaps the austerity took its toll: he died in 1584 aged just forty-six.*

Pius V (Pope from 1565 to 1572)

Between them, Pius IV and his nephew steered the Council of Trent to a conclusion, but when Pius died in December 1565, he wasn't succeeded by Borromeo, but by Cardinal Michele Ghislieri. He took the name Pius V. He was a kind of Carafa-lite. Deeply ascetic, he wore a hair shirt, regularly walked barefoot and demanded austerity from all around him. He was a hardliner who had blasphemers flogged and who forbade doctors to treat patients who had not been to regular confession or Mass. He decreed that all unmarried prostitutes and all men found guilty of sodomy should be burned at the stake: a decree which would have made uncomfortable reading for quite a number of his predecessors. He even tried to make adultery a capital offence, but was dissuaded, probably on the grounds that it would have pretty much emptied the Church of other priests and laity. In Rome, unmarried men were forbidden to employ female servants. More ludicrously, or possibly worryingly, nuns were banned from having male dogs as pets. He also prohibited bullfights. The Romans complained that he was trying to turn Rome into one huge monastery.

Like his mentor, Carafa, Pius V was a big fan of the Inquisition and spent many a happy hour enjoying the interrogations in the torture chamber and cheerfully sentencing heretics to death. When he sent a small army to France to support the government there, he gave them special instructions to kill all Huguenot

---

* Borromeo was later canonised and he is one of the few saints whom you can physically enter; there is a giant statue of him in Arona, Italy, which is 23 metres tall and stands on a plinth 12 metres in height. Visitors can climb up the inside the statue and look out through his ears.

prisoners. He extended the persecution of the Jews, banning them from all the papal territories except for the ghetto in Rome and another smaller one in Ancona.

Gregory XIII (Pope from 1572 to 1585)

Pius V died in 1572 and was succeeded by Cardinal Ugo Boncompagni, who became Gregory XIII. He had been a leading lawyer at the Council of Trent, but nowadays he is chiefly remembered for reforming the calendar. It was all a bit complicated, but the old Julian calendar, which had been used since 46 BC, was now running ten days behind the proper date since it miscalculated the length of time the earth takes to go round the sun. So Gregory decreed that the day after 5 October 1582 would actually be 15 October. There were widespread protests about this: not least by the Protestants, who refused to obey. For one thing, they were not going to have the Pope tell them what day it was, thank you very much; for another, many of them were devout readers of Revelation and they were worried that changing the dates would throw out all their calculations about the end times. In the end the English only followed suit in 1752, and the Protestant Swiss cantons in 1812. In regions where the Orthodox Church held sway – Russia, Greece and the Balkan States – they did not make the change until the twentieth century. And the Isle of Wight still hasn't caught up.

Gregory XIII carried on the reforming work of Trent, establishing colleges and seminaries. He gave over to the Jesuits the running of many of these places. (The enlarged Jesuit College became known as the Gregorian University.) He also established an English seminary in Rome, from where a steady stream of underground missionaries went forth to re-evangelise England. Several ended up as martyrs. He replaced the old system of papal legates – the Pope's 'ambassadors' – with a new order of trained diplomats called nuncios. But he was not exactly enlightened.

When he heard of the St Bartholomew's Day massacre, he held a special Mass of Thanksgiving. He spent his time trying to persuade King Philip of Spain to launch an invasion of England, plotting the assassination of Elizabeth I whom he called 'the Jezebel of the North', and organising two invasions of Ireland. In one of these he spent a lot of money outfitting an adventurer called Thomas Stukely with a ship and 800 men. He was livid when Stukely took more money from the King of Portugal and attacked Morocco instead. All this cost money and, when he died, aged eighty-three, his thirteen-year pontificate had left the papacy almost bankrupt.

Sixtus V (Pope from 1585 to 1590)
And then another swing. After Gregory XIII, welcome Sixtus V, elected on 24 April 1585. A farmworker's son from Ancona, he was a Franciscan. A brilliant preacher, he had led the Inquisition in Venice, and had a reputation as a stern, unyielding, ruthless dictator. He neutered the College of Cardinals (not literally, although he probably would have done if he thought he could have got away with it) and transferred power instead to the 'congregations' – various papal government departments.

He brought law and order to the papal lands, largely through the arbitrary arrest and execution of some seven thousand 'brigands'. Reports had it that there were more impaled heads on spikes along the Ponte Sant'Angelo than melons in the market. And through his careful, not-to-say draconian management of the finances, including punitive taxes, he made himself one of the richest princes in Europe. A significant proportion of this income was spent on Rome itself, transforming it into Europe's greatest city with a star-shaped city plan and many of the streets, piazzas, fountains and monuments that draw millions of tourists to Rome today. He wanted to use some of that money to get England back. So he promised subsidies to Philip II to pay for an invasion. But the Spanish Armada was defeated in 1588, and he refused to pay. When he died of malaria on 27 August 1590, there was widespread rejoicing.

—∾∾—

And so it continues. In the next sixteen months there were no fewer than three popes: Urban VII, Gregory XIV and Innocent IX, all of whom died with the regularity of Spinal Tap drummers.

In 1592 Pope Clement VIII came to the papal throne. A deeply pious man, he embodied many of the ideals of the Counter-Reformation. He spent hours every day in prayer, contemplation and confession. He visited the seven pilgrimage churches on foot fifteen times a year. He was a scholar who repaired the mess Sixtus V had made of the revised Vulgate. He revised the breviary, and the missal. But he also enlarged the Index of Forbidden books, adding many Jewish titles to the list. And during his reign, the Inquisition sent more than thirty heretics to the stake, including the Dominican scientist, philosopher, mathematician, cosmologist, astrologer and all-round smarty-pants Giordano Bruno. Clement recognised Henry IV of France as a Catholic, a decision he regretted when, in the Edict of Nantes, Henry granted extensive rights to the Huguenots.

In the Jubilee celebrations of 1600 some half a million pilgrims made their way to Rome. Not only was this an enormous boost to the papal coffers but it showed that rumours of Catholicism's death were greatly exaggerated. At the beginning of the seventeenth century, Rome was still the capital of Christendom. The Catholic Church had suffered major blows in the century just passed. It had lost England and Scotland, half of Germany, and the Netherlands. There were millions of French Protestants.

But the Catholic Church had survived. And Europe and the Western world was now, irrevocably, Catholic and Protestant.

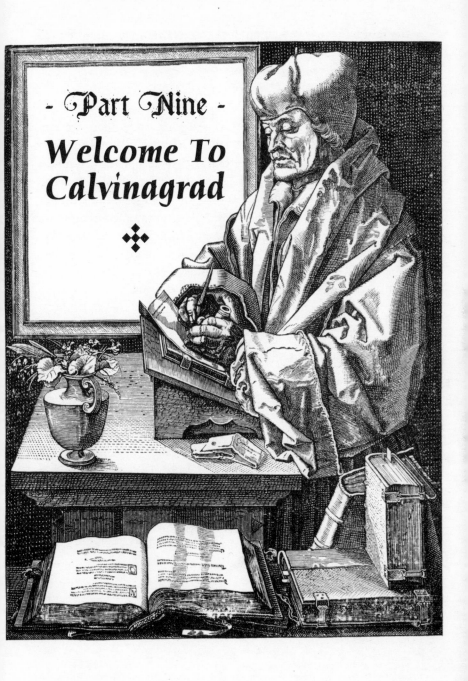

- Part Nine -
Welcome To Calvinagrad

❖

27 The return to Geneva

Strasbourg

'But what,' I hear you ask, 'of Calvin? What happened to him?'
Well remembered.

When we last met Jean, he and Farel had been evicted from Geneva after a failed attempt to Make Everyone Holy.

Farel went to Neuchâtel. Calvin reverted to Plan A and went to live in Strasbourg. It was a dark time for him: he felt that he had failed. Which he had, now I come to think of it. But in Strasbourg several things happened to encourage him.

First, he came into contact with Martin Bucer. Bucer persuaded Calvin to stay in the city and installed Calvin as pastor of Strasbourg's small French refugee church.* From Bucer, Calvin learned how to manage the civic, communal side of reform. In Strasbourg, Bucer had instilled some of the discipline which Calvin and Farel had aimed at, and actually made it work. Indeed, at one point, this discipline was turned against Calvin himself. Calvin was accused of not believing in the Trinity and summoned before Bucer. He successfully acquitted himself, although people said he went white with rage, which, given he was usually pale, must have made him virtually transparent. It wasn't the last time that he was going to get angry about the Trinity.

Second, Calvin returned to writing. He published a second,

* That is, the church was small in number. It wasn't a collection of tiny French émigrés.

much expanded version of his *Institutes*. And he also wrote the first of his commentaries; on Romans, of course. I mean, it's the Reformation. Why would you want to write about anything else?

Third, he got married. He did so largely on the advice of Bucer. 'I am not one of those infatuated lovers who, captivated by a pretty face, kiss even her vices', he wrote. 'The only beauty which interests me is that she should be modest, obliging, not haughty, not extravagant, patient and solicitous for my health.' Sounds more like he's advertising for a carer. He rejected a number of applicants for the post (the first one didn't speak French, the second didn't appear very interested, the third actually got engaged to him then broke it off in sudden horror at what she had done) before settling on Idelette de Bure. She was actually the widow of an Anabaptist, but one assumes Calvin had her thoroughly vetted and reprogrammed before marriage.

Idelette bore Calvin a son, and probably some daughters – all of whom died in infancy. Despite this, and the many other difficulties of Calvin's life, he and Idelette do seem to have been happy together. When she died in 1549, Calvin wrote that he had 'been bereaved of the best companion of my life'.

Severe laws

Calvin was happy in Strasbourg. But Geneva was in turmoil. Again. The faction which had driven Farel and Calvin from the city had been driven out itself and Farel's supporters – known as the Guillermins (i.e. Williamins) – had regained control. There had been riots and unrest; the city needed a firm hand. So the council turned to the strongest hand it knew: that attached to the arm of Calvin.

Calvin had no desire to return – he said he would prefer 'a hundred deaths to this cross' – but he was once more persuaded by Farel (who, conveniently, was too busy to accompany him) and by Bucer, who for some reason thought a Calvin-less

Strasbourg seemed an attractive proposition. So, in 1541 Calvin moved back to Geneva, to a house provided for him by the city. This time, though, he had some conditions:

> If you desire to have me for your pastor, correct the disorder of your lives. If you have with sincerity recalled me from exile, banish the crimes and debaucheries which prevail among you . . . I consider the principal enemies of the gospel to be, not the pontiff of Rome, nor heretics, nor seducers, nor tyrants, but bad Christians.

It was time to launch Geneva 2.0. Geneva would be transformed into the über-Protestant city. 'Let the severity of the laws reign in the church', Calvin wrote. And 'severe' is the word. The Church was reorganised along what Calvin believed to be a New Testament model. Churches were stripped of all their decoration. Calvin drew up a set of 'Ecclesiastical Ordinances', which governed not only the Church, but almost every aspect of ordinary life. He structured the Church along the lines he had seen in Bucer's Strasbourg: four levels of authority: pastors, doctors, elders and deacons.* Pastors carried out general ministry; teaching was the responsibility of the doctors, and the pastors and senior doctors formed a Company of Pastors. The elders – twelve laymen elected from the city council – oversaw life in every home in Geneva. The deacons looked after social care for the poor and the sick. They were all organised into committees known as presbyteries – and this became the basis of what is known as the Presbyterian system. Calvin didn't get it all his own way: he wanted a weekly celebration of the Lord's Supper, but he was only allowed a quarterly celebration, and his deacons never amounted to much, but apart from that it was all set up to his satisfaction.

---

* As opposed to the official threefold order of bishop, priest and deacon. Or the unofficial threefold order of diocesan accountant, vicar's wife and Obligatory Old Person Who Scares Everyone.

Great Moments in Reformation History

NUMBER 21: Calvin returns to Geneva.

The Ecclesiastical Ordinances were an extension of the Church's area of control. Under their guidelines, the Church had the duty of poking its nose in – sorry, overseeing – many aspects of ordinary life. Calvin established what was known as the *grabeau*, a system by which households would be visited by elders, who would helpfully critique any citizens who had fallen away. Everyone had to learn the official catechism and those who didn't were banned from the Lord's Table. Persistent or serious offenders had to face a draconian church court known as the Consistory, a group composed of pastors and elders, who met every Thursday to hear cases, tell people off and issue a range of punishments. Minor offences were punished with admonition, reprimand or exclusion from the Lord's Supper. And for more serious offences the council passed the miscreant on to the city council, for more significant 'correction'.

New laws were passed concerning divorce, blasphemy, drunkenness. Dancing, theatre and fashionable trousers were banned. Anyone found to have a rosary or 'idols to adore' was sent to the Consistory. Ditto for anyone who went on a pilgrimage. Anyone inviting another person for a drink was fined three sous. A man who refused to go and listen to sermons was evicted from the city, along with his family. The use of the name Claude was forbidden, because it might remind people of St Claude, a locally popular saint. It was estimated that in the 1560s, around five offenders were excommunicated every week.

The Consistory was feared and hated. It was accused of promoting informants or people with grudges. Certainly some of the offences seem petty. No, some of the offences *were* petty. A woman was admonished for kneeling on her husband's grave and crying 'Rest in peace'. Others were rebuked for believing in peasant cures: a woman was rebuked for sorcery for trying to cure her husband by tying a walnut around his neck with a spider in it. Anything smacking of 'popery' was cracked down on, from a Franciscan who prayed to the Virgin Mary, to merchants who made rosaries. Three young men who scoffed three dozen patés were imprisoned and forced to live on bread and water. A man charged with 'unnatural vice' was burned to death. (To be fair, some decisions were a lot more enlightened, like the man who was sent to prison for insisting on his right to beat his wife.)

It is often said that this was nothing to do with Calvin. Certainly, as a French refugee he had no right to vote or hold any secular office, and technically he was just a council employee and not in any official disciplinary position. He wasn't even a full citizen of Geneva until 1559. All this allows his supporters to claim that he was entirely detached from all this. It wasn't him, guv. But *come on* – his fingerprints are all over the job. True, he didn't operate the machinery itself. He kept his distance, kept his hands clean, mastered the art of plausible deniability. So, while it's wrong to depict Calvin as some kind of Protestant Ayatollah, he as much as anyone was responsible for Geneva becoming the World Centre of Disapproving of Things. Calvin was in charge, without actually being in charge – the best kind of 'in charge' there is.

So how did Calvin exert this influence? Simple. He did it from the pulpit. He preached Geneva into submission. The number of sermons preached in Geneva is eye-watering. There were daily sermons, and three sermons on Sunday, and you *had* to attend. Calvin alone preached 260 sermons a year. And he surrounded himself with like-minded people. It is significant that from the 1540s until 1594 not a single native Genevan was a member of the Genevan ministry: they were all immigrants.

It wasn't just the ministers who moved in, either. Geneva started to attract a lot of fans of Calvin. The population more than doubled during his time not in charge, most of the newcomers being French refugees. Calvin was good for business, since many of these people were skilled workers who established industries

Great Moments in Reformation History

NUMBER 22: In Geneva, Calvin demonstrates his new way of deciding who is in the elect.

Eeny-meeny-miny-mo . . .

like clock making. In particular, Geneva became the centre of a thriving publishing industry. The religious refugees who fled to the city included a great many writers, scholars and printers, especially from France. The French installed Geneva's presses. The sheer number of these people radically altered the nature of the city. The city established a paper-making industry. The number of printers and booksellers in the city jumped from between three and six before the Reformation, to three hundred or more.*

This being Geneva and the Reformation, naturally they specialised in Bible printing and biblical scholarship. I mean, it wasn't exactly going to specialise in racy paperbacks. In 1551, a French scholar-printer called Robert Estienne (or Stephanus) issued an edition of the Greek New Testament in Geneva which was notable for featuring verse references. A couple of others had done this before, but it was Estienne's verse division which stuck and which we follow today. Later, English refugees created one of the great monuments of English literature: the Geneva Bible, the world's first study Bible.

This influx changed the city. Geneva stopped speaking German and started speaking French. Many of the old middle-class inhabitants were forced to leave and their houses were occupied by immigrants. It was a very modern picture: immigrants accused of stealing jobs and pushing up rents. People started muttering about putting all these refugees on a boat and sailing them back down the Rhône to France. They hadn't got rid of the Italian Pope only to be lorded over by French clergy.

And the blame for most of this was laid at the feet of one

---

* Between 1550 and 1560, 130 refugee printers and booksellers settled in Geneva. The bulk of these people came from Lyons. Such was the devastating effect on the printing industry in Lyons, that by 1585 the few printers who remained in Lyons were mainly just repackaging books printed in Geneva, slapping on new title pages to disguise their point of origin, and shipping them on to Spain and Italy. The centres of the printing world changed during the Reformation: Venice went into a decline as a print centre after the Counter-Reformation put an effective end to their scholarly activities.

man: the man who was Definitely Not In Charge, Oh Dear Me No. Calvin was widely resented. In the early 1550s there were riots led by what became known as the 'Libertine' party. (At least that was the derisive nickname Calvin gave them; they called themselves 'Children of Geneva'.) People started disrupting his sermons, having sudden 'coughing fits' or moving themselves about on their seats to make farting noises. Others tried to empty their chamber pots on him as he walked beneath their windows.

Calvin was aggrieved by all this criticism. As far as he could see, all he was doing was denying people the opportunity to sin.

Emptying your chamber pot in Calvin's direction was one thing. It was openly speaking out against him that could get you in trouble. The opponents of Calvin and the authorities were ruthlessly silenced. An anonymous note was found in Calvin's pulpit threatening him with assassination. It was discovered to be the work of Jacques Gruet, a leading Libertine. Gruet's wife had been imprisoned for a few days for the crime of dancing. His father-in-law complained that the people had been enslaved by the French pastors. Gruet accused Calvin of behaving like a bishop. But worse, Gruet was found to be a radical free thinker, an advocate of free love and an atheist. He was tortured and beheaded.

In autumn 1551, Jerome Bolsec made the error of publicly challenging Calvin's doctrine of predestination, arguing that Calvin's God was 'a tyrant and an idol like the Jupiter created by Pagans'. Calvin spent an hour trying to persuade him to repent, but in the end gave up and called him 'a monster vomiting forth poison'. He ensured that Bolsec was banished from Geneva. Bolsec reconverted to Catholicism, went to France and consoled himself by writing a largely fabricated life of Calvin in which the reformer was accused of homosexuality, hypocrisy and anything else Bolsec could throw into the mix.

Then there was Servetus.

28 Preserving purity

The bloodthirsty council of the learned

The reformers had torn down many of the pillars of Catholicism. But once you start destroying things it is hard to stop. People get a taste for destruction. Thinking can become addictive. From the 1530s onwards the reformers start to talk a great deal more about 'discipline and order' – *Zucht und Ordnung* – as well as freedom. They did this because people were not just rethinking the bits of Catholicism that they were supposed to rethink, they were rethinking everything. Pamphleteers and preachers started to question the very basics of Christian belief: the Incarnation, original sin, infant baptism, the sacraments, even the Trinity. This was not reformed thinking: it was heresy.

How heresy should be treated was a topic of considerable debate in the early years of the Reformation, not least because the Reformation was, of course, a movement which was itself heretical – at least from the Catholic point of view. Some people argued that you should not punish heretics. Vergerio, a former papal nuncio-turned-evangelical-preacher, argued that heretics should be constrained, but not killed: 'I hate such disturbers more than a dog and a snake,' he wrote, 'but I prefer that they should be incarcerated in the foulest dungeon rather than they be destroyed by fire and sword.' Others, like the Anabaptist leader David Joris, spoke out against 'the bloodthirsty council of the learned', by which he meant all those who decided who was heretical and deserved to die.

In 1531 a scholar called Michael Servetus published a book called *On the Errors of the Trinity*, a treatise which denied the doctrine of the Trinity. He was a Unitarian. This meant that he was hated not just by Calvin but by Lutherans, Anglicans, Catholics, the Mother's Union, you name it. He was a universally despised heretic.

Servetus was, in some ways, responding to the monotheistic faiths in Spain, which for centuries had housed significant Jewish communities, not to mention being ruled by Muslims for a few hundred years. He argued that the Trinity was a later belief grafted onto monotheistic Judaism, and that jettisoning the idea would therefore bring unity between Jews, Christians and Muslims. (And, of course, he was right to some extent: most Christians would argue that the truth of the Trinity is inherent in the New Testament, but it is nowhere explicitly spelt out. It first occurs as a word in the writings of Tertullian, in the third century.)

Calvin had had a lengthy and fractious correspondence with Servetus, which, in the end, he gave up on in frustration. (He was particularly irritated when Servetus sent him a copy of the *Institutes* which he had heavily annotated, pointing out errors in the book.) Servetus, naively, foolishly or courageously, stated that he was willing to travel to Geneva and meet Calvin. Calvin wrote to Farel, ominously, that if Servetus did come, 'as far as my authority goes, I would not let him leave alive'.

It was the Catholics who first convicted Servetus of heresy. He was living in Vienne under an assumed name, but somehow his identity was revealed to the Inquisition. They received a letter from one Guillaume de Trie, a merchant in Geneva. Included in the letter were eight pages torn from Servetus' book. But how could that have happened? There was only one man in Geneva who had been sent a copy of that book. Then, at the first inter-rogation, Servetus was presented with further material, including, strangely, pages from Calvin's *Institutes*, bearing annotations in Servetus' handwriting. Calvin, working through de Trie, had delivered Servetus to the Inquisition. The Inquisition decided to burn Servetus, but he escaped over the rooftops, so they were reduced to burning his effigy instead.

And then, for some reason, Servetus made his way to Geneva. Probably he was trying to pass through as quickly as he could, but he went to church and was recognised. His level of self-delusion can be seen in the fact that, from his prison cell, he wrote to the Geneva city council demanding Calvin's arrest and offering to take Calvin's house and goods when Calvin was executed. The city council, though, were in no mood for charity. Calvin did try to get Servetus to repent. But Servetus refused and he was found guilty. The council was anxious to prove to the rest of Christendom that it was as orthodox as anyone, so Servetus was sentenced to death.

Apologists for Calvin argue that Calvin had no say in the sentencing (which was true) and that he argued for a lenient sentence. However, that lenient sentence was beheading, rather than burning, so, you know, it's not *much* more lenient. And he was instrumental in the whole affair. In a letter dated 20 August 1553, he wrote to Farel that 'after he [Servetus] had been recognised, I thought that he should be detained . . . I hope that sentence of death will at least be passed upon him.'

Which is exactly what happened. In the end, Servetus was taken to the city gate and burned. As the flames rose, Servetus cried, 'Oh Jesus, son of eternal God, have pity on me!'

Farel, who was in Geneva at the time, watched the execution and said that if Servetus had cried out 'Oh Jesus, eternal son of God . . .' he would have been spared. See? If he'd just turned two words around, just said things in the right order, then he would have been OK. I'm struggling to think of a more chilling example of when theology goes bad. In fact, many of the big guns of the Reformation are shown in a shoddy light by this episode. Farel was, reportedly, the one who 'bellowed most loudly' at the execution; the Scots reformer John Knox, also in attendance, applauded loudly when Servetus died.

And Calvin? Well, he might have done all that he could to persuade Servetus to change his mind, but he also did all he could to get the man arrested and killed. Certainly Melanchthon believed that Calvin was responsible; he even wrote to Calvin to thank him: 'To you also the Church owes gratitude at the present moment . . . I affirm also that your magistrates did right in punishing, after a regular trial, this blasphemous man.'

The truth is that virtually every other city, region or principality would have killed Servetus for his views. Wittenberg, Strasbourg, Geneva, Zürich, London were all places with varying degrees of intolerance for heterodox views. But even so, the Servetus case caused a backlash. Many Genevan citizens blamed Calvin for Servetus' death. Some even began to view Servetus as a 'martyr of Jesus'. The most vociferous critic was a friend and colleague of Calvin, Sebastian Castellio, whom Calvin had made rector at the Collège of Geneva. Their relationship had been deteriorating for some years. Part of the problem was that Castellio, in Calvin's eyes, was developing suspect views. He declared that the Song of Songs should not be in the Bible because it was 'simply a lascivious or obscene song describing Solomon's objectionable love affairs'. And then Castellio dared to speak out against Calvin in a public meeting. He said that the clergy should stop persecuting those who disagree with them on matters of biblical interpretation, and should be held to the same standards that all other believers were held to. Calvin charged Castellio with the offence of 'undermining the prestige of the clergy'. Under pressure, Castellio resigned from his position as rector. For a while he was reduced to begging from door to door, or doing menial jobs, but finally he was driven from the city.

His fortunes looked on the up when he was appointed to a teaching position in the University of Basel and he was there in October 1553 when Servetus was executed. Castellio launched a stinging attack: he accused Calvin of having 'hands dripping with the blood of Servetus'. Castellio argued that Calvin and the authorities had no right to execute any man for his ideas. He wrote a treatise, *On Heretics*, which argued that Christians spent far too much time arguing about doctrines like the Trinity, angels, free will and suchlike. Salvation, he pointed out, was not a matter of these kind of beliefs, but of faith in Jesus Christ. And anyway, how could Christians dare to execute heretics when they couldn't even agree among themselves who the heretics were?

Castellio wrote that, 'When Servetus fought with reasons and writings, he should have been repulsed by reasons and writings.' He even quoted Calvin's own words back at him: 'It is unchristian to use arms against those who have been expelled from the Church, and to deny them rights common to all mankind.' And he pointed out what opponents of capital punishment have been arguing ever since: 'It would be better to let a hundred, even a thousand heretics live than put a decent man to death under the pretence of heresy.'

To the reformers, obviously, Castellio was just another heretic. Calvin's right-hand man Theodore Beza (of whom more later) accused Castellio of advising 'everyone to believe what he wants, opening the door by this means to all heresies and false doctrines'. But Castellio's attack hit home. Stung, Calvin published a treatise in February 1554 entitled *Defence of the orthodox faith in the sacred Trinity* (*Defensio orthodoxae fidei de sacra Trinitate*) in which he presented arguments in favour of the execution of Servetus for diverging from orthodox Christian doctrine. And he described Castellio's ideas as 'malignant, unmanageable and pernicious'. In a particularly chilling passage he not only defended his actions, but argued that even those who opposed the sentence would be considered heretics:

> Whoever shall now contend that it is unjust to put heretics and blasphemers to death will knowingly and willingly incur their very guilt . . . Many people have accused me of such ferocious cruelty that (they allege) I would like to kill again the man I have destroyed. Not only am I indifferent to their comments, but I rejoice in the fact that they spit in my face.

339

That's Calvin for you. The more people opposed him, the more certain he was that he was right.

Castellio became known as a passionate advocate of free speech, and of the separation of church and state. He died in Basel in 1563.

Later on, his enemies unearthed the body, burned it and scattered the ashes.

Heretic.

The Children of Geneva

It's hard to get a line on Calvin. He was in many ways the opposite of Luther. Luther is all bluff and bluster and outrage and hyperbole. Zwingli is all brawn and bravado and military prowess. But Calvin is thoughtful, reserved, austere, isolated even. That's what makes him such a difficult person to like. A meal with Luther would have been enjoyable or infuriating or both at the same time. A meal *chez* Calvin would have been a little, well, *quieter*.

The thing is that despite giving it up, at heart he was always a lawyer. He was a legal system on legs. He built systems, argued logically, created watertight arguments. And there is always something a little inhuman about that. The *Institutes* are a logical systematic theology with no gaps. He could write majestically; he had an acute and impressive brain. He was as thin as pen stroke. A 'great faster', he starved himself, taking only one small meal a day. When he was moved to temper, his was a cold temper. He was an intellectual, a thinker. But also a zealot, utterly committed to the cause. In later times he would have been the chief of the secret police. He exercised power through influence, through argument, through his sheer will. He never took any official position of authority because he never needed to.

Calvin's supporters love his systematic theology. They love his sonorous prose. They love the fact that they have all been elected together. Others find in Geneva a somewhat soulless, joyless place. John Knox, one of the refugees who settled there, described the city as 'the most perfect school of Christ that ever was in the earth since the days of the Apostles'. Since John Knox was an old curmudgeon without a single joyful bone in his body, this is not really a recommendation.

Certainly it wasn't a happy place for everyone. That little comment of Calvin's about people spitting on him is revealing. Because, for all that has been said about his influence in Geneva in the early 1550s, the Dear Leader's position was by no means secure. Calvin and his supporters faced stiff opposition from the so-called 'Children of Geneva'. They managed to gain influence in the council, so much so that, at one point, a leading anti-Calvanista, Philippe Berthelier, was excommunicated by the

Consistory but the excommunication was overturned by the city council. Calvin refused to accept the decision of the council. He decided to act illegally, disobey the authorities and withhold Communion. 'I will die sooner than this hand shall stretch forth the sacred things of the Lord to those who have been judged despisers.' Berthelier did not attend the service and the council decided not to force the issue.

In the end, though, Calvin's position was strengthened by the number of religious refugees that continued to flood into the city during the 1550s, coming largely because of Calvin's reputation.* In the election of 1555 these immigrant votes were crucial in winning back council control for Calvin's supporters. In response, the anti-Calvin faction rioted. Their leader, Ami Perrin, grabbed the city's baton of authority. The council chose to interpret this action as an attempted coup and used it as an excuse to crack down. The Children of Geneva were rounded up, their ringleaders executed or exiled, and their property confiscated. And in the following year's elections, any remaining anti-Calvinists were purged.

Calvinagrad was saved.

Calvin's wife died in March 1549. For the rest of his life he was plagued by ill health. A letter to his doctor complains of kidney stones and arthritis, the colic, haemorrhoids, ulcers, discharging 'blood instead of urine', nephritis and gout. But apart from that he was fine . . . He endured the pain, as he had done all his life, and spent his days dealing with the vast amount of correspondence and working on his biblical commentaries.

Confined to his bed, he requested that all the pastors in Geneva visit him so that he could exhort them not to give up after his death. He died in 1564, and such was his hatred of shrines and relics that he was buried in an unmarked grave.

---

* Over the decade, the population nearly doubled, from about 13,000 in 1550 to 21,400 ten years later.

29 The international Brotherhood of the Elect

Inventing Calvinism

After Calvin's death it was his followers and interpreters – the Calvinists – who turned out to be the dominant species in the Protestant ecosystem. And it is they who really leave us with the textbook image of Calvinism: dour, dark, always saying 'no', and obsessed with the results of the election.*

Calvin's legacy was overseen by Théodore de Bèze aka Theodore Beza. He was the professor of the Geneva Academy, where he taught for almost forty years, and he saw it as his life's work to interpret the teachings of the master, especially the *Institutes*, Calvinism's very own *Das Kapital*. Beza also succeeded Calvin as Leader of the Company of Pastors. He kept Calvinism from splitting after the leader's death, but he did it by making Calvin's system of thought more rigid, by clarifying, crystallising, hardening all the definitions and the dogma. In a wide-ranging correspondence with pastors, theologians and political leaders, Beza became the major interpreter of what Calvinism actually was. Along the way it became more legal than ever, more scholastic, more about asserting and defending propositions and banging out proof-texts

---

* The term Calvinism was originally a term of abuse, coined by Lutherans objecting to the many displaced refugee Calvin-supporting congregations in German towns.

to, er, prove things. This was different to Calvin's basic humanist approach.

Calvinism had a power and a determination that the other brands of Protestantism lacked, and part of that was because

TOP REFORMERS

Theodore Beza

Born: Vezelay, Burgundy, France, 1519
Died: Geneva, Switzerland, 1605

AKA: Théodore de Bèze, or de Besze

A renowned humanist and Greek scholar, Beza became Professor at the academy in Geneva. After Calvin's death he became leader of the Swiss Calvinists. He wrote a life of Calvin and, if anything, became even more hardline than Calvin was. His writing was influential in developing 'Calvinism'.

Fun Fact: Before his conversion, Beza was famous for his Latin poetry.

INFLUENCE	65
THEOLOGICAL IMPORTANCE	40
FACIAL HAIR	68
GENERAL GLOOMINESS	98
ABUSIVENESS	0
HAT QUALITY	23
PROPENSITY TO VIOLENCE	75

Calvinists really *were* that bit more extreme. Under Beza, predestination became a major factor. Beza taught something called supralapsarian predestination, which means God predestined, elected and basically sorted everyone out before the fall of Adam, before, even creation itself. But this sense of being chosen and special was a key factor in the success of Calvinism. Anyone who thinks that they, and they alone, are truly chosen, has a strong devotion to the cause.

And being in the 'elect' crosses national boundaries as well. Calvinism feels close to Marxism, only instead of the Brotherhood of the Workers, they had the Brotherhood of the Elect. Lutheranism was very German, Zwinglianism was very Swiss, but Calvinism was international, founded by a Frenchman, living in a Swiss city, full of foreign refugees. From Geneva, Calvinism was exported throughout Europe. And the elect stuck together, wherever they were: Calvinists supported each other in different countries. English Calvinists supported military intervention in Scotland, France and in the Netherlands. They welcomed refugees and émigrés from the cause, and supported churches of French and Dutch 'strangers' in London. When Geneva was under attack from the Duke of Savoy in 1580, they raised a defence fund.

International mission was a key part of Calvin's plan. When the Children of Geneva were defeated in 1555, their property and goods were confiscated and sold, and the proceeds were used to fund a theological college in Geneva for ministers. Opening in June 1559, this academy became the hub for training wave after wave of Protestant missionaries and teachers. By 1564 it had 1,500 members, mostly foreign students. Its graduates were sent out as missionaries to Scotland, Italy, Poland, Hungary, the Netherlands, even South America. Calvin devoted much time to teaching, and also to writing commentaries on almost every book of the Bible (he left out Revelation). Thus, Calvinism became the driving force behind the spread of Protestantism in France, the Low Countries, Scotland – and eventually over in the colonies in North America.

So Calvinism became a truly international movement. But in each of these places it looked slightly different: in Scotland it was wrapped up in a revolution led by the nobility; in the Netherlands in the establishment of the Dutch Republic. In Germany Calvinism really established itself in the Rhenish Palatinate. Under the Elector, Frederick III, Heidelberg became another Geneva, a centre of Calvinist teaching and activity. It was in Heidelberg that they developed one of the core statements of Calvinist faith: the Heidelberg Catechism.

And it nearly caught on in France, as well.

Calvinism in France

Calvin had never returned to France after having had to leave it so hurriedly in 1536. But he never stopped thinking about it, either. From his exile in Geneva, he worked unceasingly for the reformation of his beloved homeland, establishing a network of underground churches in France, with safe houses and hiding places for those under threat. Between 1555 and 1563 nearly ninety 'Calvinist' pastors were sent to France from Geneva. Calvin's ideas were spread through travelling book distributors who distributed Calvinist propaganda specially designed for semi-literate readers. The book distributors were called colporteurs – from their ability to travel night and day, presumably.* Secret printing presses were established in Paris. And it worked: demand from France for Calvinist books was such that the Geneva publishers had to step up their output.

Henry II – the successor to Francis I – tried to stop all this Calvinist nonsense by introducing new control orders. Under the Edict of Châteaubriant in 1551, anyone accused of heresy would

---

* Actually, it's probably an amalgamation of two Latin words: *col*, which means 'neck', and porter, meaning 'carry'. They carried trays of books with straps going round their neck. It also works as a pun on the French word *comporter*, which means 'to peddle'.

347

be deprived of judicial or municipal office. But it failed to stem the tide. In 1559 the French Calvinists held their first national synod – in secret, of course – in Paris. Calvin, naturally, couldn't be there, but his spirit hovered over the proceedings. The synod adopted a Genevan Confession of Faith and Form of Discipline. By 1560 there may have been as many as two million reformed Protestants in France – 10 per cent of the population. A third of the nobility appear to have converted. Indeed, in France, Calvinism attracted people from the gentry, the men often converted by their wives or daughters. It also attracted the growing, urban middle class, who liked Calvin's emphasis on family values, hard work, thrift and telling other people what to do. These followers became known as Huguenots.* It was a mocking nickname, said to come from the German *eidgenoss* or confederate. These people did not want to hide. Calvin had always refused to sanction armed resistance, even against evil rulers, 'be their characters what they may'. Calvin believed that tyrants and dictators were God's instruments (but then again, he would). But the Huguenots wanted power. There were demonstrations, including an occupation of the Pré aux Clercs – a park on the left bank of the Seine in Paris – where they sang psalms and worshipped together. There were scuffles in the streets and attacks on congregations. Baguettes may have been hurled. Berets waved angrily. Things were getting out of hand.

Henry II died in 1559 from a jousting accident and the crown passed to Francis II. But he was only fifteen years old, so the 'burden' of ruling was taken up by the Italian queen mother – Catherine de' Medici.† She tried to broker a compromise between

---

* At one Huguenot service in 1560, of the 561 present, 36 were nobles or city elders, 24 were merchants, 87 were professionals (lawyers, apothecaries, doctors), 387 were artisans and shopkeepers, and only 27 were peasant farmers. Of the artisans, 135 were in the textile trade: Huguenots were often associated with this trade.

†Francis II died himself after a short, but eventful reign, which included surviving a kidnap attempt by twelve hundred Huguenot conspirators and

the Catholic and reformed groups and convened a meeting of theologians at Poissy in September 1561. Not surprisingly for a meeting of theologians, they couldn't agree on anything and it broke up without settlement. Next year, Catherine issued the Edict of Saint Hermaine des Près, granting the Huguenots some limited rights of assembly.

Some of the congregations grabbed their chance and actually took over Catholic churches, putting armed guards on the doors to stop them being repossessed. Catherine tried issuing another edict demanding that the Protestants should vacate the churches they had seized, in return for being allowed to worship freely outside French cities. It didn't work. Riots broke out and anti-Protestant violence spread. In March 1562 the Catholic Duke of Guise attacked a Protestant congregation, killing seventy-four people.

And this was the shape of the next forty years: conflict between the two groups with occasional periods of uneasy peace. It was never all-out civil war, rather local uprisings and sporadic outbreaks interspersed by peace agreements.

One of those agreements was worked out in 1572. It granted Protestants places of worship throughout the country and the control of four cities. The king was now Charles IX and he decided that to cement the deal, the Huguenot Henry of Navarre was to marry Marguerite of Valois, a Catholic, and the king's sister. So everybody came to the wedding, which, no doubt, was covered in the pages of *Bonjour* magazine. However, the wedding – as weddings so often do – ended up in a fight. Catherine de' Medici had by now lost influence and she hated that the king preferred the Huguenot noble Admiral de Coligny. When Coligny arrived in Paris for the wedding along with thousands of other Protestants, there was an assassination attempt. A man called

---

being married to Mary Queen of Scots for two years. Mary returned to Scotland after this tragedy, where she ran full force into the Calvinist horror that was John Knox. The poor woman never stood a chance.

Maurevert shot at the admiral; however, the bullets only tore a finger from his right hand and shattered his left elbow.

The Catholics, fearing a Huguenot backlash, decided to get their retaliation in first. Two days after the attempted shooting, Catherine ordered a massacre of all Protestants in the city. At least three thousand Protestants died in the massacre – and as many as ten thousand throughout France as it spread to other cities.

The massacre became known as the St Bartholomew's Day massacre since it was begun on 24 August – St Bartholomew's Day. Coligny was among the victims. He was stabbed in his lodgings, which is the kind of thing to bring tears to your eyes. After being knifed in the chest, he was thrown out of a window and then had his head chopped off. Clearly a hard man to kill. The St Bartholomew's Day massacre became a notorious act of premeditated violence – although that didn't stop the Pope and the Spanish king sending their congratulations. The massacre triggered a wave of violence throughout France and the peace was shattered.*

Charles IX's successor, his brother Henry III, tried to focus less on religious conflicts and more on his succession of boyfriends, but he was stabbed to death in 1589 by a Dominican friar. Catherine died the same year (although she was not the victim of killer monks). The crown fell to Henry of Navarre, and he was a Huguenot.†

The sides lined up. On one side there were Henry and the Huguenots – which is, frankly, a band name waiting to happen. These were supported by the Low Countries, much of Germany,

---

* During this period, many French Huguenots left France. Many of them went to the New World, to the French territories in Canada, where they became farmers, fur traders and very polite people.

† He was, in fact, the man who had married the king's sister in the days preceding the St Bartholomew's Day massacre. He claimed that the marriage was never consummated and it was later annulled by the Pope after Henry of Navarre became king in 1589. He then married Marie de' Medici.

and Protestant sympathisers in England. On the other side there was the French Catholic League, supported by the Spanish King Philip II. It looked like it would all kick off, but in the end Henry IV, as he now was, solved the conflict in an unusual way for a Protestant sympathiser: he became a Catholic. His conversion, in 1593, had much more to do with *realpolitik* than religion. It meant that France had a Catholic monarch – which is what all the Catholics wanted – but one who had strong links with Protestants. And it meant that Henry could be crowned in Rheims Cathedral and get his hands on all the goodies. As he is supposed to have said, 'Paris is well worth a Mass.'

A few years later, he issued the Edict of Nantes, which guaranteed liberty of conscience throughout France, and allowed Huguenots to access schools, hospitals, universities. Catholics could worship freely in Catholic towns, Huguenots in their towns. (Although Huguenots were still barred from Paris.)*

This compromise stabilised things for a century or so, until, in 1685, Louis XIV arbitrarily revoked it, which caused a mass exodus of the Huguenot artisans into England and the Low countries.

Still, it worked for a while. *C'est la vie.*

---

* Henry IV was also murdered by a fanatic called François Ravaillac, a Catholic zealot who had received a personal vision that instructed him to convince King Henry IV to convert all the Huguenots to Catholicism. Unable to secure an interview with the king to give him this good news, he decided to murder him instead.

- Part Ten -

The Disunited
Kingdom

❖

Heir Loss

- IT 'S A RIGHT ROYAL PAIN.

You know the feeling - you're the king of a major European nation, but you can't conceive a son. Try DIVORCE™ - the new shampoo from the House of Wolsey. With DIVORCE you can wash the old wife away, leaving your headship ready for new heir growth. (Warning: may not work on first application. Rinse and repeat. Up to five times.)

ALSO ANNOUNCING OUR LATEST
PRODUCT: BIGAMY™, by Philip of Hesse.
Because one wife is never enough.

30 Evangelical Eddy and scary Mary

Common prayer

'But Nick,' I hear you ask pleadingly, and yet with a hint of defiance, 'what about England and Scotland. And Ireland. And that other one.'

Good question. (Wales, by the way.)

Well, let's start with England first. The path of the English Reformation was a zigzag, not a straight line. And in the years after Henry VIII's death there was probably more zig and zag than people could cope with.

Henry died in 1546, leaving the kingdom to his son, Edward, the child of his third marriage (to Jane Seymour). But Edward was only nine, so he was granted a 'Lord Protector' in the form of Edward Seymour, 1st Earl of Somerset. Somerset was a 'convinced evangelical' who was in correspondence with many of the leading continental reformers such as Bullinger in Zürich. This was a welcome change for Cranmer, who no longer had to worry about tiptoeing around Henry's mood changes. So the pace of change increased, although Cranmer's official government-issue sermons reinforced the Lutheran scheme of salvation where righteousness had to be 'embraced by faith'. England actually moved much further towards a Swiss-style Zwinglian Reformation – especially when it came to the Eucharist and the abolition of older Catholic practices. (Sadly, it was too late for all those Zwinglians who were executed in Henry's reign, but that's the Reformation for you.)

Laws were passed abolishing chantries – the endowed chapels where 'chants' (requiem Masses) were sung for the souls of the dead. Only a generation before, the English had believed that their dead relatives needed a leg up out of purgatory in the form of prayers and Masses. Now all that was gone.

Cranmer created the first *Book of Common Prayer* in 1549. It was a masterful piece of work, in beautiful English prose. It reorganised the pattern of church services and turned everything into English as lucid and beautiful as crystal. But it did make changes: many traditional rites and rituals were omitted. And the changes were enough to provoke armed revolt in Devon and Cornwall, which was crushed by Spanish and German mercenaries.

So, clearly, there was still many who felt strongly about the 'old faith'. And there were worrying signs of 'new' beliefs as well. There were rumours that England had a touch of the Anabaptists. In 1550, Joan Bocher, a woman who lived around Romney Marsh in Kent, was burned at the stake for expressing radical ideas about the Incarnation.* She was a believer in the theory of Christ's celestial flesh – that Christ did not derive his physical body from his mother but that it was a 'divine distillation' – which sounds more like a really good whisky. Although Cranmer and Ridley made efforts to persuade her to recant, she refused, and in the end Cranmer pressed for her execution – some accounts claim that he pressurised the reluctant king (who by then was twelve) into signing the death sentence. John Foxe (of Foxe's martyrs fame) approached the king's chaplain, John Rogers (of the Matthew's Bible fame), to save Joan (of divine distillation fame). But Rogers refused, saying that burning was 'sufficiently mild'. She was burned at Smithfield on 2 May 1550.

Cranmer. Ridley. Rogers. What goes around comes around. Just sayin'.

The new evangelical climate proved fatal for some. And, indeed,

---

* Joan had previous for smuggling Tyndale's New Testament into England.

TOP REFORMERS

Edward VI

Born: Hampton Court Palace, England, 1537
Died: Greenwich, England, 1553

AKA: Edward Tudor

The son of Henry VIII and his third wife, Jane Seymour, Edward came to the throne aged only nine. He – and his various advisers – created new patterns of worship and established the first articles of the Church of England. He died aged fifteen.

Fun Fact: Edward's burial place in Westminster Abbey was unmarked until 1966.

INFLUENCE	30
THEOLOGICAL IMPORTANCE	10
FACIAL HAIR	0
GENERAL GLOOMINESS	0
ABUSIVENESS	0
HAT QUALITY	65
PROPENSITY TO VIOLENCE	45

for Somerset. He was ousted by his political opponents.* His

---

* Edward Seymour was eventually executed in 1552. The fifteen-year-old King Edward wrote in his diary that 'the Duke of Somerset had his head cut off upon Tower Hill between eight and nine o'clock in the morning'. He then added, 'Spent the day playing Super Mario Karts. Bored.'

place was taken by the Duke of Northumberland, who was a more extreme Protestant and who thought that Cranmer's 1549 *Book of Common Prayer* hadn't gone nearly far enough. So in 1552 a revision was made: now the 'Lord's Supper' or 'Communion' was purely a commemorative celebration which emphasised the once-for-all efficacy of Christ's sacrifice of himself on the cross. Towards the end of Edward's reign the official doctrine of the Church of England was defined in the Forty-Two Articles.

People weren't happy. The English don't mind change, as long as it happens really slowly and everything looks pretty similar afterwards. But here they seemed to be losing everything they had previously held sacred. Add in the effects of a dire economic collapse and the result was that there were armed uprisings in East Anglia and the south-west of England, where the leaders called not only for the restoration of the Latin Mass, but also for a ban on the English Bible.

Then, in 1553, Edward VI died without an heir, meaning that the next in line was his sister Mary Tudor, daughter of Henry VIII and Catherine of Aragon.

We've had the zig. Now it was time for a zag. A really, really, big zag.

And along came Mary

Mary was Catholic. Very, very Catholic. Not only that, but as the daughter of the divorced, maligned and embittered first wife of Henry VIII, she had some very personal grudges against all this Lutheran and Calvinist stuff. It had ruined her life.

Now it was payback time. Mary was going to return England to the true faith by whatever means necessary. As we've seen, not everyone was against this. The monasteries had been destroyed, the prayer book changed, the Bible officially translated, but many hearts and minds were yet to be fully converted. So it is possible that had Mary survived a bit longer, or had she trodden a little more gently, then England might have returned to the Catholic fold.

But Mary wasn't really into treading gently. She was more of a 'stamping on your groin' kind of girl. Not to mention 'dancing on your grave'. Within a month of ascending the throne, the English Bible was banned from being spoken in church services and Bibles placed in church were taken out and burned. She banned the import of works by Tyndale, Coverdale and Cranmer and set up the Company of Stationers, which as well as guarding the stationery cupboard, acted as a board of censorship.* Cranmer was deposed and Cardinal Reginald Pole was recalled from Rome to become Archbishop of Canterbury. Married clergy had to put away their wives. Where they put them away, we don't know. Possibly in the stationery cupboard. Services went back to being said in Latin. 'The Latin service is a plain mark of Antichrist's Catholic Synagogue,' complained the evangelical John Bradford, in a perfect storm of mixed metaphors, while William Dalby wrote, 'Here is no news but candlesticks, books, bells, censers, crosses and pipes . . . the Mass is very rife.'

And Mary started to enforce these measures in a brutal crackdown. Prominent evangelicals and reformed clergy were arrested and sent to the fire. The sheer number of executions in her reign earned her the name 'Bloody Mary' and she remains the only queen to have a cocktail named after her. Apart from Queen Bahama Mama, who hasn't been crowned yet.†

Bishop Bonner claimed the executions were necessary surgery. The authorities were acting like 'a good surgeon [who] cutteth away a putrefied and festered member; for the love he hath to the whole body lest it infect other members adjoining to it'.

* In fact, not a single Bible was printed in England during her reign. Mary's reign led to so many Protestant printers fleeing that they had to import liturgical and Catholic books from abroad.
† Although, since a lot of the executions were burnings, Fiery Mary might be a better name. Whatever the case, she was a pretty scary Mary.

The first of the festered members to be cut off was the former king's chaplain and fan of mild burning, John Rogers, aka Thomas Matthews, creator of the Matthew's Bible. He was burned to death at Smithfield on 4 February 1555. In all, around three hundred Protestants were burned during Mary's reign. That may not seem a huge number, but it represents 7 per cent of the total of all those executed for heresy throughout Europe in the course of the century. The number included bishops such as Ridley, Hooper, Latimer and Cranmer, but by far the majority of those who were amputated during this surgical operation were ordinary tradesmen and labourers who had never themselves been involved in any form of politics. They were not famous or wealthy or influential: they were housewives, clergy, lay preachers, coopers, blacksmiths. They were people like John Leaf, a twenty-year-old apprentice candle maker who was burned at the stake with John Bradford, mentioned above. Bradford turned to Leaf and said, 'Be of good comfort brother; for we shall have a merry supper with the Lord this night!'* It was one thing when rich people got beheaded or burned, but when ordinary people died in this way, that created a backlash. Mary created a wealth of Protestant martyrs whose courage did more to establish Protestantism than the Prayer Book ever did. It was celebrated in one of the all-time bestsellers, John Foxe's *Book of Martyrs*.

The most famous victim, though, was Thomas Cranmer. He was arrested and imprisoned, and initially signed a recantation of his Protestant views. He was then taken to St Mary's Church in Oxford, where it was expected that he would make a full public confession. Instead, once he got up to speak, he went completely off-script and declared that he was right all along. He was taken out and burned, plunging the hand that had signed the recantation into the fire first. As we've seen, his record is not

---

* Bradford, who had the nickname 'Holy Bradford' (for the state of his life, rather than the condition of his socks), was arrested and shared a cell for a while with Cranmer, Ridley and Latimer. They spent their time together studying the New Testament.

spotless, but like a lot of the people in this story, his courage in the face of death was impressive.

The Protestants were frightened and appalled, but there were only three choices available to them: death, exile or keeping your head down. The latter was the most popular choice, but it meant a certain amount of outward conformity and dissimulation. (Calvin, typically hardline, condemned such people as 'Nicodemites', after Nicodemus in the New Testament, who came to Jesus secretly at night. But then Calvin was safe in Geneva.)

For those that remained, life was perilous. And people began to resent the scale of the repression. Mary also made some tactical errors. In particular, she married the Roman Catholic Prince Philip II of Spain. This was officially Not A Popular Move. The English people distrusted the Spanish and saw this as portending an invasion. Or a coup. Or possibly being forced to drink San Miguel. There was unrest, and an abortive armed uprising in Kent.

Many of the evangelicals chose to leave the country. They headed for the Protestant centres in Europe, gathering first in Frankfurt where, typically, they had a massive argument about whether to use the second prayer book of Edward VI or whether to revise it in a more Calvinist direction. The pro-revision group was led by John Knox, a fiery Scottish reformer. Knox was eventually expelled from Frankfurt and went to Geneva, which was much more to his taste.

But all this violence and repression made them start to consider whether it was right to obey rulers who were clearly so violent. Not to mention Catholic. In 1556 John Ponet, former Bishop of Winchester, published a book in Strasbourg entitled *A shorte treatise of politike power, and of the true obedience which subjectes owe to kynges and other civile governours*. This book argued that opposition to secular rulers was justified, and it even justified tyrannicide. Such a shocking idea had to be published anonymously, of course. Two years later, in Geneva, another English exile called Christopher Goodman published a book with the does-exactly-what-it-says-on-the-tin title of *How superior powers ought to be obeyed of their subjects, and Wherein They May Lawfully By God's Word Be Disobeyed And Resisted*. And if that didn't make his argument clear, the subtitle ran: *Wherein also is declared the cause of all this present misery in England, and the only way to remedy the same*. The book supported Wyatt's rebellion and attacked the government of Mary I of England.* Ponet had not mentioned Mary by name, preferring to target her bishops. Goodman, however, made it clear that Mary, an 'open idolatress', deserved what was coming to her. The shocking thing about these books is that they advocated direct action against unjust governors, even to the point of assassination.

The idea of justified disobedience was taken up in, of all places, a footnote to a new edition of the Bible. The group of émigrés in Geneva produced one of the most influential, groundbreaking Bibles of all time. The Geneva Bible, produced in 1560, is the first true study Bible. It is stuffed full of notes, comment, maps, pictures, diagrams, indexes and all manner of helps for the user.† There are glossaries of proper names, a concordance of 'the principall thinges that are conteined in the Bible' with their chapter and verse references. The Geneva Bible was a real user-friendly Bible, everything designed to encourage the reader to study scripture for themselves. It was printed in roman type, rather than the eye-wateringly difficult gothic black-letter type, and was the first English Bible to use verse numbers within chapters – taken from Estienne's Bible. It was priced affordably.

---

* It wasn't just Mary: he blamed the government of women in general. In the same year, Goodman's BFF John Knox, also in Geneva, published his book *A First Blast of the Trumpet* on the same subject. Of which, more later.

† It's sometimes known as the Breeches Bible – from the translation of Genesis 3.7: 'Then the eyes of them both were opened, and they knew that they were naked, and they sewed fig tree leaves together, and made them selves breeches.'

It also had marginal notes.* One note in particular reflects the kind of radical political ideas that these émigrés were starting to think about. It occurs at Exodus 1:17, where the Hebrew midwives disobeyed Pharaoh's command to kill the children and made excuses. 'Their disobedience herein was lawful,' ran the note, 'but their dissembling evil.' Of which, more later . . .

Had Mary survived for long, things in England might have been very different. Her counter-Reformation might have stuck. We might all be wearing sombreros and speaking Spanish. But she ran out of time. As did her sidekick, Reginald Pole. They both died on the same day: 17 November 1558. And a new queen ascended the throne.

Zig.

---

* In Shakespeare's *Hamlet*, written around 1600, there is a scene where preparations are being made for the duel between Hamlet and Laertes. A courtier called Osric reels out a load of technical jargon about duelling and Horatio quips, 'I knew you must be edified by the margent ere you had done.' It's a reference to the preface of the Geneva Bible where the editors tell the readers that for 'good purpose and edification' they 'have in the margent' noted certain things.

31 Good Queen Bess

Middle of the road

The new queen was Elizabeth, the daughter of Henry VIII and Anne Boleyn. Anne, of course, had been an evangelical, and her daughter followed in that vein. Well, sort of. She was definitely not a Calvinist. She liked images and statues and she seems to have preferred her clergy celibate. She often broke out into old-fashioned Catholic oaths such as 'By God's Body!' which really annoyed the fundamentalist Protestants. (Probably one of the reasons she did it so much.) And she once ventured the opinion that two or three preachers were enough for the whole country.

So, when, on Whitsunday 1559, England returned to the Protestant fold, it did so without entirely divesting itself of all those Catholic trimmings. Yes, the Edwardian Prayer Book was reinstated as the only legal form of worship. And there were penalties for those who refused to toe the Protestant line: even casual absence from church could result in a fine of a shilling – which was a couple of weeks' wages. But there were also still robes and vestments, saints' days, stained glass and ornaments.*
The fact is Elizabeth trod a middle line. She might have seen Catholics as potential enemies, but she wasn't exactly thrilled about Protestant extremists. Her great skill, as queen, was what has been called masterly inactivity. If in doubt, wait and see. If

---

* John Knox described Elizabeth as 'neither good Protestant nor yet resolute Papist'.

you absolutely must make a choice, aim for compromise, the middle path. She embodied the *via media*, as it became known: that English genius for being – or at least, appearing to be – reasonable.

A series of compromises brought some measure of unity. The Act of Supremacy declared Elizabeth Supreme Governor of the Church of England (she couldn't, of course, be 'Head of the Church', as she was a woman). And a new Act of Uniformity merged the two prayer books of Cranmer together in such a way that it was possible to hold varied views of the Eucharist. Possibly even at the same time. It all worked, providing you didn't look too closely.

Many people *did* look closely, of course. With a Protestant on the throne, all those who had gone abroad, or underground, during Mary's reign returned. And they were like Protestant sniffer-dogs: they could smell out a false doctrine at fifty yards. They hoped and expected that Elizabeth would move from Rome to Geneva, from Popeville to Calvinagrad, but she never did. In fact, she stated outright that she 'did not want to look into her subjects' minds'. Elizabeth followed a path of extreme moderation. She and her advisers invented a brand of Christianity which didn't offend many people, but didn't excite them overly either. A brand in which virtually everyone was mildly disappointed.

Or as we call it today, Anglicanism.

In 1571 the Forty-two Articles were trimmed down to thirty-nine, and ever since then Anglican vicars have promised to obey them, before going on to do pretty much as they like. This was compromise on an industrial scale.

Of course, there were limits. Under Elizabeth's rule, Catholic priests were hunted down and Catholics were put under restrictions. Catholic recusants – those who refused to submit to the new regulations – were obliged to pay a fine if they refused to attend Church of England services. Some Jesuits and Catholic missionaries were executed – although there were certainly far fewer martyrs than in her half-sister's reign. And the main cause of those executions was not so much religious dogma, as the continued threat to the country from Spain.

Mary Tudor, you will recall, had married Philip II of Spain, so he had some claims to the throne. Initially he thought diplomacy might work, and tried to persuade Elizabeth to marry him. She delayed her reply so much that eventually he gave up on the idea. But there was still a lot of pro-Catholic sentiment in the country. Catholicism remained strong in the north of England and in pockets elsewhere.* In 1570, the Pope issued a condemnation of Elizabeth. Plots to replace her with her Catholic cousin, Mary Queen of Scots, were concocted by English Catholics and backed by the Spanish. Elizabeth was reluctant to execute a monarch, viewing – presciently as it turned out – that it would set a bad precedent, but in the end Mary was executed when letters were intercepted implying that she herself had no such scruples about the assassination of Elizabeth. In such a climate Catholic priests and aristocracy were felt to be dangerous, a threat, resolutely opposed to the idea of the crown as head of state and Church.

That threat reached its height with the launch of an attempted invasion of England by Philip II, who had clearly got fed up with Elizabeth playing hard to get. So in 1587 he launched an invasion fleet – the mighty Spanish Armada – with the intention of defeating the English and bringing the country back into the Catholic fold (among the 19,000 soldiers there were 180 monks). However, the Armada was defeated by a mixture of the English navy and some truly appalling weather. It was the beginning of Spain's decline as a superpower, and the rise of England. The English took the defeat of the Armada as a sign – the final, incontrovertible proof that God was Protestant. And, as Münster did for the Anabaptists, it handily enabled propagandists to balance the equation 'Catholic' = 'foreign enemy who wants to invade and probably smells of garlic'.

---

* Some areas of the north, such as Lancashire, didn't really become Protestant until the first half of the seventeenth century.

Great Moments in Reformation History

NUMBER 25: The Spanish Armada runs into a storm.

Worst ferry crossing *ever.*

Puritan attitudes

Anglicanism was a compromise: its doctrine, as outlined in the Thirty-nine Articles of 1563, was clearly reformed, but it kept the elaborate, solemn liturgy, the beautiful music, and such obviously papisty things as cathedrals, bishops, deans, canons, paid choirs – all the trappings of what later became known as High Church. Most people accepted this, but many of the refugees who returned from Geneva hated all this compromise stuff. They didn't want to ride the 'middle way'; they wanted the highway to heaven.

Elizabeth was deeply suspicious of this new breed of extremist Protestants. Her supporters mocked them as 'puritans' – a term of abuse which may have been invented in 1564 by the then Archbishop of Canterbury, Matthew Parker. These were, the name implies, the people who thought they were 'purer' than the rest, the holier-than-thous.* Much of our image of Puritanism comes

---

* They were also called 'precisians' in the sense of sticklers for details.

not from Elizabeth's time but from a century later. Some of our perceptions about the Puritans are just plain wrong. We imagine them as monochrome people, dressed in black, with tall stovepipe hats, but that was actually how they were painted, in their best clothes. It was their version of a dinner jacket and black tie. In normal life they wore similar clothing to everyone else.*

And like the Anabaptists, the definition is a little hazy. They were not a coherent, unified group. They differed over many points of doctrine.† What they did have in common was a belief that the Reformation still had a way to go. Deeply opposed to the Anglican establishment, the Puritans saw the Church as still being infected with the 'dregs of popery'. They wanted a 'further reformation' which would see the abolition of the Prayer Book and the bishops. They were scriptural literalists who disliked even kneeling at Communion, wearing vestments, even wedding rings. They loved nothing more than a sermon, unless it was two sermons.‡

And their movement had significant support. And, following Luther, it harnessed the power of the printing press. One best-selling book was John Foxe's *Acts and Monuments of the Church*, more popularly known as *The Book of Martyrs*, which listed in gruesome detail the martyrdoms of Protestants, not just during Mary's reign, but during Henry's – Elizabeth's father, of course – as well. It was a masterpiece of Protestant propaganda, the largest book ever published in England, and it was made all the more compelling by the gruesome pictures.§ But the engine room

---

* John Owen, the Puritan's Puritan, wore his 'hair powdered, cambric band with large costly band strings, velvet jacket, breeches set round at knees with ribbons pointed, and Spanish leather boots with cambric tops'. He later was the bass player in a 1980s New Romantic band.

† John Milton, for example, didn't even believe in the Trinity. He was a very impure Puritan. Thank heavens Calvin had died by the time he came along.

‡ Based on the Bible, they decided that there had to be two Sunday services because Numbers 28:9 speaks of two burnt offerings each Sabbath.

§ There is also evidence that the illustrations were sometimes cut out and put up on the walls. That must have cheered the room up.

of Puritanism was Cambridge University. In Cambridge, Puritan dons like Laurence Chaderton radicalised a generation of Puritan preachers by creating an East Anglian version of the Geneva seminary, which sent out trained preachers into many churches throughout the country.

Elizabeth was tolerant, but not that tolerant. In 1576, Elizabeth instructed her new Archbishop of Canterbury, Edmund Grindal, to oversee a clampdown by shutting down Puritan Bible study meetings. But Grindal was an evangelical, and to him this meant suppressing the word of God. So he refused. Elizabeth took this with the good grace usually associated with kings and queens of the time, and had him put under house arrest. He remained confined in Lambeth Palace until he died seven years later.

She replaced him with John Whitgift, who was a much more happy clamper. Many Puritans were deprived of their posts. For the Puritans this was a betrayal that engendered a deep distrust of kings and queens. (They thought back to some of those ideas that had been circulating in Geneva: maybe, just maybe, kings and queens were A Bad Idea.)

Their disgruntlement found expression in a series of tracts by one 'Martin Marprelate': a pseudonym which combined the first name of their hero, i.e. Luther, and what they wanted to do, i.e. damage prelates or bishops. These outrageous, outspoken tracts channelled the spirit of Luther in the vivid writing and wild accusations. Whitgift was accused of drunken, debauched, homosexual orgies in Lambeth Palace. The tracts referred to bishops as 'dunghills' and 'servants of Satan'.

Who produced these is uncertain. But whoever was responsible, it confirmed the link between Puritanism and sedition. The authorities started house-to-house searches to find the secret printing press, and raided many Puritans' homes. In 1593, Parliament passed an Act Against Puritans, and a massive cultural PR programme kicked in. In the theatres, Puritans were mocked as greedy, licentious hypocrites. To be fair, the Puritans had attacked the playwrights and the theatre: they saw the theatre as a place of bawdy, impure humour, not to mention a place where prostitutes plied their trade. (Defenders of the Puritans like to point out how maligned they are. But there is, undoubtedly, a certain joylessness about them. They were in favour of closing down the inns and the taverns and the theatres. They did attract their fair share of grumpy old gits. William Prynne believed that 'Christ Jesus our pattern . . . was always mourning, never laughing'. But then he'd had his ears cut off so he was bound to be a bit jaundiced about life.)

Faced with such opposition, Puritan leaders had two choices.

Some started to give up any hope of the established church. They went rogue, headed underground. They started their own independent congregations. Freed from state control, each local meeting was self-governing, free to worship in what it considered an authentic way, and empowered to elect their own ministers to lead them. This was similar to the Anabaptist meetings in continental Europe, but these were not strictly Anabaptists – many maintained Calvinist beliefs. Some congregations continued with infant baptism as well.

Collectively they became known as 'Separatists': people who had deliberately separated from the established church. Naturally, when discovered, they were harshly treated. Separatist leaders were hanged. In 1593, the two leaders of the Separatists in London were beheaded. However, the members of their congregation were spared their lives, as long as their leaders emigrated to Holland.

Others opted simply to keep their heads down. Take a long view. They started to develop a vision of an England purified from all the filth and degradation of popular culture. No more maypoles or football. Close down the theatres and shut the pubs. This was an England where 'Sunday' would become the 'Sabbath'. Morality would be legally enforced. If England would not go to Geneva, they would bring Geneva to England.

After all, Elizabeth was ageing and childless, and soon there would be a new king on the throne. And he was raised in Scotland. By Calvinists. How much more Puritan could you get?

Women, children and incompetent people

Of course, through all of this there are voices we strain to hear. The voices of the major reformers are loud enough, as are those of the popes, the kings and queens. But the voices of the common people are harder to discern. Often we only hear of them at their end. Although his *Book of Martyrs* is, of course, partisan and propagandist, Foxe does record the heroism of ordinary people.

Take one of the most notorious of the martyrdoms, the burning of thirteen people at Stratford-le-Bow on 27 June 1556. It was an event that was watched by some twenty thousand spectators. And one of the striking things about the event is the make-up of the thirteen who were killed. They were nearly all working class, and included a brewer, two blacksmiths, three labourers, a serving man, a weaver, a tailor, a sawyer, and two women: Elizabeth Peper, the wife of a weaver, and Agnes George, the wife of a husband-man.* There was also a foreigner, one 'Lion Cauche', described as a broker from Flanders, resident in the City of London.

Thirteen ordinary men and women. All given the opportunity to recant, and all chose to die instead. And they all spoke out. After they were condemned, John Feckenham, the Dean of St Paul's, preached a sermon against them – the equivalent of a public denunciation. The group responded by issuing their own joint declaration of faith.

It's significant that there were women among these victims. The Reformation certainly empowered women to hold to their own opinions, to follow their consciences even if it cost them their lives. But it also closed off other well-travelled spiritual pathways. The closure of the convents, an increasing suspicion of mystics and visionaries, and the restriction of ministry as something only available to men, meant that the only real 'voca-tion' women had was marriage or martyrdom.

---

* A sawyer is someone who saws wood. A husbandman is someone who mans husbands. Or possibly a tenant farmer.

When a monastery or a convent closed, the impact on its residents was shattering, particularly for women. Although those evicted were granted pensions, most nuns lived in poverty. Many of those 'freed' from the convents were married off, not always willingly. Sometimes the nuns fought back. In the years before Calvin arrived in Geneva, the council decided to close down the Convent of the Poor Clares. Around 1535, Sister Jeanne de Jussie, a young woman in her twenties, started writing *A Short Chronicle*, which described how they stood firm against the relentless harassment, the threats and the pressure on the Poor Clares to give up their convent.

In Strasbourg, when the Lutheran pamphleteer Matthias Wurm tried to remove his sister Anna from the convent in which she lived, she replied:

> You are neither my father nor my mother. I do not owe you obedi-ence and I will not obey you . . . I am in a good, pious, blessed, honourable, free, spiritual estate, wherein both my body and soul are well cared for . . . I want to stay here . . . I have given myself to God with full knowledge and awareness in eternal chastity here to serve him. With his help I will abide by this until my death. No one of the world can sway me. I have never asked you to take me out of the cloister and I am not asking you to do so now.

When the Peasants' War broke out in 1525 the council forced the nuns out of the convent for their own protection. Some of the nuns returned later, but Anna was not among them. She is not heard of again.

Luther believed in the priesthood of all believers, but some believers were more priestly than others. Ministers were male: 'the Holy Spirit has excepted women, children, and incompetent people from this function, but chooses (except in emergencies) only competent males to fill this office'.

Sometimes, though, this led him into some interesting seman-tics, notably in detaching 'preaching' from 'teaching', a spurious argument which you still find spouted a lot today:

> The four daughters of Philip were prophetesses. A woman can
> do this – not preach in public, but console and teach – a woman
> can do this just as much as a man. There are certainly women
> and girls who are able to comfort others and teach true words,
> that is to say, who can explain Scripture and teach and console
> other people . . . this all counts as prophesying, not preaching.

So there you go. You can teach, console, comfort, just don't call
it preaching. Of course, to be fair, virtually all the various flavours
of reformed churches agreed with him (with the exception of some
of those crazy Anabaptist types). And that was the strong social
and cultural norm of the time. Women who wanted to have their
say had, as is so often the case throughout history, to find less
obvious ways. Nevertheless, there were some who bucked the trend.

Christians like Marie Dentière, a noblewoman, wrote letters
in defence of Calvin during his exile from Geneva, and vehemently
defended the right of women to teach.

In 1523 an eighteen-year-old student called Arsacius Seehofer
was arrested in Ingolstadt for holding 'Lutheran ideas' and forced
to recant.* Ingolstadt was in Bavaria, and the Bavarian authorities had forbidden the promulgation of Lutheran ideas there.
Then a letter was received by the authorities which denounced
this shameful attack on free speech, and challenged the Catholic
establishment to a public debate. What made the letter slightly
different was that its author was a woman – Argula von
Grumbach.

Argula was born in 1492 to a noble family in Bavaria. Her
father gave her a Bible when she was only ten, despite the warn-
ings of Franciscan preachers, who claimed it would 'only confuse
her'. Far from confusing her, it fired her up, and she later became
a keen follower of Luther, and wrote that letter, in which she
poured scorn on the Catholic theologians of the university forcing
a 'lad of eighteen' to recant his beliefs:

---

* Nowadays, of course, he would be christened Bootylicious Seehofer.

Where do you read in the Bible that Christ, the apostles, and the prophets imprisoned, banished, burned, or murdered anyone? You tell us that we must obey the magistrates. Correct. But neither the pope, nor the Emperor, nor the princes have any authority over the Word of God. You need not think you can pull God, the prophets and the apostles out of heaven with papal decretals drawn from Aristotle, who was not a Christian at all . . .

This was a woman who knew her stuff.

'I would be willing to come and dispute with you in German . . .' she threatened. 'You have the key of knowledge and you close the kingdom of heaven.'

The letter caused an immediate sensation, not least because here was a woman daring to stand up to the authorities, and backing her arguments up with a mass of scripture quotations. When it was published it went through fourteen editions in the first two months. (In response, a slanderous poem was published under the pseudonym of Johannes of Lanzhut, which told her to get back in the kitchen, and claimed that she only stood up for Arsacius because she fancied him. She was called a 'shameless whore' and a 'female desperado'.) She was accused of neglecting her husband and family. Balthasar Hubmaier was a fan, saying that she 'knows more of the divine Word than all of the red hats [cardinals] ever saw or could conceive of'. She went on to engage in a considerable correspondence with Luther and other leading reformers, and subsequent letters and poems sold tens of thousands of copies.*

Since then, of course, she has hardly been mentioned at all.

Poignantly, the only words we hear of some women are those spoken as they head towards their deaths. One of the most remarkable was Anne Askew. Born to minor nobility in 1521 in a rural village in Lincolnshire, when she was fifteen she was

---

* One of her poems runs, 'May God teach me to understand / How I should act towards my man.' Clearly she also invented Country and Western.

forced into an arranged marriage to Thomas Kyme, the son of a neighbouring farmer. We get a good idea about Anne from the fact that, even though she reluctantly married Thomas, she refused to change her surname. Anne was a natural radical who turned piety into protest. When, in 1543, Henry VIII made it illegal for women to read the Bible, Anne promptly marched to Lincoln, sat down in the cathedral and spent a week reading her Bible in front of everyone. It meant the end of her marriage: either Thomas kicked her out or, more likely, Anne left him. She went to London and established a reputation as a preacher. In 1545 she was arrested for heresy, but the charges were dropped when no witnesses could be found.

What is interesting about Anne's story is her agency. She refused to be quiet and behave. She argued cogently with the lawyers at her various trials. She wrote poetry and letters from prison. Of course she could not be allowed to continue and in 1546 she was arrested again. This time she was subjected to barbaric treatment. She was taken to the Tower of London and cruelly tortured in an attempt to make her reveal the names and whereabouts of other evangelicals. Her interrogation was overseen by the Lord Chancellor, Sir Thomas Wriothesley, and another chancer with the pantomime-villain name of Sir Richard Rich. Frustrated by her refusal to betray her fellow evangelicals, they put her on the rack. In letters smuggled out of the prison, she said 'because I lay still and did not cry, my Lord Chancellor and master Rich took pains to rack me with their own hands till I was nigh dead'.

She never did give in. In the end she was sentenced to be executed. Her treatment on the rack had been so terrible that she could no longer walk and had to be carried in a chair to Smithfield.

Even then she bit back. A vicar called Nicholas Shaxton was summoned to preach a sermon to Anne and her fellow victims. What made this ironic was that he had actually been arrested for heresy at the same time as Anne, but had recanted. (Initially they sent him to visit Anne in prison to urge her to follow his example. She reported, 'I said to him, that it had been good for him never to have been born; with many other like words.') As she sat at the stake, chained at the waist, he preached a sermon. And she refused to listen passively, agreeing instead with some of the things he said, while criticising some other comments and claiming that 'he misseth, and speaketh without the book [i.e. the Bible]'.

Sir Thomas Wriothesley offered her her freedom if she agreed to recant. She refused.

She was burned alongside three men: a courtier, a priest and a tailor.

32 Our friends in the north

McLutherans

'But what,' I hear you ask, 'of our friends in the north?'

To which I reply, 'Manchester?' And you say, 'No, a bit more north.'

And then I say, 'Newcastle?'

And you say, 'No. Scotland, you fool.'

Ah, Good question. (Although you weren't very precise to be honest. Try harder.)

Well, Scotland had proved fertile ground for Luther's ideas from early on. An abbot called Patrick Hamilton had come into contact with Luther's ideas while he was studying on the continent – he studied at Paris and Leuven – and brought them back to St Andrews. Where he was welcomed with open arms. Or not. Actually, the Archbishop of Saint Andrews ordered his trial, so in 1527 Hamilton fled to Germany. It's possible he met Tyndale during his travels. But he didn't stay there – he returned to Scotland and continued preaching. He even published a small tract – the rather travelogue-named *Patricke's Places* – where he explained Luther's ideas to the Scottish.*

---

* *Patricke's Places* is the informal version of its real title *The Common Places of Divinity*, taken from Melanchthon's *Loci Communes*. It's a simple outline of Lutheran ideas of justification by faith. 'We wot [i.e. 'know'], that a man that is justified, is not justified by the works of the law, but by the faith of Jesus Christ,' he writes. 'He that hath the faith wotteth well that he pleaseth God . . .'. Hamilton clearly knew what's wot.

It couldn't last, and in 1528 he was summoned to a hearing, condemned as a heretic, and burned at the stake very quickly to stop any rescue by his friends. His execution, not to mention the fact that he had some high connections, only spread Lutheran ideas. It was said that the 'the reek of Patrick Hamilton infected all on whom it did blow'. I'm hoping 'reek' here means smoke.* Anyway, killing him certainly reeked of something. The flames of his fire lit the fuse for the Reformation in Scotland.

The King of Scotland at the time was James V, part of the Stuart family, who were devout Catholics. He never broke with Rome as his uncle Henry did in the south (James's mother, Margaret, was Henry's sister), not least because he was already effectively in control of his church. But when he died in 1542 it left the throne in the hands of his daughter Mary, and her hands weren't really that capable, since she was only a few days old. In 1548, at the grand old age of six, Mary was betrothed to Francis, son of King Henry II of France. Mind you, she was older than her fiancé, who was only four. But the main point was that the kingdoms of Scotland and France were united. Allez les bleus and hoots mon.

So power passed to a series of regents. Most notably James Hamilton, the Earl of Arran. Arran changed his religion like other people change their kilts. He was notorious for flip-flopping between Catholicism and Protestantism, depending on his mood, the weather, what he had for lunch, etc. In 1543 he decided that being Protestant was, you know, *so* in, so he launched a number of reforming initiatives, including arresting the leading Roman Catholic, Cardinal David Beaton of St Andrews and having the Bible translated into vernacular Scots (I'm really hoping they subtitled it the 'Och Aye The Good Noos'). The next year, however, he changed his mind. So he released Beaton and arrested his opposite number, the leading evangelical preacher, George Wishart.

* The place of his execution is marked by a monogram PH in the pavement. Traditionally, students at St Andrews avoid stepping on it in case it brings them bad luck in their exams. I'm not sure Hamilton would approve of such superstitious behaviour.

It was like the reigns of Edward VI and Mary Tudor wrapped up in one person. Wishart was burned as a heretic in 1546.*

It produced a backlash. A small group of violent protesters broke into St Andrews castle, murdered Beaton in reprisal and hung his body from the window. Yes, it was curtains for Beaton.†They occupied the castle and turned it into a sort of Protestant fortress. The Occupy St Andrews Movement held the castle for a year until, eventually, some French troops arrived and bombed them into surrender. The men captured in the castle were sentenced to be galley slaves aboard French ships. And among them was a man called John Knox.

Opportunity Knox

Knox had been converted in 1543 and served for a while as a bodyguard to Wishart. As a preacher he started as he meant to go on: his very first sermon had been on the topic of why the Pope was actually the whore of Babylon from Revelation. Knox was a hard man. On board the galley ship, the Protestants were faced with torture and beatings if they refused to revere an image of the Virgin Mary. Knox refused, and when they forced the image in his face he tore it from their grasp and chucked it overboard.

He was released after two years and went to England for a bit. First he went to Berwick, which is about as far north as you can go in England without drifting into Scottishness. Then he moved to London, where he spent his time trying to encourage

---

* Wishart had a long history of heresy. He was initially investigated in 1538 and fled to England, only to be accused there of heresy by Thomas Cromwell a year later. In 1543 he returned to Scotland. He was burned at the stake on 1 March 1546 at St Andrews, where his remains, presumably, were raked into a bunker.

† Knox, in recounting the story later, described how the cardinal was 'struck . . . twice or thrice through with a stog sword'. Stog means 'to stab'. Just thought you ought to know.

the slowcoach Cranmer into speeding up the Reformation. He was offered the post of Bishop of Rochester but, fortunately for the inhabitants of Rochester, refused it. Then Edward died and Mary came to the throne, and Knox had to flee. He went to the place that became his most favourite place ever on earth: Geneva.

For Knox, Geneva was 'the most perfect school of Christ that ever was in the earth since the days of the apostles'. And he started to think big: what if you took Calvinagrad and moved it to Edinburgh? What if the whole of Scotland could be one, big, happy reformed family? Only without the happiness bit, obviously. Because you sense that Knox was only really happy when he was being grumpy.* A contemporary description says,

> In bodily stature he was rather below normal height. His limbs were straight and well-proportioned; his shoulders broad; his fingers somewhat long. His head was a medium size, with black hair; his appearance swarthy yet not unpleasant. His countenance, which was grave and stern though not harsh, bore a natural dignity and air of authority; in anger his very frown became imperious.

And there was a lot in his life to get grumpy about. As a former employee of the French galleys he was grumpy about the French. As a signed-up card-carrying member of the Calvinist Party he was very grumpy about Catholics. And as a big old bloke with a beard, women irritated him immensely. So imagine his joy during this time when the ruler of Scotland was a French Catholic woman.† And in England there was another woman in charge. And both of them were called Mary.‡

---

* As we've seen, one of his happiest moments in Geneva was when Michael Servetus was executed – an event which cheered him up immensely.
† Mary, Queen of Scots, had eventually married Francis in 1558.
‡ Knox sent his English brethren a prayer to pray for Mary Tudor which began: 'Delay not thy vengeance, O Lord! but let death devour them in haste; let the earth swallow them up; and let them go down quickly into hell . . .' Would have made a lovely fridge magnet.

In the same year, therefore, that his friend Goodman wrote his book on '*How superior powers ought to be obeyed of their subjects*', Knox rolled up his sleeves, turned his misogyny up to eleven and produced a book showing that it was against God's will for women to be in charge of anything. The book was pithily titled *The First blast of the trumpet against the monstrous regiment of women* ('monstrous regiment' means unnatural rule). It was full of his typically caustic, bitter and outspoken rhetoric. In the introduction he admonishes 'the Ile of greate Brittanny' for being ruled by 'Jezabel'. 'How abominable before God, is the Empire or Rule of a wicked woman, yea of a traiteresse and bastard.' But it's not just Britain; women should not be allowed in charge anywhere: 'To promote a woman to bear rule, superiority, dominion or empire above any realm, nation, or city, is repugnant to nature, contumely to God, a thing most contrarious to his revealed will and approved ordinance, and finally it is the subversion of good order, of all equity and justice.' Or, to put it another way, Mary, Mary, quite contrarious. In Knox's view, God created women as servants and subjects to men, and only ever allowed them to rule as punishment for national sin. It was another development in the politics of resistance, although with Knox the main thing to be resisted was Women In Charge. Within a year of publication, Mary Tudor had died and England returned to Protestantism. That might have been good news for Knox were it not for the fact that Mary's successor was another monstrously regimental woman. Elizabeth I was the definite possessor of lady bits, including a brain, and there was no way that she was going to forgive Knox for blasting his trumpet in her general direction. In fact, her antipathy towards Knox's *Trumpet Blast* made her even more suspicious of anything to do with Geneva.

Meanwhile things were changing in Scotland. In 1559 Mary also became Queen of France when her husband Francis ascended the throne. Although officially Queen of Scotland, Mary lived in France while a series of regents governed Scotland, acting in her name.* In the same year, Knox returned to Scotland (his arrival was delayed because Elizabeth refused him permission to pass through England. She was so not a fan of his work). He immediately began preaching, and, such was the placid, quiet nature of his message, that it led to riots, vandalism and the looting of monasteries. Knox joined forces with a band of Scottish nobles who called themselves by the rather Game-of-Thrones-sounding name of the 'Lords of the Congregation', who vowed to defend the word of God (although they were also quite keen on the idea of taking over church property as they had seen happen down in England). Aided by English money, the pro-French forces were expelled, and in 1560 the Scottish Parliament decreed that the Pope no longer had any authority in Scotland, and instead that all doctrine and practice had to conform to a new confession of faith (the Scots Confession) drawn up by John Knox.

Scotland was now Calvinist. Welcome to McGeneva. Or maybe we should call it Knoxville.

Books of Discipline

The Scottish Parliament passed laws banning Mass, and adopting a Calvinist statement of faith. They remodelled the Church along Genevan lines, a system outlined in the very Knoxian-titled *First Book of Discipline*.† Knox established a Presbyterian system of church government, with a nationwide network of presbyters, who gathered together in a national synod, the General Assembly, to make decisions.

In the midst of all this, Mary, Queen of Scots, returned from France. Her time as Queen of France had been all too brief;

---

* Confusingly, the regent at the time was, to Knox's deep annoyance, *another* Mary, Mary of Guise. Knox wrote that her regent's crown was as fitting as 'a saddle upon the back of an unruly cow'. Such a charmer.

† Its sequels were *The Second Book of Discipline*, *My Little Book of Discipline*, *What The Book of Discipline Did Next* and *Fifty Shades of Greyfriars*.

Francis died in December 1560 and the widowed Mary returned to Scotland, arriving in Leith on 19 August 1561. Mary was very much a Catholic, but she was also very much the queen. And for the Protestant Kirk, which had been established in defiance of the monarchy, this made the position rather uncomfortable.

It all got very complicated. Mary actually granted toleration to the Kirk. But she refused to grant assent to the Scottish Parliament's law abolishing the Mass, on the grounds that, as a Catholic, she wanted to celebrate it herself. A compromise deal was worked out allowing Mary to have her own private Mass, even when it had been banned elsewhere. Knox was furious. He was a man from a poor background, he'd served as a galley slave, he was not the kind of man to allow people to act in defiance of the law, just because they were toffs. Mary's private Mass was an infection, a cancer to be rooted out. He preached incendiary sermons against the queen and even personally led a mob to Holyrood Abbey to disrupt the queen's Mass.

Great Moments in Reformation History

NUMBER 26: In Scotland, John Knox gets carried away.

And I'm going to ban haggis as well!

It's the school of hard Knox.

Mary was stubborn, over-dramatic, and possessed of extremely bad judgement. Then again, she was a teenager . . . Even so, it's possible that with a man more tolerant and understanding than John Knox in charge – a category which includes most men who have ever lived – Mary might have become enough of a Protestant for a peaceful reign to take hold. But Knox and his mates were only interested in denouncing and humiliating her. His sermons reduced her to tears. He likened her to the Emperor Nero. He told her that if monarchs exceeded the law, they could expect to be forcibly resisted. She asked if he would come to her directly with differences of opinion, rather than launching attacks in sermons, but Knox refused. He treated her with condescension and even contempt. Once when Mary tried to interrupt him he patronisingly replied, 'I began, Madam, to reason with the Secretary, whom I take to be a far better dialectician than your Grace is.' For his part, Knox thought that Mary had 'a proud mind, a crafty wit, and an indurate heart against God and his truth'. What's more she didn't clean her room up, and she spent too much time texting her friends.

The example of Henry IV of France showed that a Protestant king could not rule a Catholic people. Mary showed that a Catholic queen could not rule a Protestant people. And what this shows is that *cuius regio, eius religio* – the principle whereby the religion of the ruler was the religion of the people – actually cut both ways. It might have been designed as an ideal which showed that power flowed from the top down, but in practice the power flowed the other way. It was the people who decided that Mary's religion was not to be theirs.

Admittedly she didn't help herself very much. Her life was riven by a succession of tabloid-esque sexual scandals. She had taken another husband, Lord Darnley, with whom she had had a son, James in 1566. But the marriage was not a happy one. Darnley was arrogant and greedy for power. He thought that Mary was having an affair with her Italian secretary, Rizzio, so had him murdered in front of his pregnant wife at a dinner party. The

TOP REFORMERS

John Knox

Born: Haddington, Scotland, c.1513
Died: Edinburgh, Scotland, 1572

AKA: Mr Chuckles, The Beard which is Feared, etc.

A man of both tremendous courage and principle. Admittedly a lot of those principles were narrow and misogynistic, but you can't have everything. A powerful preacher, he established the Church of Scotland as a Presbyterian system based on Calvinist lines. His views of the authority of monarchs were to influence Puritans in England.

Fun Fact: Knox's burial place is now parking space No.23 behind St Giles' Cathedral, Edinburgh.

INFLUENCE	45
THEOLOGICAL IMPORTANCE	27
FACIAL HAIR	92
GENERAL GLOOMINESS	98
ABUSIVENESS	75
HAT QUALITY	17
PROPENSITY TO VIOLENCE	45

rumours were that it was Rizzio who was actually the father of the queen's child. Then, strangely – some might say 'conveniently' – a few months later, Darnley himself was murdered. His body and that of his valet were discovered in the orchard of Kirk o'

Field, in Edinburgh, where they had been staying.* Mary then increased the scandal by marrying one of the suspected assassins, the Earl of Bothwell.† There was an uprising against the couple, culminating in the Battle of Carberry Hill in 1567. Having found her thrill on Carberry Hill, Mary was deposed in favour of her infant son. She tried briefly to organise another uprising, but that failed, so she fled south to England.‡ This was out of the frying pan and into the barbecue. Mary had previously claimed Elizabeth's throne as her own and was considered the legitimate sovereign of England by many English Catholics. Elizabeth didn't know quite what to do with her – so did nothing, as usual – simply holding her in custody in a succession of castles. Eventually, after spending some eighteen years in custody, Mary was found guilty of plotting to assassinate Elizabeth, and was subsequently beheaded.

Mary's son, James VI of Scotland, remained in Scotland to be brought up by Scottish Calvinists in what was possibly the least fun childhood ever. Scotland was Calvinist. And it has been drinking its way out of that ever since.

Knox, whose first wife died in 1560, also controversially remarried, aged fifty, the seventeen-year-old Margaret Stewart, who was herself a distant relation of Mary Queen of Scots. But his influence had been on the wane for some time (he had called for Mary's death after the Darnley affair, but he didn't get his way). He died in November 1572. In his will he wrote that 'None have I corrupted, none have I defrauded; merchandise have I not made.' He certainly left no fortune: his death plunged his family into poverty.

---

* Darnley's murder is one of the strangest in history. First, two barrels of gunpowder were exploded in the room beneath his sleeping quarters. But that didn't kill him. His body was found outside, in the orchard, surrounded by a cloak, a dagger, a chair and a coat. And Darnley, it was revealed, had been strangled. Whoever the murderer was, clearly he – or she – had a lot of trouble working out how to do it.

† His shoes were found at the murder scene: presumably after he hotfooted it. In order to marry Mary he divorced his wife twelve days before the wedding.

‡ Bothwell went into exile in Denmark, where he died, insane, in 1578.

His legacy is hard to judge. He had integrity and courage. But he was also one of those chiefly responsible for the dour, inflexible, monochrome Calvinism which characterised Scottish religion for so long. Thanks in a large part to Knox, Scotland became Presbyterian, rather than following a form of Anglicanism. And today the members of the Presbyterian denomination number millions worldwide.

But perhaps one of his strongest legacies was that he reinforced the idea that kings and queens did not automatically command respect: they had to earn it. Position did not grant you spiritual privileges. And in Scotland, a queen had been deposed to be replaced with the choice of the Kirk and Parliament. This was a revolutionary philosophy. Knox really did believe that you could depose kings and queens. And this philosophy was to have a huge impact south of the border, and particularly on Mary's grandson.

33 God's silly vassal

The royal gift

Elizabeth died in 1603. True to her theory of avoiding difficult or divisive decisions, she had never married.* Without an heir, the throne passed to James VI of Scotland, the son of Mary Queen of Scots. He became James I of England. England, Wales and Scotland were joined together in a friendly merger and have been Completely Happy Together ever since.

For both James and the English Puritans it was a dream come true, although for totally different reasons. The Puritans believed that among the baggage which James would bring south from Edinburgh was a large consignment of Scottish Calvinism. This was someone who would be on their side. After all, he'd been raised by John Knox and all his chums. He'd even written learned treatises condemning tobacco and witchcraft and other such works of the Devil. This was their moment. He would make the changes to the Church which Elizabeth had refused them.

For James, though, ascending the throne of England meant leaving all that behind. James grew up with a hatred of Calvinism and the black-clad, beardy-McBeardy faces who force-fed him their ideology at every opportunity, and probably thought Calvin was a bit of a woolly liberal. One of his tutors was George

---

* She was known as the Virgin Queen, the earliest known branding for Richard Branson's empire.

Buchanan, the most learned Scottish humanist of his generation. Buchanan schooled James in Greek and Latin, but Buchanan had a very Knoxian attitude to kings. He thought they were basically public officials. They had a job to do for the government, but if they didn't deliver on the goals and targets, then the people had a right to dismiss them. In works like *De jure regni apud Scotos* and the more vernacular *History of Scotland* Buchanan cited the precedents of a dozen kings in Scottish history who had been deposed. Of course, a lot of this history was largely fictional and based on myths of large hairy men hitting each other with clubs, but nevertheless the point stood. Buchanan's attitude was echoed by Andrew Melville, Rector of St Andrews University, who famously told the king, 'Sirrah, ye are God's silly vassal; there are two kings and two kingdoms in Scotland: there is king James, the head of the commonwealth; and there is Christ Jesus, the king of the Church, whose subject James the Sixth is, and of whose kingdom he is not a king, not a lord, not a head, but a member.'

Let's face it, when you're the king and someone calls you 'God's silly vassal' you remember that sort of thing. You store it away in the 'payback' file. So it's hardly surprising that James became a sort of anti-Buchanan, a passionate believer in the absolute divine right of kings. He wrote two books – *The Trew Law of Free Monarchies* and *Basilikon Doron* (i.e. 'Royal Gift') – which stated that, far from being government functionaries, or 'silly vassals', kings ruled by divine appointment. A bit like, er, the pope.

And although James grew up in deepest, darkest McCalvinshire – or maybe *because* he grew up there – he was about as far removed from a Geneva Protestant as it is possible to imagine. Admittedly he made some of the right noises. He tried to present himself as a devout, reformed Protestant and he even managed a few sneers at the southern softies, claiming their Communion service was just the 'masse in English'. And it's possible that he was the man who invented the word 'Anglican' – which he meant as an insult. But his actions tell a different story. The rumours clouded about him like midges. James was reputed to have engaged in 'carnal lust'. He had, the stories said, been lured into it by the Earl of Lennox, the first of a succession of male favourites who hung around James for the rest of his life. James was even imprisoned for a time over this, while Lennox was forced to flee.

So when the news came through of the old queen's death, James couldn't wait to (a) escape Scotland; (b) free himself from the oppressive disapproval of all those Scottish presbyters; and (c) have access to a new shedload of cash. He jumped on the Gravy Train at Edinburgh Waverley and made his way south.

Meanwhile, for the English Calvinists it was Christmas come early. Or it would have been had they approved of Christmas. Which, of course, they didn't.* Anyway, they didn't even wait for him to get to London; a deputation of Puritans met him as he made his way south, and presented him with a list of requests, including reforms to church services and amendments to what they still saw as a bit of a 'popish' prayer book. James refused to commit himself to anything, merely promising to moderate a conference to be convened the next year. In the meantime, having sneered at Anglicanism, when he moved

---

* In his 1583 book *The Anatomie of Abuses*, the Puritan Philip Stubbe wrote of Christmas: 'That more mischief is that time committed than in all the year besides, what masking and mumming, whereby robbery, whoredom, murder and what not is committed? What dicing and carding, what eating and drinking, what banqueting and feasting is then used, more than in all the year besides, to the great dishonour of God and impoverishing of the realm.' Sounds like a cracking Christmas to me. Part of their opposition was because Christmas was extremely popular among the Catholic recusant community. The staunchly Catholic Dorothy Lawson celebrated Christmas 'in both kinds . . . corporally and spiritually', indulging in Christmas pies, dancing and gambling. In 1594 some imprisoned Catholic priests at Wisbech managed to celebrate Christmas and even included morris dancing. As if they hadn't already suffered enough.

south he had a Damascus Road experience, or a Great North Road experience at any rate, and he soon became a keen convert to it.

The authorised version

The conference took place in Hampton Court in 1604. And to the Puritans' dismay, James utterly refused to make any changes. For a man who'd grown up dealing with *proper* Puritans, hard nuts like Knox, these softy southerners were easy meat. James destroyed their hopes of imposing an English version of Presbyterianism by stating that such an idea 'agreeth as well with the monarch as God and the Devil'. He had absolutely no intention of allowing any system in which 'Jack and Tom and Will and Dick shall meet and at their pleasure censor me'.

However, one demand of theirs that James did agree to was to authorise a new translation of the Bible. But even here, he managed to outwit them. What the Puritans wanted was the official adoption of the Geneva Bible. But James *hated* the Geneva Bible. Well, not so much the Bible itself, but all those marginal notes which he believed to take a seditiously Buchananish approach. James called such notes 'partial, untrue, seditious and savouring of traitorous conceits'. He particularly hated the one about the midwives which implied that it was OK to disobey a monarch. To James, disobedience to a royal command – *any* royal command – was an act of sedition.

Instead, James suggested a new translation should be done by 'the best learned of both Universities'. So he appointed forty-seven scholars, working in six 'companies', and laid down careful guidelines to control their approach. It was less a new translation, more a revision of previous versions 'as little altered as the truth of the original will permit'. He ordered that 'the old ecclesiastical words to be kept, viz. the word Church not to be translated Congregation', and, crucially, that 'no marginal notes at all to be affixed, but only for the explanation of the Hebrew or Greek . . .' The result was the King James, or 'Authorised', version.

It's one of the monuments of English culture and probably the most widely read book in history, but when it was published in 1611, it was widely ignored. And those who didn't ignore it generally criticised it. Where the Geneva Bible was small and readable, the first edition of the KJV was the size of a small truck and printed in dense, Gothic, illegible black-letter type. It opened with a lengthy preface followed by the lectionary. And that's the thing. The KJV was designed to be read *to* the people, not read *by* them. James agreed with his great-uncle Henry: the Bible should be kept safe in church, chained to the lectern and only doled out in carefully controlled doses.

In accordance with his instructions, James had his old words back. *Ekklesia* was 'church', *presbutoros* was 'bishop' (instead of 'elder' – another blow for the Presbyterians) and, in one of its most celebrated passages, 'faith, hope and love' had turned back into 'faith, hope, charity . . . but the greatest of these is charity'. Which of course could easily mean almsgiving. Ker-ching!* In fact the whole thing had been artificially aged. While today we look at the KJV as a magnificent showcase of what the English language can do, for its first readers it was a bit over the top. In an attempt to make it sound properly grand, the translators dressed the text up in an archaic style that no one had ever really used. It was the world's first mock-Tudor Bible. Even some forty years later, John Selden observed that its language was 'well enough so long as scholars have to do with

---

* The translators were following the Latin version. Jerome translated it as *caritas*, because he thought the Latin word *amor* too gross. Over time, of course, charity came to represent not only the giving of alms, but the whole edifice of church giving. Tyndale used the more correct translation: 'Though I speake with the tonges of men and angels and yet had no love I were ever as soundinge brasse: or as a tynklynge Cymball . . . Nowe abideth fayth, hope and love, even these three: but the chefe of these is love' (1 Cor. 13:1, 13).

it, but when it comes among the common people, Lord, what gear do they make of it'. Anthony Johnson, writing less than ninety years later, stated that the absence of notes from the KJV led to complaints from some readers that 'they could not see into the sense of Scriptures'.*

Still, beneath this fancy, mock-Tudor panelling there's the robust masonry of Tyndale's original building. Some 94 per cent of the KJV New Testament comes from Tyndale's translation. The translators did all the fancy work, but Tyndale did all the heavy lifting.

Puritan scholars lambasted this Bible for its inaccuracies. Hugh Broughton said, 'Tell His Majesty that I had rather be rent in pieces with wild horses, than any such translation by my consent should be urged upon poor churches . . . The new edition crosseth me. I desire it to be burnt.' The rest of the people greeted the KJV with a resounding 'meh' and carried on reading and buying the Geneva Bible, with its notes and maps and pictures. They understood that. It spoke their language. In the end the authorities had to ban the sale of the Geneva Bible in order to force the KJV onto the public. Eventually the supply of Geneva Bibles ran out and the KJV took over. But if it had been a straight shootout, the KJV might never have survived.

Gunpowder, treason and plot

In 1605 an Italian called Guido Fawkes was discovered in a cellar of the Houses of Parliament with barrels of gunpowder, a box of matches, and a copy of *Teach Yourself Bomb Making*. The plot had been . . . er . . . plotted by a group of English Catholics led by Robert Catesby. The idea was to blow up the House of Lords, which would act as a signal to a mass popular uprising

---

* The American Benjamin Franklin wanted to produce a version in modern English.

somewhere in the Midlands. They would then install Princess Elizabeth – James's nine-year-old daughter – as queen, and England would return to the bosom of the old faith. Some of the conspirators were killed during a skirmish, and the remaining eight – including Fawkes – were hung, drawn and quartered. It was England's 9/11 moment – although without the actual destruction. And forever after, the remembrance of the plot was used to remind the Patriotic Protestant English of the Peril from Perfidious Papists.*

As a reaction to the plot, James appointed some Puritan bishops as a kind of counterbalance and some anti-Catholic laws were strengthened. But several loyal Catholics retained high office during James's reign. He was distressingly un-Puritan in some of his ways. He was a drunkard, profligate with money. In 1618, he published a book, *The Book of Sports*, which declared that it was perfectly all right to play sport on a Sunday afternoon, provided it was not things like hunting or bear baiting or cock fighting. To the zealously sabbatarian Puritan ministers, this was an outrage. Sunday was a day for listening to seven-hour sermons and thinking very seriously about the Direction Your Life Was Taking. Their disgust was further compounded by the royal decree which forced them to read the book out to the public from their pulpits. James's extravagance was notorious, so much so that in 1614 Parliament refused to carry on funding his extravagant court, with its sexual scandal, intrigue and licentiousness. And he had a number of male favourites with whom he seemed very, very, very close.

In the end the Puritans had to come to terms with the fact that James, like Elizabeth, was not going to give them what they wanted. They wanted the Scottish Presbyterian system introduced, but James replied 'No bishop, no king' and went on to order that all clergy should affirm their approval of bishops and

---

* In Lewes in Sussex, they still burn an effigy of Pope Paul V, who was Pope at the time of the plot.

the entire contents of the Prayer Book. When some ninety clergy refused, they were evicted from their posts.

Not surprisingly, many decided that enough was enough. They decided to leave the established church – to separate themselves. And they became known, and dismissed, as Separatists.

34 Our friends in the west

The emerald isle

But there's a question on your lips, dear reader. I can sense it. And the question is, 'You've missed two. What about Ireland. And the other one.'

All right, all right. And it's *Wales*, for heaven's sake.

Well, in England the Reformation happened in a very English way, with lots of arguments and zigzagging before everyone calmed down and had a cup of tea and agreed to be all moderate about it. In Ireland, you could say it happened in a very Irish way: i.e. completely opposite to how it happened elsewhere.

Ireland had always been regarded as a semi-wild land, inhabited by barbarians. Or the Irish, to use the technical term. Henry VIII had officially given Ireland a promotion, turning it into a proper kingdom (although, obviously, that didn't mean it got its own king: he felt there was more than enough Henry for everyone to share). Yet despite the fact that he and his successors were the Kings or Queens of Ireland, the principle of *cuius regio, wossname expelliamus* didn't seem to work at all.

Part of the problem was the language: most of Ireland spoke Gaelic so there was a communication problem. Although, it has to be said that Scotland spoke two languages as well, and when John Knoxxed, they welcomed Calvinism with open arms. The bigger problem was that the English rulers didn't see this as a problem. They didn't really make any attempt to overcome the language barrier. When the 1549 Prayer Book was introduced it was published in English and in Latin, but not in Gaelic. And although Elizabeth was keen that there should be a Gaelic translation of the Bible (she even paid for a special Gaelic typeface) the plan repeatedly stalled and it didn't appear until 1685. Another factor was the lack of an Irish university. Too many preachers were failed English clergy on the run. When Trinity College Dublin was founded in 1592 it was almost too late. And it was not until thirty years later that William Bedell, its most enlightened provost, insisted that the clergy it produced should be able to communicate in Gaelic.

But the major factor was a widespread resentment of those on the other side of the Irish Sea. This was fuelled by the English colonial policy: in order to establish more of a presence in the country, the English rulers started sending over settlers, immigrants who lived in what they called 'plantations'. (Ironically, though, the person who started this colonisation scheme was not the Protestant Edward or Elizabeth, but the Catholic Queen Mary.) The plantation strategy was deeply unpopular with the native people – unsurprisingly, since it was their land which was being grabbed. It allowed the opponents of the Reformation to characterise the Irish Reformation as an official colonial project of the English and the Scots. The Gaelic words for Protestant became 'Albanac' and 'Sasanac', i.e. Scotsman and Englishman. The evangelical John Bale was appointed as an Irish bishop. He was an eloquent preacher and communicator and should have had a lot of success, but instead of being gratefully converted, 'the wild Irish' took him hostage and he was only released after a ransom was paid. In the account he wrote of this, he put a quote from the Psalms on the title page: 'God hath delivered me from the snare of the hunter, and from the noisome pestilence.'

So, although all the various English Reformation statutes were rubber-stamped by the Irish Parliament, not many of them actually stuck. The Tudor regime banned celebration of the Catholic Mass in 1568, but nobody took any notice. The Irish monasteries were only dissolved in the areas under effective English control.

In the western, more remote parts of Ireland, they clung on, continuing a monastic tradition stretching back a thousand years or so. And, unlike in England, the chantries were never closed down either. So they still provided a steady stream of Catholic worship and, indeed, money, to the Church.

Most importantly, while almost all the Irish bishops took the Oath of Supremacy, a lot of them still kept the communication channels open with Rome just in case the whole Hexit thing didn't work out. The Irish coastline allowed easy communications with Spain, France and Portugal. And to aid that communication, Latin continued to be widely taught and spoken. A Spanish soldier shipwrecked in the ill-fated Spanish Armada was amazed to find there were peasants in a remote Irish village who spoke Latin. Although efforts to fuel revolution by sending over Spanish soldiers never came to anything, a different kind of revolution was initiated. There were six Catholic training colleges set up in Spain and Portugal for the training of Irish clergy and they sent over a steady stream of missionaries, priests and ninja Jesuits. In 1621 Catholic recusants were no longer subject to fines. In 1635 a new church was built in Dublin, a Jesuit church, complete with a high altar and confessional boxes.

Ireland, then, was a success story . . . for the Counter-Reformation.

It was only in the north that Protestantism gained any kind of hold. In a land-grabbing scheme backed by London money, James I decided that northern Ireland would be the perfect place to send a load of people, mainly from the lawless areas of the Scottish/English border. When they arrived, they brought with them all the attitudes of the reformed Scottish Calvinism: they were God's elect arriving to bring the good news to the papists of Ulster. They built a new, Protestant cathedral in Derry – or Londonderry as it was renamed.

Preserving the Welsh

Ireland is an example of How Not To Establish A Reformation. That other place – you know, the bit to the west of Birmingham. *Wales.* That's it. Wales is the complete opposite. It helped that Henry's family – the Tudors – were from Wales (although this was a fact they tended to play down while in England). This meant that they understood Wales in a way that they never even attempted to understand Ireland.

Two other factors helped. The first is that, frankly, it was a lot easier to enforce things in Wales than over the sea in Ireland. All you had to do to suppress a monastery in Wales was nip down the M4. Another factor was the state of the Church in Wales. With few exceptions, the Welsh clergy were relatively weak and ill trained. And the monastic establishments were also struggling. By 1536, the thirteen Cistercian houses of Wales had only eighty-five monks between them.

Most of the bishops appointed to Wales after 1559 were Welsh. A newly founded college in Oxford – Jesus College – was specifically intended to educate Welsh men and proved a significant source of Welsh Protestant clergy.*

Most importantly, they created a Welsh Bible. In 1551 the Denbighshire scholar William Salesbury published a Welsh translation of the main texts of the Prayer Book. In 1567 he produced a not-very-good translation of the New Testament. This was amended and incorporated into the big success story: the Welsh Bible of 1588. It's known as Bishop Morgan's Bible, after its translator – William Morgan – who became Bishop of Llandaff and then St Asaph. The success of Morgan's translation lay in exactly the same areas as those of Tyndale's and Luther's: he understood the Welsh language and he understood the people. He knew how they spoke. He loved the language itself. And his

---

* It was founded in 1571. Amazingly, despite the name, to this day they still do not offer a carpentry course.

work implied that Welsh as a language mattered. Indeed, the book was instrumental in preserving Welsh as a living language.

In his introduction, Morgan actually implied that Protestantism was the true Welsh religion and that to sign up to the Reformation was to be truly, authentically Welsh. He claimed that the Reformation was really just returning the world to the original Celtic religion, which had been corrupted by the Romans. Somehow, I find the idea of Calvinistic Druids unconvincing.

Anyway, the fact is that the Reformation was so successful in Wales that by 1603, out of a churchgoing population of some 212,000, only 3,500 were Catholics: a smaller proportion than anywhere else in Britain.

- Part Eleven -
Revolution

❖

35 The Low Countries

Calvinist pirates and orange Dutchmen

'And what,' I hear you ask, 'of Belgium?'

Blimey. Where's that one come from? Well, if you must know, Belgium didn't exist, as such. (In fact, many would say that even now it's only vaguely real.) But the region which includes what today we call Belgium was part of a confederation of provinces known as the Low Countries, due partly to the cut of their trousers, but mainly to their altitude. Seventeen provinces made up the Low Countries: the northern half were mainly Dutch and spoke . . . er . . . Dutch; the southern half were Flemish, and spoke Flem. Or possibly French. And the whole lot was owned, of course, by our old chum, Charles V, Holy Roman Wossname, King of Spain, Lord of the Flies, Land of the Free, etc.

Confused? Yep. Me too.

The proximity of the Low Countries to Germany meant that they were quickly influenced by Lutheran teachings. As we have seen, Holland had given birth to the *Devotio Moderna*,* so there was a ready and fertile soil for Luther's ideas to grow. Not only that, but as great traders, the Dutch could spot a sales opportunity when they saw it. So printers in Rotterdam and Amsterdam happily supplied books and Bibles to all parts of Europe (especially smuggling them across the channel to England). These

* See p. 23.

provinces also began to offer a safe place for more radical ideas. As we've seen, many radical Anabaptist supporters found refuge in the towns of the Netherlands. Calvinism also spread in the French-speaking parts of the Netherlands as a steady stream of missionaries arrived from the Geneva preacher factory. One estimate reckons that some sixty thousand preachers arrived in the provinces during this period. There was also a large number of refugees from France and elsewhere: there were seventeen communities of Calvinist refugees in 1572.

These, though, were quite unusual Calvinists. More violent than the Swiss brand. In the summer of 1566 the Dutch Calvinists started open-air 'hedge-preachings', which drew crowds of up to twenty-five thousand to the fields outside Antwerp. Their preaching whipped the crowd up into a frenzy of iconoclasm and over the course of two weeks many churches were sacked and their art destroyed. In Antwerp, thirty churches were attacked in two days. In Ghent, images were not just destroyed, they were tortured, mutilated, abused, executed, their eyes gouged out and their heads cut off. And when challenged as to who had given these people the right to destroy these icons, the executioners simply answered: 'God.'

Naturally, this alarmed the authorities, most notably, Charles V's son, Philip II, who was an even more ardent Catholic than his dad. Charles had abdicated in 1555, and shared out all his titles – Emperor of the Holy Roman Empire, King of Spain, Duke of Burgundy, Middle of the Road, Cock of the Walk, etc. – between his brother, Ferdinand, and his son, Philip. Philip determined to root out heresy and started to reform the church structure in the Netherlands. He replaced the moderate governor general (actually his aunt, Margaret of Parma) and, in 1567, sent in troops under the leadership of the hardline Duke of Alva. And a brutal crackdown took place.

This, in turn, sparked resentment and fear from the Dutch. They began to worry that the Inquisition would move north and start Inquisitioning all over the place. The situation was further exacerbated by widespread unemployment and economic difficulties, not to mention a long-standing resentment of Spanish influence. The put-upon Dutch decided that enough was enough. They slammed down their mugs of Hoegaarden, stubbed out their joints of pot and decided to rebel. In fact the economic situation helped them a lot, since the Spanish economy was in a pretty ropey state. Spain simply could not afford to keep underwriting all the wars that their kings – the emperors – kept launching. Alva found himself strapped for cash. In 1576 unpaid Spanish troops mutinied and sacked Antwerp. And the Spanish forces which remained loyal found it hard to advance northward because of the many dykes.

We'll pause here, while you supply your own joke.*

In the end, a compromise was reached, brokered by Alessandro, Duke of Parma, which kept the southern states Catholic and under Spanish control. And they remained that way until the nineteenth century, when they became, wait for it . . . Belgium! In the northern states, however, Calvinism continued to establish itself. Rigidly disciplined and organised Calvinist revolutionaries turned themselves into highly trained fighters. Nicknamed 'Beggars', they used sea power to dominate the northern ports of Holland: they were, essentially, Calvinist pirates. The people in these ports were anti-Spain, but they weren't always pro-Beggar, yet in town after town, control was seized by this tiny minority. In Alkmaar, in 1576, for example, the Calvinists took control, despite only numbering one hundred and sixty in a town of six thousand inhabitants. But then, as history shows time and time again, you don't need many fanatics to frighten people. In most cases the Beggars didn't even have to fight: the mere threat of force was enough to take over the town, and once in control, the Beggars imposed a strict, draconian iconoclastic rule.

---

* The dykes, of course, had been built to protect the really low bits of the Low Countries from flooding.

The northern states were also helped by allies from outside, keen to see an end to Spanish dominance. In 1581 they renounced their allegiance to the Spanish monarch and chose instead William of Orange, who was named after the town in the south of France, not because he spent a lot of time on the sunbed.* William had been a close friend and confidant of Charles V, but he had objected to the religious persecution of his own people and had converted to Calvinism in 1573. He became Stadholder of the United Provinces. Sadly, in 1584 he became more of a blood orange when he was murdered by a hired assassin called Balthazar Gérard. Philip II had offered a large cash reward for anyone who would kill William. Gérard was a Catholic Frenchman and his action is probably the first time that a gun was used to kill a head of state.

William is one of the good guys. One of the very few good guys. His last words were said to have been, 'God, have pity on my soul. Have pity on this poor people.' He was someone who argued for tolerance when he was a Catholic *and* when he was a Protestant. He was succeeded by his brother Maurice. And one has to ask, why have we not heard more of Maurice of Orange. I mean, it's almost a rhyme.

Eventually the northern provinces broke completely from Spain and declared themselves the Dutch Republic. In 1609 a truce was negotiated with Spain. Twelve years after that the northern states were granted independence. And that was the beginning of Holland. Or the Netherlands. Or whatever they're called.

So there you go. The Belgium bit in the south stayed mainly Catholic, the Holland bit in the north went Calvinist.

But there were murmurs of discontent; in particular, arguments about predestination. Well, it was bound to happen.

---

* He was also known as William the Silent, although he would never explain why.

TULIP from Amsterdam

In 1559, Calvin came out with his last, and biggest, edition of his *Institutes*. Of all the *Institutes*, this was the most Institutional. And, as we've seen, not much of it is about predestination. But then again, you don't need much strychnine to poison someone.

In Holland, the main opposition to predestination came from someone who originally set out to defend it. Jacob Arminius was a Calvinist pastor who had trained at the seminary in Calvinagrad – albeit some twenty years after Calvin died. In Amsterdam a Catholic humanist called Dirk Coornhert attacked the idea of predestination, calling it repellent, unjust and unbiblical. So, not a fan, then. Arminius, as a good graduate of Geneva, was given the task of defending the doctrine. Ironically, his life took an unexpected turn, because the more he examined the doctrine, the more Arminius found himself agreeing with Dirk. (In fact, he was the third Calvinist pastor who had been given the task and all three ended up by agreeing with Dirk.)

Arminius actually developed a new counter-theory. Arminianism, as it came to be known, keeps the idea of predestination, but in a rather different way. Arminius argued that it was all about time. God predestined people for salvation on the basis of his foreknowledge of their faith. He didn't arbitrarily pick and choose on the basis of his own divine will, as Calvin taught. Instead, Arminius argued, everyone who wanted to become a Christian was automatically saved; but God, being God, could see who would or would not become a Christian with his help. It's kind of predestination from the wrong end. For Arminius, 'God truly wills the salvation of all men', but he is not going to force them. He draws them 'through sweet persuasion'. Humans have freedom of choice, as well as God.

He kept this idea under his hat for a long time, for fear of reprisals, and, indeed, when he eventually released his ideas, they

TOP REFORMERS

Jacob Arminius

Born: Oudewater, Netherlands, 1560
Died: Leiden, Netherlands, 1609

AKA: Jakob Hermanszoon

Former Calvinist pastor turned anti-predestination campaigner. A professor at the University of Leiden, he developed the theory which came to be known as Arminianism. Although condemned at the time, his theories were later taken up by John Wesley, founder of Methodism.

Fun Fact: In 1606 Arminius delivered an address titled 'On Reconciling Religious Dissensions among Christians'. That went well, then . . .

INFLUENCE	70
THEOLOGICAL IMPORTANCE	55
FACIAL HAIR	40
GENERAL GLOOMINESS	10
ABUSIVENESS	0
HAT QUALITY	0
PROPENSITY TO VIOLENCE	0

caused a storm of controversy. After his death, his followers shaped his ideas into five principles which were debated at the Synod of Dort in 1618. The adherents of predestination won: which was a foregone conclusion, I suppose. They condemned Arminianism and forbade its preaching. They issued ninety-three canons which defined the orthodox Calvinist religion – canons which were probably more rigid than what Calvin would have come up with. And in response to the five Arminian principles, they produced their own set of 'Five Articles', which have later been summarised using the appropriately Dutch acronym TULIP, which stands for:

Total depravity: Sin has so infected humanity that we can't do anything good in our own power, nor can we do anything towards our own salvation.

Unconditional election: God unconditionally chooses some people for salvation and others for damnation. There is nothing within these people that affects that. It's all to do with the computer or something.

Limited atonement: Christ, on the cross, only paid for the sins of the elect, not for all humanity. The rest of you have to make your own plans.

Irresistible grace: If God has intended to save you, you will be saved and born again. Resistance is futile.

Perseverance of the saints: Once saved, always saved. God preserves true Christians and will not allow them to fall away from salvation.

It ought to be pointed out that this acronym does not come from Calvin himself, who probably didn't approve of tulips anyway. But this system – and a whole lot more depressingly tough theology – became one of the core beliefs of the Dutch Reformed Church.

Great Moments in Reformation History

NUMBER 27: Beza teaches his 'Introduction to Calvinism' class.

And, speaking of total depravity, I'm aware of what you've been doing behind the bike sheds.

John the Baptist

From Tyndale's time onwards, the Low Countries had offered a place of relative safety for evangelicals of all types and, under Elizabeth and James, many Separatists followed their earlier brethren to Amsterdam.

One of the most radical of the radical Separatists was John Smith, which, given it was his real name, must have made choosing an alias difficult. He was more of a kind of man-sized cell: he simply could not stop separating.

Smith is a pivotal figure in church history. He had studied for the Anglican priesthood at Christ's College, Cambridge, where, like so many, he was radicalised by the Puritans. He took a job as a private chaplain, but was sacked for his radical preaching. So, supporting himself as a physician (he had studied biology at

THE LOW COUNTRIES

Cambridge) he formed his own church, gathering around him a 'congregation' of like-minded followers. Of course, worshipping together in such a way was illegal, so they had to meet in secret locations in rural Lincolnshire. Even so, their numbers grew such that they had to meet in two groups. Smith led one group in Gainsborough, while a man called John Robinson (who, like Smith, had studied and been radicalised at Cambridge) led its sister group in the excellently named Scrooby. Then the authorities discovered Robinson's group, so in 1607 they left England for the Low Countries, in a move which surely has been immortalised as the Scrooby Do.*

Smith's group joined them a little later, their exodus financed by one of their members, Thomas Helwys, a prominent lawyer. In Holland they were offered a place to meet in a bakehouse owned by a Mennonite, Jan Munter. Although grateful for the accommodation, they were wary: the Mennonites were, of course, Anabaptists, and they had a reputation as heretics, revolutionaries and generally bad eggs.

But in Amsterdam, Smith started developing radical ideas of his own. First, he insisted that the Bible should only be read in Greek and Hebrew in church. Then, he declared the entire Anglican church to be false. In a book he wrote in 1608, *The Character of the Beast*, he argued that since the Anglican church was a false church, then all baptisms it carried out were false. 'Baptism is not washing with water,' he wrote, 'but it is the baptism of the Spirit, the confession of the mouth, and the washing with water: how then can any man without great folly wash with water which is the least and last of baptism?' As he continued to think about baptism, he decided that the Anabaptists were right – only believers should be baptised. Baptism was a matter of choice and commitment: it was adult, believer's baptism

* It took them a lot of effort to get there. Their first attempt was thwarted when they were betrayed to the authorities by the sea captain who had promised them transport. They were searched, and all their money and possessions confiscated.

which signified that you were a true believer and which allowed you to become a member of the Church.* So he decided to get baptised, and, since he could think of no one more qualified, he baptised himself. This act scandalised many of the other Separatists in the city. Richard Bernard nicknamed him a 'Se-Baptist' (self-baptiser). This derogatory term stuck, although gradually people stopped using the 'se-' bit.

And, so, John Smith invented the Baptists.

Smith was a man prone to second thoughts. Not to mention third ideas, fourth notions and fifth delusions. And eventually all the 'self-baptising' mockery got to him and he came to believe that maybe he'd been a bit presumptuous, so he had the Mennonites baptise him again. This was, technically, his third go at baptism, since he had already been baptised as an infant, and it really infuriated his fellow leader Thomas Helwys, who disagreed with the Mennonites on matters of Christology, on their rejection of oaths and on their pacifism. Helwys retaliated in the only way he knew how: he separated from Smith. So it was that the Baptists – who at this point had only been going for a year – split up. Smith was excommunicated, thus establishing another key practice of Baptist congregations: sacking the minister.

Smith ended up joining the Mennonite Church. Helwys decided that he would return to England, on the grounds that it was wrong to stay safe in exile when others were living in ignorance back home. So along with ten other fellow believers, he returned to London, and founded the first Baptist congregation on British soil in Spitalfields, which at that time was just outside the city. He died in prison in about 1615.

---

* This emphasis on a personal choice and commitment also led Smith to reject predestination. Later on, different Baptist groups appeared who, unlike him, adopted Calvinism. These became known as the Particular Baptists, to differentiate them from those vague, not-very-particular wishy-washy General, or non-Calvinist Baptists.

TOP REFORMERS

John Smith

Born: Nottinghamshire, England, c.1554
Died: Amsterdam, Netherlands, 1612

AKA: John Smyth

A Puritan preacher, he left the Church to found his own Separatist congregation. They fled to Holland in 1609 where he founded the first modern Baptist church. Later he became a Mennonite.

Fun Fact: His church in Holland was called 'The Brethren of the Separation of the Second English Church at Amsterdam'.

INFLUENCE	35
THEOLOGICAL IMPORTANCE	20
FACIAL HAIR	40
GENERAL GLOOMINESS	10
ABUSIVENESS	0
HAT QUALITY	0
PROPENSITY TO VIOLENCE	5

That is the thing about separatism. Once you start, you can't stop.

Indeed, the idea of 'separating' is one of the most long-lasting legacies of the Reformation. Luther made a man's religious convictions his fixed point. Whether he said it or not, 'Here I stand' does sum up his approach. But one man's religious convictions are another man's heresies. For centuries, rightly or wrongly, it had been the practice of Christians – their engagement with the sacraments of the Church – which had defined 'membership' as such. But after Luther it becomes not only the practices, but what you believe about those practices.

Nevertheless, Luther, Calvin and Zwingli all believed in infant baptism, in babies being baptised into the Church. Their church was still largely inclusive. Adult baptism kills that one off. Separatist churches rejected the idea that all 'Christians' in any given area were members of the Church. You had to sign up, subscribe. The Church, in their eyes, could not include 'all the profane of the parish'. Naturally this put them at odds with the established churches, many of which had appointed the profane of the parish to serve as the vicar. But it also separated them from their neighbours, from their friends, their families. The idea of separatism implies, by its very nature, a division between true believers and non-believers. It implies membership.

Some of the Separatists decided to separate themselves even further. After arguments had broken out among his group of Separatists (see what I mean), John Robinson drove his Scrooby mobile from Amsterdam to Leiden, which at that time was an important centre of learning, with a renowned university. Under his leadership the church grew steadily. He even studied at the university and wrote many pamphlets defending separatism. But the years were hard and, in the end, Robinson and others decided that what they needed was some place they could truly call their own. The political situation was deteriorating. War was brewing between Spain and Holland and they didn't want to be caught when the Spanish invaded.

In early 1619, they decided to emigrate further than any had gone before. They would go to the New World. Or, as civilised people the world over now call it: that bit south of Canada.

They negotiated the hire of two ships: the *Mayflower* and the

Speedwell. However, *Speedwell* proved to be something of an ironic name: the ship was so unseaworthy that it barely made the short hop from Holland to London. So as many as could, transferred to the other ship, the *Mayflower.* Only thirty-five members of Robinson's congregation actually sailed on the *Mayflower.** The rest of the passengers were made up of sixty-six others who weren't going for religious reasons but who probably just wanted to go to Disneyland.

To those early pilgrim fathers, what they were doing was full of biblical symbolism. It reminded all those involved of that bit in the Bible with Moses and the Red Sea and the marginal note that James hated. It was a second exodus. They told themselves that they would all go to New England and build a New Jerusalem. It would all be terribly . . . new.

Of course it didn't quite work out that way. While the Puritan Separatists did find a home in the New World, they did what all Separatists love to do, and rapidly separated from each other, dividing into a bewildering number of Protestant groups and sub-sects.

And they've been happily separating ever since.

---

* Robinson was not among them. Robinson's farewell sermon included a swipe at the Lutherans who, he claimed, 'cannot be drawn to go beyond what Luther saw. Whatever part of His will our God has revealed to Calvin, they [Lutherans] will rather die than embrace it; and the Calvinists, you see, stick fast where they were left by that great man of God, who yet saw not all things.'

36 Religious wars

Through the Prague window

Bohemia had long maintained its Hussite church, which pre-dated Luther. Although it had been ruled by Catholic Habsburgs – members of the Imperial family – various internal divisions among the ruling family members had allowed the state to maintain its relative freedom of religion. But then the ageing Emperor Matthias made his cousin Archduke Ferdinand his heir and had him elected King of Bohemia in 1617.

Ferdinand, who was also next in line as Holy Roman Emperor, decided that he, personally, would put things right. A devout Catholic, he let his subjects know that things had to change, and that they were no longer going to get the relative religious liberty that they had taken for granted for so long. When the local dukes, earls and assorted nobility protested, he had their assembly dissolved. He sent representatives to Prague with a 'sharp letter' to the assembled Bohemian nobles telling them exactly what he was going to do. The Bohemians were so outraged by the letter they chucked the Imperial representatives out. Literally. Through a window. The three men survived the seventy-foot drop: Catholics said they were rescued by angels; Protestants claimed they landed in a dung heap.* The event, known as the 'defenestration of

---

* It seems that they landed on a handily placed heap of straw. One of them – a secretary called Philip Fabricius – was later granted the title *Baron von Hohenfall* by the Emperor. Hohenfall means 'high fall'.

Prague', launched a revolt and a reformed Protestant – the Elector Palatine, Friedrich V – was put on the throne of Bohemia. Seeing an opportunity, the militantly Calvinist Prince Gábor Bethlen of Transylvania made an attempt to gain the throne of next-door Hungary, by attacking the Imperial Habsburg armies and taking over their land. And he was supported by the Turks – the Ottoman sultan offered to support the Transylvanians, on the basis that my enemy's enemy is my friend. Surely the only Calvinist–Muslim alliance in history.

The empire struck back. By now, Ferdinand had been promoted and was the fully fledged Holy Roman Emperor. He launched a counter attack to regain the crown. And that was the start of the Thirty Years' War. Because, although he retook Bohemia very easily and started dismantling the Hussite Church, in other nations alarm bells started ringing: they didn't want to see a resurgently powerful empire. So they started to join in. Lutheran Sweden and Catholic France both attacked the empire's forces and eventually the war sucked in Spain and Germany as well.

The Thirty Years' War was a horrible, energy sapping, deeply unholy holy war. Gradually the original religious causes of the war were forgotten, submerged beneath a protracted, attritional fight for territory, during which Germany was pretty much brought to its knees. Shades of wars to come.

More than ten million people are estimated to have died through the war. By the time the exhausted powers signed the Treaty of Westphalia in 1648, no one had really won anything very much. But one thing seemed to have crystallised in the European mind: religion was not really worth fighting over. The French *éminence grise*, Cardinal Richelieu, said: 'The interests of the state and the interests of religion are completely different things.' For the best part of 120 years Europe had been wracked by the wars of religion. They were worn out by it. From now on, Europe was going to become gradually, but increasingly, secular. And the religious boundaries which were fixed at the end of the war are pretty much the same today.

The death of the king

In the same year that the Thirty Years' War concluded, the Puritans finally got what they had always longed for: power.

After a bloody, traumatic, civil war, King Charles I surrendered to Parliamentary forces and Oliver Cromwell turned the whole country Puritan and instigated what he termed 'Godly reformation'.

Perhaps it was his stutter, perhaps it was his shyness, perhaps because he had been brought up with his father's obsessive belief in the divine right of kings, but James I's son Charles was a reserved, distant, authoritarian, aloof figure. He was never liked. Or even admired. His father had concocted a brilliant plan: he would reconcile Protestantism and Catholicism by marrying his son Charles to the Catholic daughter of the King of Spain. It only showed how remote he was from the feelings of ordinary people. Not only had they not forgotten all that Armada business; this idea merely confirmed their belief that the royalty were a bunch of stuck-up, immoral crypto-papists. Charles had the good sense to dodge that bullet; although, since he went on to marry the Catholic daughter of the King of France, you could argue that he didn't dodge it by much. When the Princess Henrietta Maria arrived from Paris, she brought with her a large retinue of Catholic priests and was allowed to keep her own court and her own form of worship in Somerset House, a little piece of Catholic France right in the middle of Protestant London. The people assumed that she was luring the king in the same direction.

Their view was only confirmed when, following his coronation, Charles started to restore a more traditional ritual to British churches. He promoted William Laud to be Archbishop of Canterbury, and Laud began to move the Church back towards a more Catholic style.* It was what people would term Anglo-

---

* Laud, like Charles, was not a loveable man. He was, though, very fond of his cats and a giant tortoise, the skeleton of which can still be seen on display in Lambeth Palace.

Catholic. Yes, it kept the liturgy and creed intact, but it added a whole lot of what its enemies called 'popery'. It had vestments and incense and ceremonies.* Communion rails were installed in churches and people were expected to kneel at them. Laud maintained that England had never actually stopped being Catholic, nor had it *really* split from Rome. In his view, England wasn't really so much a Protestant country as a highly reformed Catholic one. Once again, the Puritans found themselves being pushed out. Their preachers were banned. Calvinism was out, Arminianism was in.

This had the effect of energising even the most moderate of the Protestants. For the first time people began to choose to call themselves Puritan. It became a badge of honour, rather than a term of abuse. And the people began to sympathise and even support them. In 1637, three Puritan critics were arrested and brought before the Star Chamber – an extra-judicial court which served as a kind of English version of the Inquisition. William Prynne had criticised Queen Henrietta Maria, and the other two, Henry Burton and John Bastwicke, had spoken out against the bishops. (Burton described all bishops, rather brilliantly, as 'upstart mushrumps' – which is going to be my new insult of choice.) They were duly punished – parts of their ears were cut off, and they were branded with the letters SL, standing for 'seditious libel'.† They were then put in the stocks in the expectation that people would throw rubbish at them. But instead they were supported, even cheered. Suddenly Puritans were faced with something that had never happened to them before: they were popular. Or, at least, less unpopular than the king.

The tension rose between them. Parliament contained a large number of Puritan sympathisers. And when they started to voice their objections, Charles decided to dissolve Parliament and rule

---

* The return of ornate vestments confused people. When one old lady in Norwich saw her minister wearing scarlet vestments, she wondered why the mayor was serving Communion.
† Prynne claimed that it really stood for 'Stigmata Laudis'.

himself. The problem was that he was broke. Without Parliament he couldn't raise taxes. That was, after all, why kings *had* parliaments – it wasn't for advice or law making or anything like that, it was just (a) to keep up appearances; and (b) to get the tax laws passed. Charles tried to raise money himself, using long-forgotten laws and levies, but that just plunged him to new depths of unpopularity. Amazingly, he responded to this by plunging to new depths of ineptitude. Between them, Laud and Charles managed to alienate all of the most significant leaders in Britain.

In 1637 Charles tried to impose a version of the English Prayer Book on Scotland without any consultation. The first time this was used in a service, a Scots woman was so annoyed she threw a stool at the bishop. A riot then broke out.* The Scottish General Assembly then convened and threw out not only the Prayer Book, but all the bishops as well. They signed a covenant (some of them, in a rather over-Scottish macho way signed it in their own blood). Charles refused to acknowledge the authority of the assembly and the Scots then invaded England.

Charles had no money to pay an army to defend England because he had abolished Parliament. So he was forced into a humiliating climb-down. He recalled Parliament. In return for raising money, they forced the king to abolish all the 'Catholic' innovations which Charles had introduced. Then the Irish, not wanting to be left out, rebelled in 1641 in an attempt to throw off English rule while the English were dealing with the Scots. Parliament pressed for deeper and more radical reform. Charles dug his heels in. Conflict and rebellion spiralled and grew, and in 1642 the two sides went to war. It did not begin as a religious war. It was about the role of Parliament and the power of the king, but the religious outlook of the two sides increasingly played a huge part. As Cromwell himself said, 'Religion was not the

---

* In Brechin, the bishop had no such trouble, but then again, he did lead the service from the new Prayer Book with a pair of loaded pistols pointed at the congregation.

thing at first contested for, but God brought it to that issue at last.'

For many of the Puritans, this was the moment. This was their time. So, from 1643 to 1649, while the war was still in progress, over a hundred Puritan theologians gathered in Westminster to create the constitution for a new, reformed, reformation Church. They scrapped the Prayer Book, and, in return for support from the Scottish, promised that England would do the full Presbyterian and abolish bishops. (One of the first to be abolished was Archbishop Laud, who was tried and executed in 1645 on charges of treason – charges which were palpably not true.) John Milton, one of the chief propagandists of the Puritan cause, said that 'God is decreeing to begin some new and great period in his Church, even to the reforming of the Reformation itself.' This Puritan council created a new Calvinist statement of belief, the *Westminster Confession of Faith*.*And they replaced the *Book of Common Prayer* with the extremely dull-sounding *Directory for Public Worship*.†

But just as in other Protestant conflicts, there was an irresistible move towards radicalism, and the decades around the Civil War saw a flourishing of small sects. The Baptists, particularly, flourished. The sect had been relatively small before the war, but now grew rapidly.

There was a bewildering variety of new movements: the Diggers, who argued for the redistribution of land; Levellers, who preached equality for women, and called for all working men to have the vote, for one-year parliaments, the abolition of

---

* The confession is Calvinistic at heart, but it also emphasised Luther's ideas of *sola scriptura* and *sola fide*. It advocated a minimal form of worship, strict sabbatarianism and affirmed that the Pope was definitely the Antichrist.
† It was known in Scotland as the Westminster Directory, which makes it sound like a phone book. Its full title was *A Directory for Public Worship of God throughout the Three Kingdoms of England, Scotland, and Ireland. Together with an Ordinance of Parliament for the taking away of the Book of Common Prayer, and the Establishing and Observing of this Present Directory throughout the Kingdom of England and the Dominion of Wales.* Snappy.

the House of Lords, religious toleration. They also called for MPs to have no outside interests. Four hundred years later and we're still waiting on that one . . .

Then there were the Muggletonians, who believed that anyone who knowingly rejected their teachings was going to hell. So, to avoid inflicting this terrible fate on others, they decided it was best not to tell anyone what they believed. They were the first Christian sect actively to ban evangelism.* There were the Adamites who certainly met for worship, but were accused of doing so in the nude. The Grindletonians from Yorkshire believed that true Christians could achieve perfection on earth, although how that was possible in Yorkshire they didn't say. The Ranters, a kind of catch-all bogey-man heretical sect, believed that God had granted them an inner light and prophetic gifts, and took this as the opportunity to discard all worldly moral rules and publicly embrace nudity, adultery and even blasphemy. It's argu-able whether the Ranters actually existed or whether they were made up.

The longest-lasting and most influential of these sects was founded in 1643 by a cobbler called George Fox. He became a wandering preacher after seeing God in a dream. Fox knew Christ 'experientially', he had had a direct experience of Christ, bypassing all the institutions of the Church. What's more, he argued that *everyone* had this ability: everyone had an inner light from God. He called his movement the Friends, or the 'Society of Friends', but their enemies looked at the way they shook when under the inspiration of the inner light and dubbed them the Quakers.

These groups were, in a way, the distant offspring of the Anabaptists. They were outliers, freaks, and what they all had in common was that they were viewed with hatred. In the dour

---

* Amazingly they survived until the 1970s. They didn't even worship together, choosing just to meet up for discussions. Their leader, John Reeve, taught that only Jesus was God. That meant that when he died on the cross, he had to hand over the running of the universe to Moses and Elijah for a few days.

English Commonwealth that was introduced after the war, there weren't many entertainment options, but you could always gather a crowd to see a Quaker being beaten up.

The man in charge by then was a Congregationalist called Oliver Cromwell. He rose to prominence through his policy of rewarding actual ability in his soldiers and commanders. His New Model Army brought military success after early Parliamentary setbacks. And in 1648, Charles surrendered.

And now the Parliamentarians had a bit of a problem. What do you do with an ex-king? Most of them weren't in favour of executing him, but the radical fringes demanded the king's execution and drove out every MP who disagreed.

In defeat Charles seemed to find a new strength. He refused to admit the authority of the court arranged to try him. And when, in the end, the radical elements of the Parliamentarians took over, and the king was sentenced to death, he went with equanimity and courage. He was pretty useless as a king, but in the end he proved himself a courageous man.

In many ways, the culmination of Reformation ideas took place on 30 January 1649, when the English Puritan Parliament beheaded the king. The event was driven through by a group of radical Puritans who finally had taken to a logical conclusion all those theories of the right to resist tyranny that had begun over a century before. This was the natural, logical conclusion of Luther's *Freedom of a Christian Man*, of the Magdeburg Confession and the Geneva Bible, from the writings of Goodman and Knox, of the belief in the conscience and liberty of the individual.

To them they were acting in a thoroughly biblical way: dispatching an evil king had been done in the pages of the Old Testament.

But to many others, in Britain and abroad, the effect was profound. The king was not just another leader, but a divinely appointed individual. And to them, the Puritans in killing the king had beheaded God.

Epilogue: The world on fire

History doesn't really do 'endings'. Like a movie, no sooner have the credits rolled than someone comes along with a sequel. Or worse, a remake. History isn't often as simple as linear cause and effect. It's a bit more all over the place. Everything leads to everything else.

So when did the Reformation end? Perhaps it ended with the Peace of Augsburg in 1555, when Charles V, Holy Roman Emperor, King of Spain, Angel of the North, Top of the Milk and Ship of the Desert effectively admitted that he was never going to be able to reset the Holy Roman Empire to its default setting. From then on, the princes of these territories were able to determine their own religions, whether it be Catholic or Lutheran. Or perhaps it was that point in 1588 when the divinely ordained wind (to the British anyway) drove away the Spanish Armada, ending Spanish hopes of recovering England for the Old Faith, and leading to the enormous blessing to the world known as the British Empire. Or maybe we should end it with the Peace of Westphalia and the closure of the Thirty Years' War, which meant, from then on, that the major nations were able to determine dominance over their own territories, and to decide on the education, the religious observance, and, as far as they ever could, the cultural norms.

Maybe for some people, though, it ended a lot earlier. In 1525, with the defeat of the peasants' revolt. They'd hoped it would lead to a better, freer life, but it didn't. They were still muddy, cold and oppressed. It was just that instead of going to confession, they now had to listen to endless sermons.

I think a good ending point is 1649. The death of King Charles I of England, Scotland, Ireland and Sundry Other Places is an event that could never have occurred had it not been for the Reformation. And, although it led to a Puritan government, almost from day one that government was in decline. Because of its tendency to close things down – theatres, inns, alehouses, the House of Lords, Sunday sports – the Puritans were ever after to be characterised as the 'No Fun At All' party.* In the end, though, the People's Puritan Republic of England failed. People were fed up of Puritanland. They resented soldiers patrolling London houses on Christmas Day and removing any meat which they found being cooked. They wanted their theatre back. And their beer. And, presumably, their adultery. So when Cromwell died, they invited Charles II, son of the executed king, to return. Christmas was welcomed back with open arms, a revamped prayer book was reintroduced in 1662. Charles was so un-Puritan that he had fourteen illegitimate children by seven different mistresses.

And it was all Merrie England again.

Or perhaps the Reformation hasn't really ended at all. Because many of the basic cultural, social and political assumptions we work under today are the product of those turbulent years. Certainly the arguments of the Reformation were the crucible in which the modern nation state was formed. Those who took part in those momentous events argued for the rights of the individual, and for freedom of conscience, freedom of worship and freedom of speech. The Reformation played a huge role in all of that.

But for Luther, at least, this freedom of conscience was always subject to his reading of scripture. Luther's great declaration of independence before the Emperor at Worms was not actually a statement about individual right of conscience alone, but about

---

* They did do some good things. Under Cromwell, for the first time in nearly four hundred years, Jews were allowed back into England. It was hoped that they would be converted, because everyone knew that the conversion of Israel precipitated the Second Coming. That didn't happen, but they were allowed to worship freely.

conscience in conformity to scripture. 'My conscience is captive to the Word of God,' he said. And that last bit is crucial. It's not just about being an individual, but about being an individual in relationship with God through scripture.

The problem is this: who gets to decide what scripture says? Well. There's the paradox. Because, in that case, it was Luther. In Geneva it was Calvin, in Zürich, Zwingli. Or we could go further: in Amsterdam it was John Smith, and it depended on how he was feeling that day. Or maybe it was Melchior Hoffman. Or, worse, Jan Matthijs.

William Chillingworth wrote in 1638, 'The Bible only is the religion of Protestants.' But that was the issue. Because by the time he was writing there were many, many forms of Protestantism. We tend to think that the Reformation divided Europe into two religious camps, but actually it divided Europe into far more groups than that. One side, there was still a broad lump that was known as Catholicism; but on the other side there was not just one kind of Protestantism, but many forms: Lutheran, Calvinist, Zwinglian, Presbyterian, Anabaptist, Separatist, Rastafarian. No, all right, maybe not the last one. But loads of different groups. And they would all claim to be Bible-based.

And that is why, perhaps, the main legacy of the Reformation is schism. Splintering. People arguing over different verses of the Bible and then storming off to form their own denominations. If you want to see the legacy of the Reformation, walk down a street in Nairobi, or London, or New York. Look at the sheer number of different denominations. According to the *World Christian Encyclopaedia*, there are 33,000 denominations in the world, of which 9,000 are termed Protestant and 22,000 Independent (not to mention the 168 denominations termed 'Anglican'). The honey-tongued preacher Richard Sibbes called the Reformation 'that fire which all the world shall never be able to quench'. Today any number of bush fires are burning around the world, and new ones are igniting all the time.

One of the key lessons to be learned from the Reformation is this: if you ask people to think for themselves, don't be surprised when they do exactly that.

It's not all about disunity though. In some cases it's leading in the opposite direction.

In a recent bout of Doing Anything to Get Some Attention, the *Church Times* – the *Pravda* of the Anglican church – made a list of the '100 Best Christian books'. (I'm not bitter. No, really.) Anyway, it made for interesting reading, but looking at it again in the light of this history, it's interesting as much for who it leaves out as for who it includes. There is no Luther. Calvin's *Institutes* is nowhere to be seen. The top five books are all by Catholic writers, as are seven out of the top ten. And that's the *Anglican* church choosing.

Today, many of the certainties of the Reformation seem a lot less certain. Catholics and Protestants are often to be found on the same side of the barricades, arm-in-arm against secularism, relativism, atheism, Islam, globalisation, and many other threats. Increasingly, Catholics are adopting Protestant approaches to worship and their study of the Bible, while many Protestants are discovering the riches of Catholic spirituality and embracing the mysteries of ritual and liturgy. They go on retreats, and embrace disciplines like fasting and confession. And Christians on both sides of the fence obey their leaders if and when they want to.

It's this kind of thing that gets some Protestants – and, indeed some Catholics – very angry.

But I'm not sure why. All that people are doing is making their own stand, on the basis of their own conscience and their own reading of the Bible.

What could be more Reformation than that?

The Reformation: a chronology

1304	Petrarch, 'the father of humanism', born.
1324?	John Wycliffe born.
1372	Jan Hus born.
1378	'Great Schism' of the papacy begins. One too many popes.
1384	John Wycliffe dies in exile (i.e. Leicestershire).
1414	Council of Constance meets to end the Great Schism. Takes three years. Well, it was a *great* schism.
1415	Jan Hus executed on the orders of the Council of Constance.
1417	Election of Pope Martin V ends the Great Schism.
1440	Lorenzo Valla proves the *Donation of Constantine* to be a forgery.
1452?	Johannes Gutenberg invents the printing press.
1453	Constantinople falls to the Ottoman Turks. End of the Byzantine Empire.
1466?	Erasmus of Rotterdam born.
1483	Martin Luther born.
1484	Huldrych Zwingli born.
1492	Columbus sails to the Americas.
1505	Luther caught in a thunderstorm. St Anne mistakenly answers his prayer. He enters the monastery at Erfurt.
1509	John Calvin born.
1510	Luther travels to Rome and is unimpressed.
1511	Luther moves to Wittenberg. Gasparo Contarini discovers justification by faith but keeps it to himself.

1512	Luther takes his doctorate and begins lecturing at Wittenberg.
1513	Election of Pope Leo X. Champagne all round!
1515	Luther lectures on Romans.
1516	Publication of Erasmus' *Greek New Testament*.
1517	(31 October) Luther 'posts' the Ninety-five Theses. Maybe by nailing them, definitely by using the actual post.
1518	(April/May) Luther defends his theology to the Augustinian order.
	(October) Luther meets with Cardinal Cajetan in Augsburg.
	(December) Zwingli moves to Zürich.
1519	(1 January) Zwingli begins systematic preaching in Zürich.
	(June) Election of Charles V.
	(July) Leipzig. Luther debates his ideas with Johann Eck.
	Luther has his 'tower experience'.
1520	(August/September) Luther publishes the *Address to the Christian Nobility of the German Nation* and *The Babylonian Captivity of the Church*.
	(November) Luther publishes *The Freedom of a Christian*.
1521	(January) Luther excommunicated from the Roman Catholic Church and made an 'enemy of the Holy Roman Empire'.
	(April) Diet of Worms.
	(May) Luther taken into protective custody in Wartburg Castle. (Until March 1522.)
1522–3	Ignatius Loyola convalesces at Manresa (near Barcelona) during which he has Very Deep Religious Experiences, later formulated as his *Spiritual Exercises*.
1522	Luther completes his German translation of the New Testament.

1523	(January) First public debate about the Reformation in Zürich.
	(October) Second public debate in Zürich. Zürich goes all Zwingli. Sausages all round!
1523–5	Beginnings of the Anabaptist movement in Zürich.
1524–5	Peasants' War in Germany.
1525	Anabaptists celebrate first adult baptisms in Zürich.
	(June) Luther marries Katharina von Bora.
1526	William Tyndale's English *New Testament* printed at Worms.
1527	Sack of Rome by troops of the Emperor.
	Schleitheim Confession attempts to unite early Anabaptists.
	Council of Västerås in Sweden grants powers to the king who immediately starts to confiscate church property.
1528	Patrick Hamilton burned for heresy in St Andrews.
1529	Iconoclastic riots in Basel. Abolition of the Mass in Strasbourg.
	(July) Diet of Speyer orders the enforcement of the Edict of Worms. The Protestation of the Evangelical Estates gives us the term 'Protestant'.
	Colloquy of Marburg. Luther and Zwingli argue about what happens during Communion. Among other things.
1530	Diet of Augsburg; Confession of Augsburg prepared by Philip Melanchthon and presented to the Diet. Nobody likes it.
1531	Formation of the Schmalkaldic League.
	(11 October) Battle of Kappel. Zwingli is killed. Replaced by Heinrich Bullinger.
1534	Act of Supremacy acknowledges Henry VIII as 'supreme head of the church in England'. First complete edition of Luther's translation of the Bible. Election of Alessandro Farnese as Pope Paul III.

	A load of posters go up in Paris. Calvin leaves in a hurry.
1534–5	Anabaptist rule in Münster.
1536	First edition of Calvin's *Institutes*.
	(July) Calvin is persuaded to stay in Geneva by Guillaume Farel.
	Erasmus dies. William Tyndale executed.
	Sweden abolishes canon law, marking final break with Rome.
1536–40	Dissolution of the English monasteries.
1537	Calvin presents the Genevan magistrates with the first version of his *Ecclesiastical Ordinances*.
	Report on abuses in the Catholic Church presented to Paul III. It is suppressed. Then leaked.
1538	Calvin and Farel expelled from Geneva.
1539	Publication of the second, expanded edition of Calvin's *Institutes*.
1540	Society of Jesus (the Jesuits) officially recognised.
1541	Diet of Regensburg nearly pulls off the impossible by getting Catholics and Protestants to agree on the doctrine of justification by faith. Naturally Luther and the Pope veto it.
	(September) Calvin returns to Geneva. The city goes full Calvinist. Fondue all round!
	(November) *Ecclesiastical Ordinances* issued in Geneva.
1545	(December) Opening of the Council of Trent. It goes on in phases until 1563. No, really.
1546	Schmalkaldic War begins. Luther dies.
1547	Henry VIII dies. Succeeded by his evangelical son, Edward VI.
1548	First English Prayer Book.
1551–2	Second session of the Council of Trent.
1552	English Prayer Book version 2.0.
1553	Evangelical Eddy dies. Mary Tudor becomes queen

and tries to restore Roman Catholicism to England. Bloody Marys all round!

1553 Servetus killed in Geneva.

1555 Peace of Augsburg – *cuius regio, eius religio* and all that. Establishes rulers' right to decide the religion of their states.

Calvin's opponents defeated in Geneva. A city rejoices. (Quietly.) First Geneva-trained pastors dispatched into France.

Election of Gian Pietro Carafa as Pope Paul IV.

1558 Elizabeth I becomes Queen of England and restores England to Protestantism.

1559 Foundation of the Geneva Academy.

(March) First national synod of the French reformed churches in Paris.

Creation of Index of Prohibited Books.

Calvin produces his final, definitive, enormous edition of the *Institutes*. John Knox returns to Scotland. Haggis all round!

Henry II (France) dies. His widow, Catherine de' Medici, becomes the regent for his three sons who succeed him: Frances II (d. 1560), Charles IX (d. 1574) and Henry III (d. 1589).

1560 Revolution in Scotland led by the Lords of the Congregation. Scotland goes Calvinist. Nobody rejoices, on principle.

1562 Outbreak of the first of the Wars of Religion in France.

1562–3 Third and final session of the Council of Trent.

1564 Death of Calvin.

1566 Beginning of the Dutch revolt.

1572 (August) St Bartholomew's Eve massacre. Three thousand Huguenots killed in Paris over three days.

1584 (July) William the Silent is shot. Presumably the gun had a silencer on it.

1585	Election of Pope Sixtus V.
1587	(February) Execution of Mary, Queen of Scots.
1588	Spanish Armada attacks England but fails. Cups of tea all round!
1589	Assassination of French King Henry III; accession of Calvinist Henry of Navarre as Henry IV.
1593	Calvinist Henry IV becomes Catholic Henry IV and is crowned King of France.
1598	Henry IV grants Edict of Nantes, giving French Huguenots the right to worship in France. (Eventually overturned in 1685.)
1603	Death of Elizabeth I. James VI heads south and becomes James I of England.
1604	Hampton Court Conference.
1605	Gunpowder, treason and plot!
1609	Establishment of Dutch Republic. Oranjeboom all round!
1610	(14 May) Assassination of Henry IV.
1618–19	Synod of Dort debates predestination and other Calvinist things.
1618	In Prague some guys are thrown through a window, beginning the Thirty Years' War. It goes on for . . . er . . . thirty years.
1620	The *Mayflower* sails from Plymouth to Massachusetts with a cargo of Calvinists.
1625	James I dies. Charles I succeeds him. There may be trouble ahead . . .
1637	Charles tries to impose the English Prayer Book on Scotland. Stools are thrown. Riots ensue.
1639	Charles I sends his first army against Scotland. It doesn't go well.
1642	The English revolutionary war begins.
1643–49	Westminster Assembly produces the Westminster Confession of Faith, two catechisms, a Directory of Public Worship and No Fun Whatsoever.

1648   The Treaty of Westphalia ends the Thirty Years' War. It gives religious rights to Calvinists, Lutherans and Roman Catholics in the Holy Roman Empire.

1649   Charles I executed. England is proclaimed a republic.

1658   Oliver Cromwell, Lord Protector of England, dies.

1660   Charles II proclaimed King of England. Spaniels all round!

Index

Also by Nick Page

A Nearly Infallible History of Christianity

ISBN 978 1 444 75013 3
eBook ISBN 978 1 444 75014 0

I'm not angry, just
very disappointed

THINGS YOU LEARN FROM CHRISTIAN HISTORY

NO. 1

It's the resurrection, stupid

The history of the church begins on a Sunday morning in AD 33, when a man whom everyone thought was dead was found walking about in a graveyard. Christianity's core business is resurrection. There is always life after death. There is always hope.

Given some of the places we are going to go on this journey, it might be worth holding on to that fact.

1 Resurrection, Rome and Revelation

Er... no

It was AD 33 and the people in charge of Jerusalem were *extremely* annoyed.

This was not new. There was a lot in life to annoy them – the workload, the pressures of responsibility, the sheer cost of buying the position of high priest from the ruling Romans, remembering to wear the right robes for the festivals, not to mention the fact that everyone hated them and viewed them as collaborators.

And now there was this: two Galilean fishermen who had been teaching and causing a disturbance in the temple. That was not the problem, the temple was always full of religious agitators of one sort or another: Pharisees, Essenes, would-be-Messiahs, Young Conservatives. Nor was it the fact that these men were rumoured to have performed miracles. That was *supposed* to happen in Jerusalem and was officially Very Good for Tourism. No, what really annoyed them was that these men were claiming that their leader had come back from the dead. And since the temple elite had gone out of their way to organise the man's death in the first place, this was a flagrant threat to their authority.

His name was Jesus of Nazareth. Yeshua – to give him his real name – was a miracle-worker, teacher, radical preacher from Galilee. He had led his followers to Jerusalem, caused a riot in the temple, and said a lot of things the authorities found very hurtful, actually. So they had arrested him, taken him to the Roman prefect Pontius Pilate, and persuaded Pilate to have him killed. (They weren't allowed to execute him themselves. Which was *another* annoying thing.)

Now the followers of this Jesus were claiming that he had risen from the dead, which was not only impossible, but was directly in contravention of their theology.* More, they claimed that he was the long-awaited Jewish Messiah. (Later on, his followers used the Greek word for Messiah – *Christos* – which means 'anointed one'. Hence 'Jesus Christ'. It's not his surname; just his job description.)

The two men – Peter and John – were instructed by the high priest and the other people in charge of the temple 'not to speak or teach at all in the name of Jesus'. And here is their reply: 'Whether it is right in God's sight to listen to you rather than to God, you must judge; for we cannot keep from speaking about what we have seen and heard' (Acts 4.18–20).

Or, in other words, 'No.'

And there you have it. Right at the start of Christianity we have one of its most characteristic acts: a lack of respect for authority. A refusal to be silenced. The truth is that, right from the start, authentic Christianity has been deeply, *deeply* annoying.

Dead man walking

The account of the hearing comes from the book of Acts. But the earliest account we have of these resurrection appearances comes from a letter written around AD 54 to a group of Christians misbehaving in Asia Minor:

> Christ died for our sins in accordance with the scriptures, and that he was buried, and that he was raised on the third day in accordance with the scriptures, and that he appeared to Cephas, then to the twelve. Then he appeared to more than five hundred brothers and sisters at one time, most of whom are still alive, though some have died. Then he appeared to James, then to all the apostles. Last of all, as to one untimely born, he appeared also to me. (1 Cor. 15.3–8)

The 'me' in question here is a man called Paul of Tarsus, aka Saul, of whom more, later. He's reminding the badly behaved Christian community

* The ruling parties in Jerusalem were Sadducees, who didn't believe in the resurrection of the dead. They also didn't believe in fate, angels or the immortality of the soul. Or Father Christmas.

in Corinth that witnesses to this resurrection were still around. A number of these were key leaders of the church – Cephas, aka Peter, and James; but he also mentions the 'apostles', an amorphous group that generally refers to anyone who saw the risen Jesus. Twenty years later, according to Paul, many of these were still alive. By then they were telling the story to anyone who would listen (and many who wouldn't).

The first time the wider world heard about the resurrection was forty days after the event. The followers of Jesus had gathered together in one place to pray, during the Jewish festival of Pentecost, when the Holy Spirit descended on them. The city was full of Jews from other parts of the world: Parthians, Asians, Egyptians, Romans, Welsh – they were all there.* And with the outpouring of power Jesus' followers started to speak about Jesus in the visitors' languages. From the start, the Jesus movement was international.

Many people joined the new movement that day. But what, exactly, were they joining? The church itself, let alone many of its core doctrines, hadn't been invented. These converts didn't go home with an informative tract, a copy of the Gideons' Bible and a newsletter giving times of the church services. All they had was the story of what happened: what people had seen Jesus do and heard him say. Things that had been passed on.

Pass it on

Paul says of Jesus' resurrection appearances that he didn't invent them: they have been 'handed on' to him. He is quoting a Christian statement of faith – a kind of creed. He learned other things as well:

> For I received from the Lord what I also handed on to you, that the Lord Jesus on the night when he was betrayed took a loaf of bread, and when he had given thanks, he broke it and said, 'This is my body that is for you. Do this in remembrance of me.' In the same way he took the cup also, after supper, saying, 'This cup is the new covenant in my blood. Do this, as often as you drink it, in remembrance of me.' For as often as you eat this bread and drink the cup, you proclaim the Lord's death until he comes. (1 Cor. 11.23–26)

* Not the Welsh, obviously. Pay attention.

From the start Christians *learned* the story of Jesus. This was an age when, for the most part, you couldn't look anything up. Most people couldn't read. That, and the fact that the internet wouldn't be invented for another two thousand years or so made Googling something pretty tricky. There were libraries but these were for posh people with togas. So ordinary Christians learned by memorising and repeating. And, in one of Christianity's best innovations, they also learned through eating, which is absolutely my favourite kind of learning. The story was embedded in a meal, which Paul calls 'the Lord's supper'. It became known as 'the Eucharist' – from the Greek word for thanksgiving. It was a thank-you meal.

The meal was both symbolic and practical. Christians from all social classes shared the food, to demonstrate that 'we who are many are one body' (1 Cor. 10.17). And it was a proper meal. Today, when communion consists of something that claims to be wine but that manifestly isn't, and something that claims to be bread but is either (a) a day-old Hovis, or (b) a bit of cardboard called a *wafer*. We forget this. Their meal was actually, you know, a *meal*.

In their meetings they did other things as well. They prayed, read and discussed the Scriptures, and sang stuff as well. Indeed, from another of Paul's letters we get what is probably an ancient Christian hymn. The lyrics tell about Jesus being 'in the form of God' but choosing to become a slave, taking human form and dying on the cross. And therefore God 'highly exalted him' and every knee will bow, 'every tongue confess that Jesus Christ is Lord, to the glory of God the Father'.*

These are radical views. And though Paul is writing a couple of decades after the events, very early on the central contradictions of all this must have been clear. These people were following a man who had died on the cross – a death reserved for slaves and foreign rebels. They claimed that he was not just *their* Lord, but the Lord of everything and everybody, which would come as a bit of a shock to a few Romans, to say the least. Most of all, Jesus was, in some way, 'in the form of God'.

These were not the kinds of views that were going to go down well. As Paul admitted, Jesus was 'a stumbling-block to Jews and foolishness to Gentiles' (1 Cor. 1.23). Which has everyone more or less covered.

* It's in Philippians 2.5–11.

As the conflict with the Jerusalem temple authorities shows, some Jews reacted badly to all this. But not all Jews, of course. Because these first followers of Jesus were Jewish. And they carried on with many Jewish practices – going to synagogue, praying at the set times, eating ritually clean food, feeling guilty, phoning their mothers regularly, etc. This was to cause conflict once non-Jews started to adopt the faith. But Jesus' first followers did not know that they were starting a new religion: they thought they were fulfilling the old one.

Indeed, the relationship of Christianity to Judaism lies behind much of the writing of their most influential early thinker: Paul of Tarsus.

PAUL

Paul, from a third-century medallion. Presumably this must have been after one of his shipwrecks, as he appears to have some kind of squid attached to his jaw

Name: Paul of Tarsus.
Aka: Saul.
Nationality: Greek-speaking Jew from Cilicia.
Dates: c.1–c.68.
Appearance: Bald, bandy-legged, monobrowed, hook nosed. But apart from that, curiously attractive.
Before he was famous: Tent-maker. Rabbinic student.
Famous for: Letter writing. Planting churches. Being very hard to understand.
Why does he matter? Defined many of the fundamental theological ideas of Christianity.
Could you have a drink with him down the pub? Definitely. Although he would probably try to convert someone, and there might be a fight.

The bandy-legged, monobrowed angel

Paul's life is a microcosm of the transformative power of early Christianity. He was born in Tarsus, a cosmopolitan city on the south coast of Cilicia in what is today Turkey. He was a Roman citizen by birth, and a tent-maker or leather-worker by trade. His family were orthodox Jews, and Paul went to Jerusalem and studied under rabbi Gamaliel. (Not *literally*, obviously. Although, having said which, the life of rabbinic students did involve copying their teacher closely: there is an account of one rabbinical student who followed his master so closely that he actually hid under the bed of the rabbi and his wife. When the rabbi protested, the student said, 'But this is Torah [the law] and I must learn it.' It's certainly an approach that would make the TV show *The Apprentice* a lot more interesting.)

Anyway, soon after the Pentecost experience the Jewish authorities lost patience with this new sect. Riots broke out and one of their number – a Greek-speaking Jew called Stephen – was killed. Paul was part of this persecution. But then his life changed. On the way to Damascus to close down a new Christian group there, he was hit by a kind of spiritual speed camera: a light flashed around him and he heard the risen Jesus saying, 'Why do you persecute me?' This orthodox Jewish persecutor of Christians became the leading apostle to the Gentiles.

Fig. I. *On the Damascus Road, Paul initially mistakes the cause of the supernatural event*

His background fitted him perfectly for missionary work: he was a Roman citizen from a Greek city, who was trained as a Jewish Pharisee. His first language was Greek, but he spoke Hebrew and had studied Torah – the Jewish law. He had other important qualities as well, notably an irresistible passion, drive and sheer bloody-mindedness and an ability to endure a large amount of personal violence. He had the talent for getting into hot water that is the sign of the true radical. Unusually for these apostolic figures, we may even know what he looked like. An early church story called the *Acts of Paul and Thecla* is a made-up story, but it contains a portrait of Paul that is so unflattering it very well may be original: 'Paul . . . a man small in size, bald-headed, bandy-legged, well-built, with eyebrows meeting, rather long-nosed, full of grace. For sometimes he seemed like a man, and sometimes he had the countenance of an angel.'

After his conversion he didn't go to Jerusalem to consult any of the embryonic church leadership (probably because he realised that the authorities would not be hugely delighted that he had joined the enemy. Or maybe his bandy legs were giving him trouble). Instead, he went to Arabia for a few years – which means the region around Damascus, rather than somewhere on a great big sand dune eating Turkish Delight. We don't know much about what Saul got up to, but it seems to have made him some enemies. Because he was forced to flee Damascus in the night, escaping over the wall in a laundry basket.* After three years he finally went to Jerusalem where he met Peter, James and the other leaders of the church. Unsurprisingly, they were nervous – but Paul was vouched for by Barnabas.

Once this meeting was over he did what he did best: he got into trouble. Acts records that he went out from the meeting and started 'speaking boldly' with the Hellenists. These were Greek-speaking residents of Jerusalem: the immigrant community, in fact. It was not what you'd call a success: the Hellenists responded to Paul's message by trying to kill him. So Paul was 'encouraged' to leave Jerusalem by the rest of the apostles. He went north, back to Tarsus, for a while.

---

* Hence the origin of the phrase 'He got clean away.'

HODDER &
STOUGHTON

Hodder & Stoughton is the UK's
leading Christian publisher,
with a wide range of books from
the bestselling authors in the UK
and around the world ranging from
Christian lifestyle and theology to
apologetics, testimony and fiction.
We also publish the world's
most popular Bible translation
in modern English, the New
International Version, renowned
for its accuracy and readability.

Hodderfaith.com   Hodderbibles.co.uk
@HodderFaith   /HodderFaith